Shall I compare thee to a Sommers day?
Thou art more lovely and more temperate:
Rough windes do shake the darling buds of Maie,
And Sommers lease hath all too short a date:
Sometime too hot the eye of heaven shines,
And often is his gold complexion dimm'd,
And every faire from faire some-time declines,
By chance, or natures changing course untrim'd:
But thy eternall Sommer shall not fade,
Nor loose possession of that faire thou ow'st,
Nor shall death brag thou wandr'st in his shade,
When in eternall lines to time thou grow'st,
  So long as men can breath or eyes can see,
  So long lives this, and this gives life to thee.

SHAKESPEARE: Sonnet 18

Rigby Heinemann
A division of Reed International Books Australia Pty Ltd
22 Salmon Street, Port Melbourne, Victoria 3207
World Wide Web http://www.heinemann.com.au
Email info@heinemann.com.au

Offices in Sydney, Brisbane, Adelaide and Perth. Associated companies, branches and representatives throughout the world.

First published 1992
Reprinted 1993, 1994 (twice), 1995
Second edition 1996

2000 1999 1998 1997
10 9 8 7 6 5 4 3 2

First edition edited by Jenny Craig
Second edition edited by Adrienne Ralph
Cover illustration by Tim Claeys
Text illustrations by Luisa Laino
Designed by Jane Pennells

Typeset in 11/13pt Perpetua by Total Image Makers
Film supplied by Type Scan
Printed in Australia by Griffin Press, Adelaide

National Library of Australia
cataloguing-in-publication data:

Lines to time: a senior poetry anthology.

Includes index
ISBN 0 85859 916 3.

1. English poetry. I. McKenzie, J.K. (John K.)

821.008

CONTENTS

CONTENTS

CONTENTS

CONTENTS

PREFACE

This second edition of *Lines to Time* is in response to the reaccreditation of the Literature study design for the VCE, and a substantial change to the poets and poems set for Units 3 and 4 in 1996.

The present selection includes all of the poets and poems set for 1996.

The Part A list is of poets who might be used for Common Assessment Task 1, Views and Values, or for Common Assessment Task 2, Creative Response. That is, *Lines to Time* now includes a substantial selection of poems from each of:

Ben Jonson, Andrew Marvell, Alexander Pope, Alfred Lord Tennyson, John Keats, Wallace Stevens, T.S. Eliot, W.H. Auden, Judith Wright, Rosemary Dobson, Dimitris Tsaloumas, Fay Zwicky, and Philip Hodgins.

The Part B list is of poems which might be used for Common Assessment Task 3, Written Examination. *Lines to Time* now includes all of the poems set for 1996 by:

Geoffrey Chaucer, Thomas Wyatt, John Donne, Thomas Hardy, Gerard Manley Hopkins, John Shaw Nielson, Robert Frost, Stevie Smith, Gwen Harwood, Adrienne Rich, and Seamus Heaney.

Also included for CAT 3 is the group of single poems by a range of Australian authors:

A.D. Hope – 'Australia'; Kate Jennings – 'Couples'; Les Murray – 'The Broad Bean Sermon'; Judith Rodriguez – 'Nu-Plastik Fanfare Red'; Fay Zwicky – 'Jack Frost'; Gwen Harwood – 'Mother Who Gave Me Life'; Ern Malley – 'Night Piece'; James McAuley – 'Envoi'; Oodgeroo Noonuccal – 'We Are Going'; Lionel Fogarty – 'Remember Something Like This'; Kenneth Slessor – 'Five Bells'.

Lines to Time also includes substantial selections from other major poets: British, American, and Australian.

The poems in *Lines to Time* are presented chronologically, according to the year of each poet's birth.

Brief biographical notes on each author are provided.

ACKNOWLEDGEMENTS

The editor and publishers would like to thank the following for permission to reprint copyright material:

W.H. Auden: Six poems from *Collected Shorter Poems*, 1930–1944, W.H. Auden. Faber and Faber Limited, London 1950; 'In Praise of Limestone' from *W.H. Auden, The Penguin Poets*, Penguin Books in association with Faber and Faber, Harmondsworth, 1958.

Geoffrey Chaucer: 'The Prologue' from *Chaucer: The Prologue and Three Tales*, eds King and Steele, Longman Cheshire, Melbourne, 1969.

Bruce Dawe: Six poems from *Sometimes Gladness* by Bruce Dawe, Longman Cheshire, Melbourne, 1978.

Emily Dickinson: Fourteen poems from *Final Harvest: Emily Dickinson's Poems*, edited by Thomas H. Johnson, Little Brown and Company, Boston, who acknowledged permission of the President and Fellows of Harvard College and of the Trustees of Amherst College, 1961, and of Mary A. Hampson and Martha Dickinson Bianchi; 'A narrow Fellow in the Grass' from *A Choice of Emily Dickinson's Verse* by Ted Hughes, Faber and Faber, London, 1968.

Rosemary Dobson: Eight poems from Rosemary Dobson, *Collected Poems*, Angus and Robertson Modern Poets, 1991.

T.S. Eliot: Four poems from *Collected Poems 1909–1962* by T.S. Eliot, Faber and Faber Limited, 1974.

Lionel Fogarty: One poem from *Ngutji*, 1984, acknowledgement to Cheryl Buchanan.

Robert Frost: Twelve poems from *The Poetry of Robert Frost*, ed. Edward Connery Latham, the estate of Robert Frost and Jonathan Cape Ltd, 1971.

Gwen Harwood: Nine poems from *Selected Poems Gwen Harwood*, Collins/Angus and Robertson, North Ryde, Sydney, 1990.

Philip Hodgins: 'Death Who', 'Making Hay', 'Ich Bin Allein' from *Blood and Bone*, Collins/Angus and Robertson Publishers, 1986; 'Shooting the Dogs' from *Down the Lake With Half a Chook*, ABC Books, 1988; 'Milk Cream Butter', 'After a Dry Stretch', 'The New Floor', 'A Memoral Service', 'The Pier' from *Up On All Fours*, Harper Collins, 1993.

Seamus Heaney: Fourteen poems from *Seamus Heaney, New Selected Poems 1966–1987*, Faber and Faber, London, 1990.

A.D. Hope: One poem from *Collected Poems A.D. Hope*, Collins/Angus and Robertson, 1972.

Ted Hughes: Six poems from *Selected Poems 1957–1981* by Ted Hughes, Faber and Faber, 1982.

Kate Jennings: One poem by Kate Jennings from *Me My Melancholy Baby*, Outback Press and the author, 1979.

Robert Lowell: Three poems from *Life Studies* by Robert Lowell, Faber and Faber, 1959.

'Ern Malley': One poem from *The Darkening Ecliptic* from *Angry Penguins* magazine, Max Harris, 1994.

James McAuley: One poem from *Collected Poems* by James McAuley, Collins/Angus and Robertson, 1971.

Les Murray: 'The Conquest' from *Collected Poems* by Les Murray, Collins/Angus and Robertson, 1991; four poems from *The Vernacular Republic* by Les A. Murray, Collins/Angus and Robertson, 1976.

Oodgeroo Noonuccal: Four poems from *My People* by Oodgeroo Noonuccal, Jacaranda Wiley Ltd, 1981.

Wilfred Owen: Six poems from *Collected Poems of Wilfred Owen*, ed Jan Stallworthy, estate of Wilfred Owen and Hogarth Press.

Sylvia Plath: Eight poems by Sylvia Plath from her *Collected Poems*, Faber and Faber, 1981.

Adrienne Rich: Eleven poems from *The Fact of a Doorframe. Poems Selected and New 1950–1984* by Adrienne Rich, W.W. Norton and Company, New York, 1984.

Judith Rodriguez: One poem from *New and Selected Poems by Judith Rodriguez*, University of Queensland Press, 1988.

Stevie Smith: Eight poems from *Stevie Smith Selected Poems*, ed James MacGibbon, Penguin Books, 1978. Requests for permission to reprint should be sent to James MacGibbon, The Cellars, Landscove, Ashburton, Devon TQ13 7LY. 'Pad, Pad' and 'Thoughts About the Christian Doctrine of Eternal Hell' from *Selected Poems* by Stevie Smith, Longmans, London, 1962.

Wallace Stevens: Seven poems from *The Collected Poems of Wallace Stevens*, Faber and Faber Limited, 1953.

Kenneth Slessor: Four poems from *Selected Poems* by Kenneth Slessor, Collins/Angus and Robertson, 1976.

Bobbi Sykes: Two poems from *Love Poems and Other Revolutionary Actions* by Bobbi Sykes, University of Queensland Press, 1988.

Dimitris Tsaloumas: 'A Progressive Man's Indignation', 'Nocturne', 'Prodigal', 'The Return' from *The Book of Epigrams*, University of Queensland Press, 1985; 'Falcon Drinking' from *Falcon Drinking*, University of Queensland, 1988; Press. 'The Debate', 'Waiting For War', 'Rhapsodic Meditation on the Melbourne Suburb of St Kilda' parts 1, 2, 4, from *The Barge*, University of Queensland Press, 1993.

Judith Wright: Nine poems from *Judith Wright Collected Poems 1942–1970*, Collins/Angus and Robertson, 1971.

Fay Zwicky: Eight poems from *Fay Zwicky Poems 1970–1992*, University of Queensland Press, 1992.

GEOFFREY CHAUCER
(1340?–1400)

Born London, son of a wine merchant. Chaucer was variously a soldier in France, a diplomat to Italy and France, and a senior public servant in England.

from THE CANTERBURY TALES
from **THE GENERAL PROLOGUE**

sweet — Whan that Aprill with his shoures soote▲
The droghte of March hath perced to the roote
every root in that liquid — And bathed every veyne in swich licour▲
by whose power — Of which vertu▲ engendred is the flour,
Spring's westwind; also — Whan Zephirus▲ eek▲ with his sweete breeth
breathed into; wood — Inspired▲ hath in every holt▲ and heeth
delicate new shoots — The tendre croppes▲, and the yonge sonne
Aries — Hath in the Ram▲ his half cours yronne,
birds — And smale foweles▲ maken melodye
That slepen al the nyght with open eye,
stirs, arouses them; hearts — So priketh hem▲ nature in hir corages▲,
go — Thanne longen folk to goon▲ on pilgrimages
pilgrims, especially to Jerusalem; strands, shores — And palmeres▲ for to seken straunge strondes▲
known — To ferne halwes kouthe▲ in sondry londes,
And specially from every shires ende
Of Engelond to Caunterbury they wende
The holy blisful martir for to seke
helped; sick — That hem hath holpen▲ whan that they were seeke▲.

1. his: suggesting personification of April.
14. ferne halwes: ancient, distant shrines known.
17. holy blisful martir: holy blessed martyr, Thomas à Becket who was murdered in Canterbury Cathedral and who is buried there.

Bifel that in that sesoun on a day
In Southwerk at the Tabard as I lay
Redy to wenden on my pilgrimage
with very devout purpose, spirit To Caunterbury, with ful devout corage▲,
At nyght was come into that hostelrye
Wel nyne and twenty in a compaignye
Of sondry folk, by aventure yfalle
In felaweshipe, and pilgrimes were they alle
were intending to ride That toward Caunterbury wolden ryde▲.
spacious The chambres and the stables weren wyde▲
And wel we weren esed atte beste.
briefly And shortly▲, whan the sonne was to reste,
everyone So hadde I spoken with hem everichon▲
immediately That I was of hir felaweshipe anon▲,
made plans And made forward▲ erly for to ryse
To take oure wey ther as I yow devyse.
nevertheless But nathelees▲ whil I have tyme and space
before; proceed Er▲ that I ferther in this tale pace▲,
Me thynketh it acordant to resoun
appearance and character To telle yow al the condicioun▲
Of ech of hem so as it semed me
what they looked like; position in society And whiche they weren▲ and of what degree▲
And eek in what array that they were inne;
then will And at a knyght than wol▲ I first bigynne.

☆ ☆ ☆

A KNYGHT ther was, and that a worthy man
That fro the tyme that he first bigan
To riden out he loved chivalrye,
Trouthe and honour, fredom and curteisye.
his king's or God's war Ful worthy was he in his lordes werre▲,
farther And thereto hadde he riden, no man ferre▲,
As wel in cristendom as in hethenesse
And evere honoured for his worthynesse.

20. An inn on the south bank of the Thames at Southwark, the approach to old London Bridge, and beside the road to Canterbury.
25. aventure: by chance, but also implying adventure.
29. esed atte beste: accommodated in comfort.
34. to the place of which I told you: i.e. Canterbury.
46. Integrity, honour, generosity of spirit, and courteous behaviour were the four main tenets of a knight's chivalric code.
49. hethenesse: heathendom, where people are not Christians.

3

GEOFFREY CHAUCER

At Alisaundre he was whan it was wonne;
Ful ofte tyme he hadde the bord bigonne
Aboven alle nacions in Pruce▲; *Prussia*
In Lettow▲ hadde he reysed▲ and in Ruce▲, *Lithuania; campaigned; Russia*
No Cristen man so ofte of his degree.
In Gernade▲ at the seege eek hadde he be *Granada*
Of Algezir▲ and riden in Belmarye▲. *Algeciras; Benmarin, Morocco*
At Lyeys was he and at Satalye
Whan they were wonne and in the Grete See▲ *the Mediterranean*
At many a noble armee hadde he be.
At mortal batailles hadde he been fiftene,
And foghten for oure feith at Tramyssene▲ *Tlemcen in North Africa*
In lystes thryes and ay slayn his foo.
This ilke worthy knyght hadde been also
Som tyme with the lorde of Palatye▲ *Palathia in modern Turkey*
Agayn another hethen in Turkye.
And evere moore he hadde a sovereyn prys▲, *renown*
And though that he were worthy he was wys
And of his port▲ as meeke as is a mayde. *demeanour*
He nevere yet no vileynye▲ ne sayde *foul language*
In al his lyf unto no maner wight▲: *person*
He was a verray parfit gentil knyght.
But for to tellen yow of his array,
Hise hors were goode but he was nat gay▲: *finely dressed*
Of fustian he wered a gypoun
Al bismotered▲ with his habergeoun▲ *stained; coat of mail*
for he was late ycome from his viage▲ *journey*
And wente for to doon his pilgrimage.
With hym▲ ther was his sone, a young SQUYER▲, *the knight; trainee for knighthood*
A lovere and a lusty bacheler
With lokkes crulle▲ as they were leyd in presse▲; *curly; held in curling irons*
Of twenty yeer of age he was I gesse.
Of his stature he was of evene lengthe
And wonderly delyvere▲ and of greet strengthe. *agile*

51. Alisaundre: Alexandria, captured by Christians from Muslims in 1365.
52. He had been honoured by being placed at the head of the table.
58. Lyeys: Ayas in Armenia; Satalye: Attalia.
75. fustian: a coarse cotton cloth; gypoun: a tunic worn under chain mail armour.

cavalry raid And he hadde been som tyme in chivachye▲
In Flaundres, in Artoys and Picardye,
in so little time on campaign And born hym wel, as of so litel space▲,
lady's In hope to stonden in his lady▲ grace.
embroidered Embrouded▲ was he as it were a meede
red Al ful of fresshe floures white and reede▲,
playing the flute Syngynge he was or floytynge▲ al the day:
He was as fressh as is the month of May.
Short was his gowne with sleves longe and wyde.
Wel koude he sitte on hors and faire ryde,
compose music and words He koude songes make and wel endite▲,
joust, fight in a tournament; draw Juste▲ and eek daunce and wel purtreye▲ and write.
hotly; at night So hoote▲ he lovede that by nyghtertale▲
He slepte namoore than dooth a nyghtyngale.
Curteys he was, lowely and servysable,
And carf biforn his fader at the table.

☆ ☆ ☆

A YEMAN hadde he and servantz namo
pleased At that tyme for hym liste▲ ryde so,
And he was clad in cote and hood of grene.
arrows A sheef of pecok arwes▲ bright and kene
carried Under his belt he bar▲ ful thriftily—
Wel koude he dresse his takel yemanly,
His arwes drouped noght with fetheres lowe—
And in his hand he bar a myghty bowe.
closely cropped skull A not heed▲ hadde he with a broun visage.
he knew well Of wodecraft wel koude▲ he al the usage.
armguard Upon his arm he bar a gay bracer▲
a small round shield And by his syde a swerd and a bokeler▲
And on that oother syde a gay daggere
embellished Harneysed▲ wel and sharp as point of spere;

99. courteous, humble, helpful.
100. carf biforn his fader: carve before his father at table, as a duty and as a mark of respect.
101. The 'Yeman' (Yeoman) is an independent commoner who acts as the Knight's military servant. The 'he' is the Knight.
106. He kept his gear in best working order, as might be expected of one who is able and who takes pride in his craft.

A Cristofre on his brest of silver sheene, *belt worn transversely*
An horn he bar, the bawdryk▲ was of grene: *over one shoulder*
A forster▲ was he soothly▲ as I gesse. *forrester; truly*

☆ ☆ ☆

Ther was also a nonne, a PRIORESSE,
That of hir smylyng was ful symple and coy▲; *modest and restrained*
Hir gretteste ooth was but by Seint Loy▲, *a very modest oath*
And she was cleped Madame Eglentyne▲. *Eglantine, briar rose*
Ful wel she soong the service dyvyne
Entuned▲ in hir nose ful semely, *intoned*
And Frenssh she spak ful faire and fetisly▲ *neatly, gracefully*
After the scole of Stratford atte Bowe▲ *in Essex, East London*
For Frenssh of Parys was to hire unknowe.
At mete▲ wel ytaught was she with alle: *meals*
She leet▲ no morsel from hir lippes falle *allowed, let*
Ne wette hir fyngres in hir sauce deepe;
Wel koude she carie a morsel and wel keepe
That no drope ne fille▲ upon hire brest. *fell*
In curteisye▲ was set ful muchel hir lest▲: *courtliness of manner;*
Hir over lippe wyped she so clene *desire, pleasure*
That in hir coppe▲ ther was no ferthyng▲ sene *cape; morsel, speck*
Of grece▲ whan she dronken hadde hir draughte; *grease*
Ful semely after hir mete she raughte▲, *reached, stretched out*
And sikerly▲ she was of greet desport▲ *certainly; merriment*
And full pleasaunt and amyable of port▲, *demeanour*
And peyned hire to countrefete▲ cheere *imitate*
Of court and to been estatlich▲ of manere *stately*
And to been holden digne▲ of reverence. *worthy*
But for to speken of hir conscience▲, *tender feeling*
She was so charitable and so pitous▲ *merciful*
She wolde wepe if that she sawe a mous
Caught in a trappe if it were deed▲ or bledde. *dead*
Of smale houndes hadde she that she fedde
With rosted flessh or milk and wastel breed▲, *a fine white bread*

115. St Christopher, patron saint of foresters and travellers.
118. The Prioress is the mother superior of her nunnery.
123. ful seemly: very modestly, self consciously decorous.
126. Hers was the French of one who'd learned the language academically and had never experienced the living, best French, that of Paris.

But soore wepte she if oon of hem were deed
stick Or if men smoot it with a yerde▲ smerte,
And al was conscience and tendre herte.
pleated Ful semely hir wympel pynched▲ was,
finely proportioned; eyes Hir nose tretys▲, hir eyen▲ greye as glas,
moreover; red Hir mouth ful smal and therto▲ softe and reed▲,
truly But sikerly▲ she hadde a fair forheed—
It was almoost a spanne brood I trowe,
truly For hardily▲ she was nat undergrowe.
aware Ful fetys was hir cloke as I was war▲.
dainty Of smal▲ coral aboute hir arm she bar
gaudies, large beads of a rosary A peyre of bedes gauded▲ al with grene
And theron heng a brooch of gold ful sheene
On which ther was first writen a crowned A
in Latin: love conquers all And after *Amor vincit omnia*▲.
Another NONNE with hire hadde she
secretary; three That was hir chapeleyne▲, and preestes thre▲.

☆ ☆ ☆

capable of leadership, mastery A MONK ther was, a fair for the maistrie▲,
hunting An outridere that lovede venerie▲,
vigorous, aggressive A manly▲ man, to been an abbot able.
valuable, fine, delightful Ful many a deyntee▲ hors hadde he in stable
rode And whan he rood▲ men myghte his brydel heere
jingling Gynglen▲ in a whistylynge wynd as cleere
And eek as loude as dooth the chapel belle
master of a small house subordinate to the abbey Ther as this lord was kepere of the celle▲.
The reule of Seint Maure or of Seint Beneit
narrow By cause that it was old and som del streit▲,
pass, go, lapse This ilke monk leet olde thynges pace▲
held; room, opportunity And heeld▲ after the newe world the space▲.
plucked hen He yaf nat of that text a pulled hen▲,
are That seith that hunters been▲ nat holy men
careless, neglecting duty Ne that a monk whan he is recchelees▲
to Is likned til▲ a fissh that is waterlees,

151. wympel: wimple, covering head, cheeks, chin and neck.
155. A hand's breadth wide.
166. outridere: he rode out to supervise the abbey's estates.
173. St Maurus and St Benedict were founders of the Benedictine Order which required strict observance of hard physical work and living continuously within a monastery.

	This is to seyn, a monk out of his cloystre;
this	But thilke▲ text heeld he nat worth an oystre,
	And I seyde his opinioun was good:
mad	What sholde he studie and make hym selven wood▲
	Upon a book in cloystre alwey to poure,
labour	Or swynken▲ with his handes and laboure
	As Austyn bit? How shal the world be served?
	Lat Austyn have his swynk to hym reserved!
hard rider using spurs	Ther fore he was a prikasour▲ aright:
	Grehoundes he hadde as swift as fowel in flight;
riding	Of prikyng▲ and of huntyng for the hare
desire, delight	Was al his lust▲, for no cost wolde he spare.
saw; trimmed	I saugh▲ his sleves ypurfiled▲ at the hond
costly grey squirrel's fur	With grys▲ and that the fyneste of a lond,
	And for to festne his hood under his chyn
unusual	He hadde of gold wroght a ful curious▲ pyn:
larger	A love knotte in the gretter▲ encle ther was.
bald	His heed was balled▲ that shoon as any glas
in condition,	And eek his face as he hadde been enoynt;
plump	He was a lord ful fat and in good poynt▲;
large, prominent	Hise eyen stepe▲ and rollynge in his heed
	That stemed as a fourneys of a leed,
supple; condition	His bootes souple▲, his hors in greet estat▲,
an important churchman	Now certeynly he was a fair prelat▲:
tormented	He was nat pale as a forpyned▲ goost,
	A fat swan loved he best of any roost,
saddle horse	His palfrey▲ was as broun as is a berye.

☆ ☆ ☆

wanton	A FRERE ther was, a wantowne▲ and a merye,
ceremonious, pompous	A lymytour, a ful solempne▲ man:
	In alle the ordres foure is noon that kan
flirtation and seductive talk	So muche of daliaunce and fair langage▲;

187. St Augustine had written that monks should perform manual labour.
202. That steamed like a furnace with molten lead in it.
208. The 'Frere' (Friar) is a member of one of four religious orders whose members live by begging; as a 'lymytour' he was granted exclusive begging rights in a certain limited area.
210. ordres foure: Carmelites, Dominicans, Franciscans, Augustinians.

He hadde maad ful many a mariage
Of yonge wommen at his owene cost.
pillar, with an obscene Unto his ordre he was a noble post▲.
connotation Ful wel biloved and famylier was he
With frankeleyns over al in his contree
And with worthy wommen of the toun,
For he hadde power of confessioun,
As seyde him self, moore than a curat,
For of his ordre he was a licenciat.
Ful swetely herde he confessioun
And plesaunt was his absolucioun:
He was an esy man to yeve penaunce
offering of food or money Ther as he wiste to have a good pitaunce▲,
For unto a poure ordre for to yive
forgiven Is signe that a man is wel yshryve▲;
gave; boast For if he yaf▲, he dorst make avaunt▲,
He wiste that a man was repentaunt:
For many a man so hard is of his herte
it pains him sorely, he He may nat wepe althogh hym soore smerte▲;
feels very guilty Ther fore in stede of wepynge and preyeres
might Men moote▲ yeve silver to the poure freres.
hood; stuffed His typet▲ was ay farsed▲ ful of knyves
And pynnes for to yeven faire wyves.
And certeynly he hadde a murye note:
stringed instrument Wel koude he synge and pleyen on a rote▲;
songs, ballads Of yeddynges▲ he bar outrely the prys.
fleur-de-lis, lily His nekke whit was as the flour-delys▲,
Therto he strong was as a champioun.
He knew the tavernes wel in every toun
barmaid And every hostiler▲ and tappestere

212–213. He found husbands for young women he had himself seduced.

216. frankleyns: wealthy landowners, often generous with their food and lodgings to visitors and travellers.

219. an assistant parish priest, trusted with the curing of souls.

220. licenciat: licenced to hear confessions of a more serious nature than local priests could absolve.

230. Before granting absolution, the confessor must be sure the sinner is contrite; moreover the absolution is contingent upon the sinner's performance of an act of contrition. In the case of Chaucer's Friar, a liberal contribution served as both proof of contrition and as satisfaction for the Friar.

Bet than a lazar▲ or a beggestere, *leper*
For onto swich a worthy man as he
Acorded nat as by his facultee▲ *ability, profession*
To have with sike▲ lazars aqueyntaunce, *sick*
It is nat honeste▲, it may nat avaunce▲ *respectable; advance*
For to deelen with no swich poraille▲, *poor people*
But al with riche and selleres of vitaille▲. *food*
And over al ther as profit sholde arise
Curteys he was and lowely of servyse;
Ther nas no man no wher so vertuous.
He was the beste beggere in his hous,
[And yaf a certeyn ferme▲ for the graunt▲: *rent; grant, territory*
Noon of his bretheren cam ther in his haunt▲;] *haunt, the area he frequented*
For thogh a widwe▲ hadde noght a sho▲, *widow; shoe*
So plesaunt was his *In principio*,
Yet wolde he have a ferthyng▲ er he wente: *a small gift*
His purchas was wel bettre than his rente.
And rage▲ he koude as it were right a whelpe. *play wantonly*
In lovedayes ther koude he muchel▲ helpe: *very much*
For ther he was nat lyk a cloystrer
With a thredbare cope as is a poure scoler,
But he was lyk a maister or a pope:
Of double worstede was his semycope▲ *short clerical cape*
That rounded as a belle out of the presse.
Som what he lipsed for his wantownesse
To make his Englissh sweete upon his tonge,
And in his harpyng▲ whan that he hadde songe *playing the harp*
Hise eyen twinkled in his heed aryght
As doon the sterres▲ in the frosty nyght. *stars*
This worthy lymytour was cleped Huberd▲. *like a kite or bird of prey*

☆ ☆ ☆

251. Hard working, for his own gain, not out of virtue. Chaucer is sarcastic.
256. *In principio*: from *John I, 1*, 'In the beginning was the word . . .' People took these words as a sort of magic charm to protect them.
258. His dishonest income was greater than his honest income.
260. lovedays: days for the settlement of disputes, often with clergy arbitrating and making financial gain from the deal.
263. maister: with a Masters degree which conferred great dignity.
265. rounded as a belle out of the presse: rounded like the shape of a bell out of a bell moulding press.
266. He lisped as a deliberate display of lasciviousness.

A MARCHANT was ther with a forked berd,
In mottelee▲, and hye on hors he sat; — *wearing multicoloured clothing*
Upon his heed a Flaundryssh▲ bevere hat, — *in the style of Flanders*
His bootes clasped faire and fetisly.
Hise resons▲ he spak ful solempnely — *opinions*
Sownynge▲ alwey th'encrees of his wynnyng▲. — *proclaiming; profits*
He wolde the see were kept for any thyng
Bitwixe Middelburgh and Orewelle.
Wel koude he in eschaunge sheeldes selle.
This worthy man ful wel his wit bisette▲: — *used intently*
Ther wiste no wight that he was in dette,
So estatly▲ was he of his governaunce▲, — *dignified; conduct of his business*
With his bargaynes▲ and with his chevysaunce. — *sly deals*
For soothe he was a worthy man with alle,
But sooth to seyn I noot▲ how men hym calle. — *not*

☆ ☆ ☆

A CLERK ther was of Oxenford also
That unto logyk hadde longe ygo▲. — *gone, taken to*
As leene was his hors as is a rake
And he nas nat right fat I undertake
But looked holwe▲ and therto sobrely. — *hollow*
Ful thredbare was his overeste courtepy▲ — *outer short cloak*
For he hadde geten hym yet no benefice▲ — *church appointment*
Ne was so wordly for to have office▲, — *secular appointment*
For hym was levere▲ have at his beddes heed — *prefer*
Twenty bookes clad in blak or reed
Of Aristotle and his philosophye
Than robes riche or fithele▲ or gay sautrye▲. — *fiddle; psaltery, small harp*
But al be that he was a philosophre▲ — *philosopher may mean alchemist*
Yet hadde he but litel gold in cofre▲, — *chest*
But al that he myghte of his frendes hente▲ — *get*
On bookes and on lernynge he it spente,
And bisily gan for the soules preye
Of hem that yaf hym wherwith to scoleye▲. — *study*

278. He desired the coast to be protected against any enemy, such as pirates.
280. The implication is of illegal trading in French currency.
284. chevysaunce: dishonest trading is implied.
287. The Clerk is a student of Oxford. To become a student he would have had to signify his intention of becoming a cleric, but he was not bound to proceed to the position of responsibility in the church.

Of studye took he moost cure and moost heede;
Noght o word spak he moore than was neede
And that was seyd in forme and reverence
And short and quyk and ful of hy sentence▲: — *elevated throughout*
Sownynge▲ in moral vertu was his speche — *full of*
And gladly wolde he lerne and gladly teche.

☆ ☆ ☆

A SERGEAUNT OF THE LAWE, war and wys▲, — *cautious and prudent*
That often hadde been at the Parvys,
Ther was also, ful riche of excellence.
Discreet he was and of greet reverence:
He seemed swich, hise wordes weren so wise.
Justice he was ful often in assise▲ — *circuit courts*
By patente and by pleyn commissioun.
For his science▲ and for his heigh renoun, — *knowledge*
Of fees and robes hadde he many oon.
So greet a purchasour was nowher noon:
Al was fee symple▲ to hym in effect, — *absolute possession*
His purchasyng myghte nat been infect▲. — *invalidated*
Nowher so bisy a man as he ther nas▲ — *was not*
And yet he semed bisier than he was.
In termes hadde he caas and doomes alle
That from the tyme of Kyng William▲ were falle. — *William the Conqueror*
Therto he koude endite and make a thyng
Ther koude no wight pynchen▲ at his writyng, — *find fault*
And every statut koude he pleyn by rote▲. — *knew by heart*
He rood but hoomly▲ in a medlee cote▲ — *informally; multicoloured coat*
Girt with a ceint of silk with barres smale;
Of his array telle I no lenger tale.

☆ ☆ ☆

308. quyk: insightful.
311. One of the high justices of the nation.
317. patent: letter authorising his appointment as justice of assizes.
pleyn commission: giving him jurisdiction over all cases.
320. buyer of land for himself, not his clients.
322. It is implied that he is able to convert doubtful land titles into secure titles for his own benefit.
325. doomes: judgements.
327. Compose and make up a legal document.

A FRANKELEYN was in his compaignye. — *wealthy landowner*
Whit was his berd as is the dayesye▲; — *daisy*
Of his complexioun he was sangwyn.
Wel loved he by the morwe▲ a sop in wyn▲; — *in the morning; wine containing pieces of bread*
To lyven in delyt▲ was evere his wone▲ — *pleasure; custom*
For he was Epicurus owene sone
That heeld opinioun that pleyn delit
Was verray felicitee parfit.
An housholdere and that a greet was he;
Seint Julian▲ he was in his contree. — *patron saint of hospitality*
His breed, his ale was alweys after oon,
A bettre envyned▲ man was no wher noon; — *stocked with wine*
Withoute bake mete was nevere his hous,
Of fissh and flessh and that so plentevous▲ — *plentiful*
It snewed▲ in his hous of mete and drynke — *abounded*
Of alle deyntees that men koude thynke.
After▲ the sondry sesons of the yeer — *in the manner of*
So chaunged he his mete▲ and his soper▲. — *dinner; supper*
Ful many a fat patrich hadde he in muwe▲ — *coop*
And many a breem▲ and many a luce in stuwe▲. — *pike; pond*
Wo was his cook but if his sauce were
Poynaunt▲ and sharp, and redy al his gere. — *piquant*
His table dormaunt▲ in his halle alway — *a permanent side table*
Stood redy covered al the longe day.
At sessiouns ther was he lord and sire;
Ful ofte tyme he was knyght of the shire.
An anlaas▲ and a gipser▲ al of silk — *dagger; pouch*
Heeng at his girdel, whit as morne▲ milk. — *morning, therefore fresh*
A shirreve hadde he been and a countour.
Was nowhere swich a worthy vavasour▲. — *country gentleman*

☆ ☆ ☆

335. His temperament, as well as his face, was dominated by blood.
338. Epicurus: Greek philosopher, believed in freedom from pain and fear. He was later misinterpreted as advocating pleasure seeking: pleyn delit.
356. The implication is that he was always ready to receive guests and to entertain them sumptuously.
357. Meetings of Justices of the Peace.
358. Represented his county in parliament.
361. The sheriff was the king's administrative officer in a shire or county. As counter, he would also be the auditor.

An HABERDASSHERE and a CARPENTER,
A WEBBE, a DYERE and a TAPYCER
the particular mode of dress of an organisation And they were clothed alle in o lyveree▲
Of a solempne and a greet fraternitee.
adorned Ful fressh and newe hir geere apyked▲ was,
tipped Hir knyves were chaped▲ noght with bras
But al with silver, wroght ful clene and wel,
every one Hire girdles and hir pouches everydel▲.
Wel semed ech of hem a fair burgeys
guildhall; dais To sitten in a yeldehalle▲ on a deys▲;
Everich for the wisdom that he can
magistrate, councillor Was shaply for to been an alderman▲,
property; income For catel▲ hadde they ynogh and rente▲
And eek hir wyves wolde it wel assente,
And ellis certeyn were they to blame:
It is ful fair to been ycleped 'Madame'
And goon to vigilies al bifore
borne, carried And have a mantel roialliche ybore▲.

☆ ☆ ☆

occasion A COOK they hadde with hem for the nones▲
marrow bones To boile the chiknes with the marybones▲
And poudre marchaunt tart and galyngale.
Wel koude he knowe a draughte of Londoun ale.
boil He koude rooste ad seethe▲ and broille and frye,
a thick soup Maken mortreux▲ and wel bake a pye,
as it seemed to me But greet harm was it as it thoughte▲ me
a scabbed ulcer That on his shyne a mormal▲ hadde he;
For blankmanger, that made he with the beste.

☆ ☆ ☆

364. webbe: weaver, tapycer: maker of tapestries.
371. member of the governing body of a town.
379. saints day vigils at which alderman's wives took precedence.
383. marchaunt: a seasoning; galyngale: a spice.
384. recognise that a particular ale was London ale and therefore expensive and of good quality.
389. blankmanger: creamed capon.

living A SHIPMAN was ther wonyng▲ fer by weste:
know For aught I woot▲ he was of Dertemouthe.
He rood upon a rouncy as he kouthe
a coarse woollen fabric In a gowne of faldyng▲ to the knee;
cord A daggere hangynge on a laas▲ hadde he
Aboute his nekke under his arm adoun.
colour, complexion The hoote somer hadde maad his hewe▲ al broun.
And certeinly he was a good felawe:
Ful many a draughte of wyn hadde he drawe
wine merchant Fro Burdeuxward whil that the chapman▲ sleep;
scrupulous, fussy; regard Of nyce▲ conscience took he no keep▲;
If that he faught and hadde the hyer hond
By water he sente hem hoom to every lond.
But of his craft, to rekene wel his tydes,
currents; immediate dangers His stremes▲ and his daungers hym bisydes▲,
His herberwe and his moone, his lodemenage,
Ther nas noon swich from Hulle to Cartage.
Hardy he was and wys to undertake;
With many a tempest hadde his berd been shake.
safe ports He knew alle the havenes▲ as they were
Fro Gootlond to the cape of Fynystere,
inlet And every cryke▲ in Britaigne and in Spayne.
His barge ycleped was the *Maudelayne*.

☆ ☆ ☆

With us ther was a DOCTOUR OF PHISIK:
In al this world ne was ther noon hym lik
To speke of phisik and of surgerye,
astrology For he was grounded in astronomye▲:
He kepte his pacient a ful greet del
In houres by his magyk naturel;

391. Dartmouth, in Devon, was a refuge for smugglers and pirates.
392. He rode as best he could on a sturdy horse, of a sort an experienced rider would not have chosen.
398. drawn from the casks he was transporting: he stole from his clients.
399. Burdeuxward: on the way from Bordeaux, then an English possession known for its wine.
405. shelter; phases of the moon; navigation.
406. from Hull in England to the Mediterranean.
410. from the Baltic to northern Spain.
411. Britanny, the north west coast of France.
417–18. He managed his patients by dosing according to the timing prescribed by his natural magic—astrology.

Wel koude he fortunen the ascendent
Of his ymages for his pacient.
He knew the cause of every maladye,
Were it of hoot or coold or moyste or drye
And where engendred and of what humour:
a truly complete practitioner He was a verray, parfit practisour▲.
known The cause yknowe▲ and of his harm the roote,
remedy Anon he yaf the sike man his boote▲.
Ful redy hadde he hise apothecaries
syrupy medicines To sende hym drogges and his letuaries▲,
to profit For ech of hem made oother for to wynne▲;
Hir friendshipe nas nat newe to bigynne.
Wel knew he the olde Esculapius
And Deyscorides and eek Rufus,
Olde Ypocras, Haly and Galyen,
Serapion, Razis and Avycen,
Averrois, Damascien and Constantyn,
Bernard and Gatesden and Gilbertyn.
moderate Of his diete mesurable▲ was he
For it was of no superfluitee
nutriment But of greet norissyng▲ and digestible.
His studye was but litel on the Bible.
red; blue In sangwyn▲ and in pers▲ he clad was al
fine, expensive silk Lyned with taffata and with sendal▲,
cautious in spending And yet he was but esy of dispence▲:
time of plague He kepte that he wan in pestilence▲,
tonic For gold in phisik is a cordial▲;
Ther fore he loved gold in special.

☆ ☆ ☆

418. The use of astrology.
419–420. Medallions inscribed with zodiacal signs. The skill was in knowing which signs to inscribe. This depended upon which signs were ascendant, above the horizon.
422–423. Human health was thought to be dominated by four humours: melancholy—cold and dry; phlegm—cold and moist; blood—hot and moist; bile—hot and dry.
431–436. medical authorities, from the legendary founder of medicine, Aesculapius, to Hippocrates of Greece in the 5th century BC, to authorities of Chaucer's own time.

	A good WYF was ther of biside BATHE
somewhat; a pity	But she was som del▲ deef and that was scathe▲.
knowledge	Of clooth makyng she hadde swich an haunt▲
surpassed	She passed▲ hem of Ypres and of Gaunt.
	In al the parisshe wyf ne was ther noon
offering in Church	That to the offrynge▲ bifore hire sholde goon,
	And if ther dide, certeyn so wrooth was she
	That she was out of alle charitee.
texture	Hir coverchiefs ful fyne were of ground▲,
dare; weighed	I dorste▲ swere they weyeden▲ ten pound
	That on a Sonday weren upon hir heed;
stockings	Hir hosen▲ weren of fyn scarlet reed
tightly; supple	Ful streite▲ yteyd, and shoes ful moyste▲ and newe.
	Boold was hir face and fair and reed of hewe.
respectable	She was a worthy▲ womman al hir lyve:
	Housbondes at chirche dore she hadde fyve
	Withouten oother compaignye in youthe,
now	But therof nedeth nat to speke as nouthe▲.
	And thries hadde she been at Jerusalem;
foreign	She hadde passed many a straunge▲ strem:
Boulogne	At Rome she hadde been and at Boloyne▲,
Galicia; Cologne	In Galice▲ at Seint Jame and at Coloyne▲;
knew	She koude▲ muche of wandrynge by the weye:
gap toothed, implying lustiness	Gat tothed▲ was she soothly for to seye.
saddle horse	Upon an amblere▲ esily she sat
	Ywympled wel and on hir heed an hat
small round shield; target	As brood as is a bokeler▲ or a targe▲,
outer protective skirt	A foot mantel▲ aboute hir hipes large
spurs	And on hir feet a peyre of spores▲ sharpe.
chatter	In felawshipe wel koude she laughe and carpe▲;
from random experience	Of remedies of love she knew par chaunce▲,
love making	For she koude of that art the olde daunce▲.

☆ ☆ ☆

452. parishioners went up to the altar rail to make offerings in order of social precedence.
455. coverchiefs: kerchiefs, a linen covering for the head built up on a framework of wire.
462. The marriage ceremony was performed at the church door, not inside the church. A nuptial service was then held inside.
472. wearing a wimple, a covering for the neck.

A good man was ther of religioun
parish priest And was a poure PERSOUN▲ of a toun
But riche he was of holy thoght and werk.
He was also a lerned man, a clerk
conscientiously That Cristes gospel trewely▲ wolde preche:
His parisshens devoutly wolde he teche.
wondrously Benygne he was and wonder▲ diligent
And in adversitee ful pacient
proved; times And swich he was preved▲ ofte sithes▲.
to excommunicate Ful looth were hym to cursen▲ for his tithes,
certainly But rather wolde he yeven out of doute▲
Unto his poure parisshens aboute
Of his offryng and eek of his substaunce;
He koude in litel thyng have suffisaunce.
Wyd was his parisshe and houses fer asonder,
But he ne lefte nat for reyn ne thonder,
mishap In siknesse nor in meschief▲ to visite
farthest; prominent and humble The ferreste▲ in his parisshe, muche and lite▲,
Upon his feet, and in his hand a staf.
example This noble ensample▲ to his sheep he yaf
acted That first he wroghte▲ and afterward he taughte;
those; took Out of the gospel he tho▲ wordes caughte▲,
And this figure he added eek therto
That if gold ruste, what shal iren do?
For if a preest be foul on whom we truste,
ignorant No wonder is a lewed▲ man to ruste;
heed, realise And shame it is, if a preest take keep▲,
foul A shiten▲ shepherde and a clene sheep;
Wel oghte a preest ensample for to yive
By his clennesse how that his sheep sholde lyve.

482. It was worth mentioning that he was learned because parish priests were often ignorant, even of the Bible.
484. parishioners: people who lived in the area for which he was responsible.
491. The offering he received at Easter and his regular income.
491. He could manage on little.
494. He was not deterred by anything from visiting his parishioners.

He sette nat his benefice to hyre
And leet his sheep encombred in the myre
And ran to Londoun unto Seint Poules
To seken hym a chauntrye for soules
retained Or with a bretherhede to been witholde▲,
But dwelte at hoom and kepte wel his folde
So that the wolf ne made it nat myscarye:
He was a shepherde and noght a mercenarye.
And thogh he holy were and vertuous,
contemptuous He was to synful men nat despitous▲
neither arrogant nor superior Ne of his speche daungerous ne digne▲,
But in his techyng discreet and benigne;
To drawen folk to hevene by fairnesse,
By good ensample, this was his bisynesse;
if But it▲ were any persone obstinat,
What so he were, of heigh or lowe estat,
rebuke; on the occasion Hym wolde he snybben▲ sharply for the nonys▲.
warrant A bettre preest I trowe▲ that nowher noon ys:
expected or sought He waited after▲ no pompe and reverence
over scrupulous conscience Ne maked him a spiced conscience▲,
teaching But Cristes loore▲ and his apostles twelve
He taughte but first he folwed it hym selve.

☆ ☆ ☆

With hym ther was a PLOWMAN, was his brother,
led; cartload That hadde ylad▲ a dong ful many a fother▲;
honest labourer A trewe swynkere▲ and a good was he
peace Lyvynge in pees▲ and parfit charitee.
whole God loved he best with al his hoole▲ herte
whether it was pleasant or painful At alle tymes thogh him gamed or smerte▲,
And thanne his neighebore right as hym selve:
make ditches; dig He wolde thresshe and therto dyke▲ and delve▲
For Cristes sake, for every poure wight,
Withouten hire, if it lay in his myght;
His tithes payde he full faire and wel
labour; goods Both of his propre swynk▲ and his catel▲.
a smock; mare In a tabard▲ he rood upon a mere▲.

509–16. Some priests left the hard work of their own parish to a poorly paid curate, and themselves sought easier well paid work, such as being chaplain to a guild (bretherhede), or in a chapel (chauntrye) in a great church, such as St Paul's.

19
GEOFFREY CHAUCER

Ther was also a REVE and a MILLERE,
A SOMNOUR and a PARDONER also,
A MAUNCIPLE and my self, ther were namo.

☆ ☆ ☆

The MILLERE was a stout carl▲ for the nones▲, — *strong fellow; for the occasion*
Ful byg he was of brawn▲ and eek of bones; — *muscles*
That proved wel, for over al ther he cam
At wrastlynge he wolde have alwey the ram▲. — *the usual prize*
He was short sholdred, brood▲, a thikke knarre: — *thickset fellow*
Ther was no dore that he nolde heve of harre▲ — *heave off its hinges*
Or breke it at a rennyng▲ with his heed▲. — *running; head*
His berd as any sowe or fox was reed▲ — *red*
And therto brood as thogh it were a spade;
Upon the cop right▲ of his nose he hade — *very top*
A werte▲, and theron stood a tuft of herys — *wart*
Reed as the bristles of a sowes erys▲; — *ears*
His nosethirles▲ blake were and wyde. — *nostrils*
A swerd and bokeler▲ bar▲ he by his syde. — *small round shield; carried*
His mouth as greet was as a greet fourneys,
He was a janglere▲ and a goliardeys▲, — *loudmouth; obscene storyteller*
And that was moost of synne and harlotries▲. — *ribald jests*
Wel koude he stelen corn and tollen thries▲ — *charge three times as much*
And yet he hadde a thombe of gold, pardee▲. — *a common oath—by God*
A whit cote and a blew hood wered▲ he, — *wore*
A baggepipe wel koude he blowe and sowne▲ — *sound*
And therwithal▲ he broghte us out of towne. — *with it*

☆ ☆ ☆

A gentil MAUNCIPLE was ther of a temple,
Of which achatours▲ myghte tale exemple — *purchasers*
For to be wise in byynge of vitaille▲: — *provisions*
For wheither that he payde or took by taille▲ — *on account*
Algate he wayted so in his achaat
That he was ay biforn▲ and in good staat▲. — *ahead; financial position*

551. literally a thick knot, a rough formidable fellow, physically.
564–565. He was a good judge of corn and could, therefore, make a good living as a miller either honestly or dishonestly.
569. A buyer of provisions for one of the Inns of Court, London courts.
573. He always waited for the right moment to buy.

	Now is nat that of God a ful fair grace
unlearned	That swich a lewed▲ mannes wit shal pace
	The wisdom of an heep of lerned men?
superiors, learned men	Of maistres▲ hadde he mo than thries ten
skilful	That weren of lawe expert and curious▲,
	Of whiche ther were a dozeyne in that hous
chief managers of estates	Worthy to been stywardes▲ of rente and lond
	Of any lord that it in Engelond
within his income	To make hym lyve by his propre good▲
useless; mad	In honour dettelees▲, but if he were wood▲,
economically	Or lyve as scarsly▲ as hym list desire;
	And able for to helpen al a shire
event; befall	In any caas▲ that myghte falle▲ or happe;
	And yet this maunciple sette hir aller cappe.

☆ ☆ ☆

	The REVE was a sclendre colerik man.
short	His berd was shave as neigh▲ as ever he kan,
	His heer was by his erys ful round yshorn,
cut very short	His top was dokked▲ lyk a preest biforn,
	Ful longe were his legges and ful lene
to be seen	Ylyk a staf, ther was no calf ysene▲.
manage; granary; corn bin	Wel koude ke kepe▲ a gerner▲ and a bynne▲,
	Ther was noon auditour koude on him wynne;
knew	Wel wiste▲ he by the droghte and by the reyn
	The yeldynge of his seed and of his greyn.
cattle	His lordes sheep, his neet▲, his dayerye,
livestock	His swyn, his hors, his stoor▲ and his pultrye
wholly	Was hoolly▲ in this reves governynge,
contract; presented the accounts	And by his covenant▲ yaf the rekenynge▲
	Syn that his lord was twenty yeer of age;
show him to be in arrears with his debts	Ther koude no man brynge hym in arrerage▲.
herdsman; farm labourer	Ther nas baillif ne hierde▲ nor oother hyne▲
cunning; fraud	That he ne knew his sleighte▲ and his covyne▲;
dreaded, feared; the plague	They were adrad▲ of hym as of the deeth▲.

588. Tipped the caps of all of them, ie. made fools of them all.
589. A reeve was manager of part of an estate; colerik: choleric and, therefore, having the qualities of leanness, sharp wits, and irritability.
596. He saw himself as in competition with auditors. They couldn't catch him out in his dishonest tricks.

house His wonyng▲ was ful faire upon an heeth;
With grene trees shadwed was his place.
buy or acquire He koude bettre than his lord purchace▲;
stocked; secretly Ful riche he was astored▲ pryvely▲;
His lord wel koude he plesen subtilly
lend; goods To yeve and lene▲ hym of his owene good▲
reward of coat and hood And have a thank and yet a cote and hood▲.
trade In youthe he hadde lerned a good mister▲:
craftsman He was a wel good wrighte▲, a carpenter.
steed This reve sat upon a ful good stot▲
dappled; called That was al pomely▲ grey and highte▲ Scot;
outer coat; a rich light blue A long surcote▲ of pers▲ upon he hade
carried And by his syde he bar▲ a rusty blade.
Of Northfolk was this reve of which I telle,
Bawdswell in northern Norfolk Biside a toun men clepen Baldeswelle▲.
Tukked he was as is a frere aboute
And evere he rood the hyndreste of oure route.

☆ ☆ ☆

A SOMNOUR was ther with us in that place
That hadde a fyr reed cherubynnes face,
pimples, inflamed skin; narrowed by swelling For saucefleem▲ he was with eyen narwe▲;
fervent, hot; sparrow As hoot▲ he was and lecherous as a sparwe▲,
scaly, scabby With scalled▲ browes blake and piled berd;
afraid Of his visage children were aferd▲:
Ther nas quyk silver, lytarge ne brymstoon,
various ointments; none Boras, ceruce ne oile of tartre▲ noon▲
Ne oynement that wolde clense and byte
large pimples that hym myghte helpen of his whelkes▲ white
lumps, pimples Nor of the knobbes▲ sittynge on his chekes.
Wel loved he garleek, oynons and eek lekes
And for to drynken strong wyn reed as blood;
mad Thanne wolde he speke and crie as he were wood▲,

608. heeth: an open place, so he could see who approached.
623. His outer coat was tucked into his girdle for ease of movement.
625. Summoners called offenders to the Archdeacons' courts which tried moral cases. In this work, Summoners were notoriously open to corruption.
626. He looked like a corrupt angel.
629. piled berd: a beard from which much of the hair had fallen.
632. Ointments for diseases of the skin.

And whan that he wel dronken hadde the wyn
Thanne wolde he speke no word but Latyn.
 A fewe termes hadde he, two or three
That he had lerned out of som decree:
No wonder is, he herde it al the day,
And eek ye knowen wel how that a jay
Kan clepen 'Watte'▲ as wel as kan the pope. — *birds were taught to say this*
But whoso koude in oother thyng hym grope▲, — *test*
Thanne hadde he spent al his philosophye▲: — *'philosophy', such as it was*
Ay *Questio quid juris* wolde he crie.
 He was a gentil harlot▲ and a kynde, — *rogue*
A better felawe sholde men noght fynde:
He wolde suffre▲ for a quart of wyn — *allow, permit*
A good felawe▲ to have his concubyn — *good mate*
A twelf month and excuse hym atte fulle;
Ful prively a fynch eek koude he pulle.
And if he foond owher▲ a good felawe — *found anywhere*
He wolde techen him to have noon awe
In swich caas of the ercedeknes curs▲, — *Archdeacon's curse, excommunication*
But if▲ a mannes soule were in his purs, — *unless*
For in his purs he sholde ypunysshed be:
Purs is the ercedeknes helle, seyde he;
But wel I woot he lyed right in dede:
Of cursyng▲ oghte ech gilty man him drede — *excommunication*
For curs wol slee▲ right as assoillyng▲ savith, — *kill the soul; absolution*
And also war hym of a *significavit*.
 In daunger hadde he at his owene gise▲ — *in his power*
The yonge gerles▲ of the diocise, — *young people of either sex*
And knew hir conseil and was al hir reed▲. — *their adviser in all things*
 A gerland hadde he set upon his heed
As greet as it were for an ale stake;
A bokeler hadde he maad hym of a cake▲. — *a round, flat loaf of bread*

☆ ☆ ☆

648. Ay: always; *Questio quid juris*: in Latin: The question is which (part) of the law (applies). This was one of the 'fewe termes' he had heard in court.

654. This implies that the summoner secretly had illicit relationships like those of other 'good fellows'.

664. *significavit*: the first Latin word of the order assigning an offender to imprisonment by the civil authorities.

669. ale stake: a pole outside a tavern from which a garland was suspended.

With hym ther rood a gentil PARDONER
companion Of Rouncivale, his freend and his comper▲
the Vatican, source of indulgences That streight was comen fro the court of Rome▲.
sang Ful loude he soong▲ *Com hider love to me.*
This somnour bar to hym a stif burdoun,
Was nevere trompe of half so greet a soun.
wax This pardoner hadde heer as yelow as wex▲,
flax But smothe it heeng as dooth a strike of flex▲;
wisps By ounces▲ henge his lokkes that he hadde
overspread And therwith he his shuldres overspradde▲,
in shreds But thynne it lay by colpons▲ oon and oon;
comfort; wore But hood, for jolitee▲ wered▲ he noon
bag For it was trussed up in his walet▲;
the latest fashion Hym thoughte he rood al of the newe jet▲:
unkempt Dischevelee▲ save his cappe he rood al bare.
Swiche glarynge eyen hadde he as an hare.
A vernycle hadde he sowed upon his cappe,
His walet biforn hym in his lappe
brimful; hot Bretful▲ of pardoun comen from Rome al hoot▲.
high; goat A voys he hadde as smal▲ as hath a goot▲;
No berd hadde he ne nevere sholde have,
As smothe it was as it were late yshave:
warrant I trowe▲ he were a geldyng or a mare.
from North to South of England But of his craft, fro Berwyk into Ware▲
Ne was ther swich another pardoner,
bag; pillow case For in his male▲ he hadde a pilwe beer▲
Which that he seyde was Oure Lady veyl;
scrap He seyde he hadde a gobet▲ of the seyl
That Seint Peter hadde whan that he wente
called Upon the see til Jesu Crist hym hente▲;

671. Pardoners sold papal indulgences which temporarily pardoned people from penance. Although only God could pardon the sin itself, the difference between the two kinds of pardon became blurred.
672. Rouncivale: The Order of St Mary Roncevalles, notorious for its trading in 'pardons'.
675–676. stif burdoun: bass part, also a cudgel; trompe: short trumpet. The two lines imply a homosexual relationship between the summoner and the pardoner.
687. vernicle: a copy of the handkerchief of St Veronica, with Christ's face on it, token of a pilgrimage to Rome.
690. implying lustful effeminacy.

cross of latten,	He hadde a croys of latoun▲ ful of stones
a cheap metal	And in a glas he hadde pigges bones;
relics; found	But with thise relikes▲, whan that he fond▲
parson	A poure persoun▲ dwellynge upon lond,
on any day he got	Upon a day he gat▲ hym moore moneye
two	Than that the persoun gat in monthes tweye▲;
insincere; tricks	And thus with feyned▲ flaterye and japes▲
	He made the persoun and the peple his apes.
	But trewely to tellen atte laste
	He was in chirche a noble ecclesiaste:
history, story of a saint,	Wel koude he rede a lessoun or a storie▲
or the like	
best; anthem during offering	But alderbest▲ he song an offertorie▲,
knew	For wel he wiste▲ whan that song was songe
must; sharpen	He moste▲ preche and wel affile▲ his tonge
	To wynne silver, as he ful wel koude;
more merrily	Ther fore he song the murierly▲ and loude.
briefly	Now have I toold you soothly in a clause▲,
social rank	Th'estaat▲, th'array, the nombre, and eek the cause
	Why that assembled was this compaignye
	In Southwerk at this gentil hostelrye
close to The Bell, another inn	That highte the Tabard, faste by the Belle▲.
	But now is tyme to yow for to telle
what we did, behaved; same	How that we baren▲ us that ilke▲ nyght
	Whan we were in that hostelrye alyght;
journey	And after wol I telle of our viage▲
	And al the remenaunt of oure pilgrymage.
	But first I pray yow of youre curteisye
rough language, ill breeding	That ye n'arette it nat my vileynye▲
	Thogh that I pleynly speke in this mateere
behaviour	To telle yow hir wordes and hir cheere▲,
precisely, in their own words	Ne thogh I speke hir wordes proprely▲,
	For this ye knowen al so wel as I,
	Whoso shal telle a tale after a man,
might rehearse	He moot reherce▲ as neigh as evere he kan
if it be his task	Everich a word, if it be in his charge▲,
Although he speaks;	Al speke he▲ nevere so rudeliche▲ and large▲,
crudely; unrestrainedly	Or ellis he moot telle his tale untrewe

708. made fools, apes, of them.

invent; find Or feyne▲ thyng or fynde▲ wordes newe;
He may nat spare althogh he were his brother,
He may as wel seye o word as another.
in common speech Crist spak hym self ful brode▲ in holy writ
And wel ye woot no vileynye is it;
Greek philosopher Eek Plato▲ seith, whoso kan hym rede,
cousin The wordes mote be cosyn▲ to the dede.
  Also I prey yow to foryeye it me
even though; social order Al▲ have I nat set folk in hir degree▲
Heere in this tale as that they sholde stonde:
My wit is short ye may wel understonde.
  Greet cheere made oure hoost us everichon
And to the souper sette he us anon.
He served us with vitaille at the beste:
we were pleased Strong was the wyn and wel to drynke us leste▲.
  A semely man oure HOOST was with alle
For to been a marchal in an halle:
prominent A large man he was with eyen stepe▲,
prosperous, respected citizen A fairer burgeys▲ is ther noon in Chepe,
Boold of his speche and wys and wel ytaught
And of manhode hym lakked right naught.
  Eek therto he was right a murye man,
to be sociable And after souper pleyen▲ he bigan
entertainment And spak of myrthe▲ amonges othere thynges
paid the bill Whan that we hadde maad oure rekenynges▲,
And seyde thus: "Now lordynges, trewely
heartily Ye been to me right welcome hertely▲,
For by my trouthe if that I shal nat lye,
I saugh nat this yeer so murye a compaignye
inn At ones in this herberwe▲ as is now.
Fayn wolde I doon yow myrthe, wiste I how;
And of a myrthe I am right now bythoght
pleasure To doon yow ese▲, and it shal coste noght.
  Ye goon to Caunterbury, God yow speede;
give you your reward The blisful martir quyte yow youre meede▲!

749. The 'Hoost' is the landlord of the Tabard Inn.
754. Host in a house of a lord.
756. Cheapside: a commercial area of London.
768. I would dearly like to give you amusement, if I knew how.

And wel I woot as ye goon by the weye
Ye shapen yow to talen and to pleye;
For trewely confort ne myrthe is noon
stone To ride by the weye domb as a stoon▲,
And ther fore wol I maken yow disport
before As I seyde erst▲, and doon yow som confort;
And if yow liketh alle by oon assent
abide by For to stonden at▲ my juggement
And for to werken as I shal yow seye,
Tomorwe whan ye ryden by the weye,
father's Now by my fader▲ soule that is deed,
unless; head But▲ ye be myrie I wol yeve yow myn heed▲.
Hoold up youre hondes withouten moore speche."
seek Oure conseil was nat longe for to seche▲,
a serious matter Us thoughte it was noght worth to make it wys▲,
advise And graunted hym withouten moore avys▲
verdict; choose And bad him seye his voirdit▲ as hym leste▲.
"Lordynges," quod he, "now herkneth for the beste,
But taketh it not, I preye yow, in desdeyn;
This is the pynt, to speken short and pleyn,
That ech of yow to shorte with oure weye
In this viage shal telle tales tweye
To Caunterburyward, I mene it so,
And homward he shal tellen othere two,
once upon a time Of aventures that whilom▲ han bifalle;
And which of yow that bereth hym best of alle,
That is to seyn, that telleth in this cas
moral truth; amusement Tales of best sentence▲ and moost solas▲,
at the expense of all of us Shal have a souper at oure aller cost▲
Here in this place, sittynge by his post,
Whan that we come agayn fro Caunterbury.
merry And for to make yow the moore mury▲
generously, gladly I wol my self goodly▲ with yow ryde
Right at my owene cost, and be youre gyde;
dispute And whoso wol my juggement withseye▲
Shal paye al that we spenden by the weye.

774. You intend to tell stories and to amuse yourselves.
793. With which to shorten our way, pass the time pleasantly.

And if ye vouche sauf that it be so
Tel me anon withouten wordes mo▲ — *more*
And I wol erly shape me▲ ther fore." — *prepare myself*
  This thyng was graunted and oure othes swore
With ful glad herte, and preyden▲ hym also — *prayed, asked*
That he wolde vouche sauf for to do so
And that he wolde been oure governour
And of oure tales juge and reportour▲ — *explain his judgement*
And sette a souper at a certeyn prys▲ — *price*
And we wol reuled been at his devys▲ — *planning*
In heigh and lough; and thus by oon assent
We been acorded to his juggement.
And therupon the wyn was fet▲ anon, — *fetched*
We dronken and to reste wente echon
Withouten any lenger▲ taryynge. — *further*
  A-morwe▲ whan that day bigan to sprynge, — *next morning*
Up roos oure hoost and was oure aller cok
And gadred us togidre in a flok
And forth we riden a litel moore than pas — *the horses could drink there,*
Unto the wateryng of Seint Thomas▲; — *at the second mile post*
And there oure hoost bigan his hors areste▲ — *rein in*
And seyde, "Lordynges, herkneth if yow leste▲! — *will*
Ye woot youre foreward and it yow recorde▲. — *agreement*
If evensong and morwesong acorde▲, — *morningsong agree*
Lat se now who shal telle the firste tale.
As evere mote I drynke wyn or ale,
Whoso be rebel to my juggement
Shal paye for al that by the wey is spent.
Now draweth cut er that we ferrer twynne:
He which that hath the shortese shal bigynne.
Sire knyght", quod he, "my mayster and my lord,
Now draweth cut, for that is myn acord▲. — *the agreement I settled upon*
Cometh neer", quod he, "my lady prioresse,
And ye sire clerk, lat be youre shamefastnesse▲ — *modesty*
Ne studieth noght; ley hond to, every man."

825. Our cock, he roused us all.
827. A little more than foot pace.

Anon to drawen every wight bigan,
And shortly for to tellen as it was,
luck; lot; chance Were it by aventure▲ or sort▲ or cas▲
truth; fell The sothe▲ is this, the cut fel▲ to the knyght,
Of which ful blithe and glad was every wyght;
must; appropriate And telle he moste▲ his tale, as was resoun▲
agreement By foreward and by composicioun▲
As ye han herd; what nedeth wordes mo?
And whan thos goode man saugh that it was so,
As he that wys was and obedient
To kepe his foreward by his free assent,
He seyde, "Syn I shal bigynne the game,
What, welcome be the cut, a Goddes name!
Now lat us ryde and herkneth what I seye."
And with that word we ryden forth oure weye,
cheerful manner And he bigan with right a myrie cheere▲
His tale anon, and seyde as ye may heere.

THE WIFE OF BATH'S TALE

In th'olde dayes of the king Arthour,
have spoken Of which that Britons speken▲ greet honour,
troops of fairies Al was this land fulfild of fayerye▲.
The elf-queen, with hir joly companye,
Daunced ful ofte in many a grene mede;
as I understand it This was the olde opinion, as I rede▲.
I speke of manye hundred yeres ago;
But now can no man see none elves mo.
For now the grete charitee and prayeres
Of limitours and othere holy freres,
That serchen every lond and every streem,
As thikke as motes in the sonne-beem,
Blessinge halles, chambres, kichenes, boures,
boroughs; high towers Citees, burghes▲, castels, hye toures▲,

10. Limitours: friars licensed to beg within a limited area.
13. living rooms, rooms, kitchens, bedrooms.

Thropes, bernes, shipnes, dayeryes,
This maketh that ther been no fayeryes.
For ther as wont to walken was an elf,
Ther walketh now the limitour himself
afternoons In undermeles▲ and in morweninges,
And seyth his matins and his holy thinges
his assigned area As he goth in his limitacioun▲.
safely Wommen may go saufly▲ up and doun,
In every bush, or under every tree;
evil spirit Ther is noon other incubus▲ but he,
And he ne wol doon hem but dishonour.
  And so bifel it, that this king Arthour
Hadde in his hous a lusty bacheler,
That on a day cam rydinge fro river;
And happed that, allone as she was born,
He saugh a mayde walkinge him biforn,
Of whiche mayde anon, maugree hir heed,
took By verray force he rafte▲ hir maydenheed;
For which oppressioun was swich clamour
such And swich▲ pursute un-to the king Arthour,
That dampned was this knight for to be deed
By cours of lawe, and sholde han lost his heed
perhaps Paraventure▲, swich was the statut tho;
But that the quene and othere ladies mo
So longe preyeden the king of grace,
Til he his lyf him graunted in the place,
And yaf him to the quene al at hir wille,
choose To chese▲, whether she wolde him save or spille.
  The quene thanketh the king with al hir might,
And after this thus spak she to the knight,
saw her opportunity Whan that she saugh hir tyme▲, up-on a day:
said 'Thou standest yet,' quod▲ she, 'in swich array,
you have no certainty That of thy lyf yet hastow no suretee▲.
I grante thee lyf, if thou canst tellen me
desire What thing is it that wommen most desyren▲?
neck bone; anger Be war, and keep thy nekke-boon▲ from yren▲.

15. thropes: small villages; shipnes: stables, sheds.
31. In spite of all she could do.

And if thou canst nat tellen it anon,
Yet wol I yeve thee leve for to gon
seek and learn A twelf-month and a day, to seche and lere▲
An answere suffisant in this matere.
And suretee wol I han, er that thou pace,
Thy body for to yelden in this place.'
sighed Wo was this knight and sorwefully he syketh▲;
But what! he may nat do al as him lyketh.
And at the laste, he chees him for to wende,
And come agayn, right at the yeres ende,
With swich answere as god wolde him purveye;
And taketh his leve, and wendeth forth his weye.
He seketh every hous and every place,
Wher-as he hopeth for to finde grace,
To lerne, what thing wommen loven most;
coast But he ne coude arryven in no cost▲,
Wher-as he mighte finde in this matere
together Two creatures accordinge in-fere▲.
Somme seyde, wommen loven best richesse,
Somme seyde, honour, somme seyde, jolynesse;
Somme, riche array, somme seyden, lust abedde,
And ofte tyme to be widwe and wedde.
Somme seyde, that our hertes been most esed,
flattered; given pleasure Whan that we been y-flatered▲ and y-plesed▲.
He gooth ful ny the sothe, I wol nat lye;
A man shal winne us best with flaterye;
And with attendance, and with bisinesse,
Been we y-lymed, bothe more and lesse.
And somme seyn, how that we loven best
For to be free, and do right as us lest,
And that no man repreve us of our vyce,
prudent; foolish But seye that we by wyse▲, and no-thing nyce▲.
For trewely, ther is noon of us alle,
If any wight wol clawe us on the galle,
That we nil kike, for he seith us sooth;
Assay, and he shal finde it that so dooth.

78. Caught, like birds with bird lime.
84. Rub us on the sore spot.

For be we never so vicious with-inne,
We wol been holden wyse, and clene of sinne.
And somme seyn, that greet delyt han we
able to keep secrets For to ben holden stable and eek secree▲,
And in o purpos stedefastly to dwelle,
betray, reveal And nat biwreye▲ thing that men us telle.
the handle of a rake But that tale is nat worth a rake-stele▲;
conceal Pardee, we wommen conne no-thing hele▲;
Midas Witnesse on Myda▲; wol ye here the tale?
Ovid Ovyde▲, amonges othere thinges smale,
Seyde, Myda hadde, under his longe heres,
Growinge up-on his heed two asses eres,
The whiche vyce he hidde, as he best mighte,
Ful subtilly from every mannes sighte,
That, save his wyf, ther wiste of it na-mo.
He loved hir most, and trusted hir also;
He preyede hir, that to no creature
She sholde tellen of his disfigure.
She swoor him 'nay, for al this world to winne,
She nolde do that vileinye or sinne,
To make hir housbond han so foul a name;
She nolde nat telle it for hir owene shame.
she would die But nathelees, hir thoughte that she dyde▲,
secret That she so longe sholde a conseil▲ hyde;
Hir thoughte it swal so sore aboute hir herte,
escape, burst out That nedely som word hir moste asterte▲;
And sith she dorste telle it to no man,
nearby marsh Doun to a mareys faste▲ by she ran;
Til she came there, hir herte was a-fyre,
And, as a bitore bombleth in the myre,
She leyde hir mouth un-to the water doun:
'Biwreye me nat, thou water, with thy soun,'
Quod she, 'to thee I telle it, and namo;
Myn housbond hath longe asses eres two!
sound Now is myn herte all hool▲, now is it oute;
I mighte no lenger kepe it, out of doute.'
Heer may ye se, thogh we a tyme abyde,

116. as a bittern booms in the mire.

must Yet out it moot▲, we can no conseil hyde;
The remenant of the tale if ye wol here,
learn Redeth Ovyde, and ther ye may it lere▲.
This knight, of which my tale is specially,
Whan that he saugh he mighte nat come thereby,
This is to seye, what wommen loven moost,
then became With-inne his brest ful sorweful was the goost▲;
home But hoom▲ he gooth, he mighte nat sojourne.
The day was come, that hoomward moste he tourne,
And in his wey it happed him to ryde,
beside a forest In al this care, under a forest-syde▲,
Wher-as he saugh up-on a daunce go
Of ladies foure and twenty, and yet mo;
drew near Toward the whiche daunce he drow ful yerne▲,
In hope that som wisdom sholde he lerne.
But certeinly, er he came fully there,
knew not Vanisshed was this daunce, he niste▲ where.
No creature saugh he that bar lyf,
Save on the grene he saugh sittinge a wyf;
person A fouler wight▲ ther may no man devyse.
began to rise Agayn the knight this olde wyf gan ryse▲,
And seyde, 'sir knight, heer-forth ne lyth no wey.
faith Tel me, what that ye seken, by your fey▲?
Paraventure it may the bettre be;
Thise olde folk can muchel thing,' quod she.
dear 'My leve▲ mooder,' quod this knight certeyn,
'I nam but deed, but-if that I can seyn
What thing it is that wommen most desyre;
reward Coude ye me wisse, I wolde wel quyte▲ your hyre.'
pledge; promise 'Plight▲ me thy trouthe▲, heer in myn hand,' quod she,
'The nexte thing that I requere thee,
Thou shalt it do, if it lye in thy might;
And I wol telle it yow er it be night.'
'Have heer my trouthe,' quod the knight, 'I grante.'
boast 'Thanne,' quod she, 'I dar me wel avante▲,
Thy lyf is sauf, for I wol stonde therby,
Up-on my lyf, the queen wol seye as I.

148. We old folk understand many things.

Lat see which is the proudeste of hem alle,
caul, a net to confine the hair That wereth on a coverchief or a calle▲,
That dar seye nay, of that I shal thee teche;
Lat us go forth with-outen lenger speche.'
whispered; message Tho rouned▲ she a pistel▲ in his ere,
And bad him to be glad, and have no fere.
Whan they be comen to the court, this knight
Seyde, 'he had holde his day, as he hadde hight,
And redy was his answere,' as he sayde.
Ful many a noble wyf, and many a mayde,
And many a widwe, for that they ben wyse,
The quene hir-self sittinge as a justyse,
Assembled been, his answere for to here;
commanded And afterward this knight was bode▲ appere.
person To every wight▲ comanded was silence,
And that the knight sholde telle in audience,
What thing that worldly wommen loven best.
not still; beast This knight ne stood nat stille▲ as doth a best▲,
But to his questioun anon answerde
With manly voys, that al the court it herde:
'My lige lady, generally,' quod he,
'Wommen desyren to have sovereyntee
As wel over hir housbond as hir love,
And for to been in maistrie him above;
This is your moste desyr, thogh ye me kille,
Doth as yow list, I am heer at your wille.'
In al the court ne was ther wyf ne mayde,
Ne widwe, that contraried that he sayde,
But seyden, 'he was worthy han his lyf.'
started And with that word up stirte▲ the olde wyf,
Which that the knight saugh sittinge in the grene:
'Mercy,' quod she, 'my sovereyn lady quene!
Er that your court departe, do me right.
I taughte this answere un-to the knight;
For which he plighte me his trouthe there,
The firste thing I wolde of him requere,
He wolde it do, if it lay in his might.
Bifore the court than preye I thee, sir knight,'

Quod she, 'that thou me take un-to thy wyf;
For wel thou wost that I have kept thy lyf.
If I sey fals, sey nay, up-on thy fey!'
like alas, an exclamation of dismay This knight answerde, 'allas! and weylawey▲!
I woot right wel that swich was my biheste.
choose For goddes love, as chees▲ a newe requeste;
Tak al my good, and lat my body go.'
curse 'Nay than,' quod she, 'I shrewe▲ us bothe two!
For thogh that I be foul, and old, and pore,
I nolde for al the metal, ne for ore,
That under erthe is grave, or lyth above,
also But-if thy wyf I were, and eek▲ thy love.'
'My love?' quod he; 'nay, my dampnacioun!
Allas! that any of my nacioun
mismatched Sholde ever so foule disparaged▲ be!'
But al for noght, the ende is this, that he
Constreyned was, he nedes moste hir wedde;
And taketh his olde wyf, and gooth to bedde.
Now wolden som men seye, paraventure,
I care not That, for my necligence, I do no cure▲
To tellen yow the joye and al th'array
That at the feste was that ilke day.
To whiche thing shortly answere I shal;
I seye, ther nas no joye ne feste at al,
Ther nas but hevinesse and muche sorwe;
a morning soon after For prively he wedded hir on a morwe▲,
owl And al day after hidde him as an oule▲;
So wo was him, his wyf looked so foule.
Greet was the wo the knight hadde in his thoght,
Whan he was with his wyf a-bedde y-broght;
rolled about He walweth▲, and he turneth to and fro.
His olde wyf lay smylinge evermo,
Bless the Lord And seyde, 'o dere housbond, *ben'cite*▲!
Fareth every knight thus with his wyf as ye?
Is this the lawe of king Arthures hous?
hard to please Is every knight of his so dangerous▲?
I am your owene love and eek your wyf;
I am she, which that saved hath your lyf;

And certes, yet dide I yow never unright;
Why fare ye thus with me this firste night?
Ye faren lyk a man had lost his wit;
What is my gilt? for godd's love, tel me it,
And it shal been amended, if I may.'
  'Amended?' quod this knight, 'allas! nay, nay!
It wol nat been amended never mo!
odious Thou art so loothly▲, and so old also,
And ther-to comen of so lowe a kinde,
twist and turn That litel wonder is, thogh I walwe and winde▲
burst So wolde god myn herte wolde breste▲!'
  'Is this,' quod she, 'the cause of your unreste?'
  'Ye, certainly,' quod he, 'no wonder is.'
  'Now, sire,' quod she, 'I coude amende al this,
If that me liste, er it were dayes three,
conduct yourself So wel ye mighte bere yow▲ un-to me.
gentility   But for ye speken of swich gentillesse▲
As is descended out of old richesse,
That therfore sholden ye be gentil men,
Swich arrogance is nat worth an hen.
Loke who that is most vertuous alway,
publicly Privee and apert▲, and most entendeth ay
To do the gentil dedes that he can,
And tak him for the grettest gentil man.
Crist wol, we clayme of him our gentillesse,
Nat of our eldres for hir old richesse.
For thogh they yeve us al hir heritage,
birth For which we clayme to been of heigh parage▲,
Yet may they nat biquethe, for no-thing,
To noon of us hir vertuous living,
That made hem gentil men y-called be;
And bad us folwen hem in swich degree.
  Wel can the wyse poete of Florence,
named Dante That highte Dant▲, speken in this sentence;
Lo in swich maner rym is Dantes tale:
"Ful selde up ryseth by his branches smale
Prowesse of man; for god, of his goodnesse,

271–2. Very rarely does a human rise in society out of his own ability.

Wol that of him we clayme our gentillesse;"
For of our eldres may we no-thing clayme
But temporel thing, that man may hurte and mayme.
  Eek every wight wot▲ this as wel as I, *person knows*
If gentillesse were planted naturelly
Un-to a certeyn linage, doun the lyne,
Privee ne apert▲, than wolde they never fyne▲ *openly, publicly; cease*
To doon of gentillesse the faire offyce;
They mighte do no vileinye or vyce.
  Tak fyr▲, and ber it in the derkeste hous *fire*
Bitwix this and the mount of Caucasus▲. *Caucasus, the edge of the world*
And lat men shette the dores and go thenne;
Yet wol the fyr as faire lye and brenne,
As twenty thousand men mighte it biholde:
His office naturel ay wol it holde,
Up peril of my lyf, til that it dye.
  Heer may ye see wel, how that genterye▲ *gentility*
Is nat annexed to possessioun,
Sith folk ne doon hir operacioun
Alwey, as dooth the fyr, lo! in his kinde.
For, god it woot, men may wel often finde
A lordes sone do shame and vileinye
And he that wol han prys of his gentrye
For he was boren of a gentil hous,
And hadde hise eldres noble and vertuous,
And nil him-selven do no gentil dedis,
Ne folwe his gentil auncestre that deed is,
He nis nat gentil, be he duk or erl;
For vileyns sinful dedes make a cherl.▲ *churl, boor*
For gentillesse nis but renomee▲ *renown*
Of thyne auncestres, for hir heigh bountee
Which is a strange thing to thy persone.
Thy gentillesse cometh fro god allone;
Than comth our verray gentillesse of grace,
It was no-thing biquethe us with our place.
  Thenketh how noble, as seith Vlaerius,
Was thilke Tullius Hostilius,

289. Fire will behave according to its nature.

That out of povert roos to heigh noblesse.
read; Seneca; Boethius Redeth▲ Senek▲, and redeth ekk Boëce▲,
Ther shul ye seen expres that it no drede is,
That he is gentil that doth gentil dedis:
dear And therfore, leve▲ housbond, I thus conclude,
of humble birth Al were it that myne auncestres were rude▲,
Yet may the hye god, and so hope I,
Grante me grace to liven vertuously.
Thanne am I gentil, whan that I biginne
put aside To liven vertuously and weyve▲ sinne.
reprove And ther-as ye of povert me repreve▲,
The hye god, on whom that we bileve,
chose In wilful povert chees▲ to live his lyf.
And certes every man, mayden, or wyf,
May understonde that Jesus, hevene king,
Ne wolde nat chese a vicious living.
Glad povert is an honest thing, certeyn;
scholars This wol Senek and othere clerkes▲ seyn.
Who-so that halt him payd of his poverte,
I holde him riche, al hadde he nat a sherte.
poor creature He that coveyteth is a povre wight▲,
For he wolde han that is nat in his might.
But he that noght hath, ne coveyteth have
Is riche, al-though ye holde him but a knave.
Verray povert, it singeth proprely;
Roman poet Juvenal▲ seith of povert merily:
"The povre man, whan he goth by the weye,
Bifore the theves he may singe and pleye."
Povert is hateful good, and, as I gesse,
A ful greet bringer out of bisinesse;
wisdom A greet amender eek of sapience▲
To him that taketh it in pacience.
miserable Povert is this, al-though it seme elenge▲:
wealth; slander Possessioun▲, that no wight wol chalenge▲.
Povert ful ofte, whan a man is lowe,
Maketh his god and eek him-self to knowe.

329. Whoever accepts his poverty.
340. A great incentive to activity.

an eye-glass Povert a spectacle▲ is, as thinketh me,
Thurgh which he may his verray frendes see.
And therfore, sire, sin that I noght yow greve,
rebuke Of my povert na-more ye me repreve▲.
Now, sire, of elde ye repreve me;
authority And certes, sire, thogh noon auctoritee▲
Were in no book, ye gentils of honour
person Seyn that men sholde an old wight▲ doon favour.
And clepe him fader, for your gentillesse;
author And auctours▲ shal I finden, as I gesse.
Now ther ye seye, that I am foul and old,
cuckold, man whose wife is unfaithful Than drede you noght to been a cokewold▲;
For filthe and elde, al-so mote I thee,
Been grete wardeyns up-on chastitee.
But nathelees, sin I knowe your delyt,
I shal fulfille your wordly appetyt.
two 'Chees now,' quod she, 'oon of thise thinges tweye▲,
To han me foul and old til that I deye,
And be to yow a trewe humble wyf,
And never yow displese in al my lyf,
Or elles ye wol han me yong and fair,
And take your aventure of the repair
That shal be to your hous, by-cause of me,
Or in som other place, may wel be.
Now chees your-selven, whether that yow lyketh.'
considered; groaned This knight avyseth▲ him and sore syketh▲,
But atte laste he seyde in this manere,
'My lady and my love, and wyf so dere
control I put me in your wyse governance▲;
Cheseth your-self, which may be most plesance,
And most honour to yow and me also.
I care not I do no fors▲ the whether of the two;
For as yow lyketh, it suffiseth me.'
I have mastery over you 'Thanne have I gete of yow maistrye▲,' quod she,
control 'Sin I may chese, and governe▲ as me lest?'
'Ye certes, wyf,' quod he, 'I holde it best.'
angry 'Kis me,' quod she, 'we be no lenger wrothe▲;

368–369. And take your chance upon what might befall your house because of me.

For, by my trouthe, I wol be to yow bothe,
This is to seyn, ye, bothe fair and good.
die mad I prey to god that I mot sterven wood▲,
But I to yow be al-so good and trewe
As ever was wyf, sin that the world was newe.
see And, but I be to-morn as fair to sene▲
As any lady, emperyce, or quene,
That is bitwixe the est and eke the west,
Doth with my lyf and deeth right as yow lest.
Cast up the curtin, loke how that it is.'
And whan the knight saugh verraily al this,
That she so fair was, and so yong ther-to
held For joye he hente▲ hir in his armes two,
His herte bathed in a bath of blisse;
one after the other A thousand tyme a-rewe▲ he gan hir kisse.
And she obeyed him in every thing
That mighte doon him plesance or lyking.
And thus they live, un-to hir lyves ende,
In parfit joye; and Jesu Crist us sende
Housbondes meke, yonge, and fresshe a-bedde,
wait over And grace t'overbyde▲ hem that we wedde.
And eek I preye Jesu shorte hir lyves
That wol nat be governed by hir wyves;
grudging of the cost And olde and angry nigardes of dispence▲,
God sende hem sone verray pestilence.

BALLADS

The ballads presented here are from southern Scotland and northern England. Originating in about Elizabethan times, they were passed orally from generation to generation, gradually being modified, so that when they were written down in the eighteenth and nineteenth centuries, there were sometimes many versions of the original ballad.

THE DOUGLAS TRAGEDY

'Rise up, rise up, now, Lord Douglas,' she says,
'And put on your armour so bright;
Let it never be said that a daughter of thine
Was married to a lord under night▲.

under cover of night

'Rise up, rise up, my seven bold sons,
And put on your armour so bright,
And take better care of your youngest sister,
For your eldest's awa the last night.'

He's mounted her on a milk-white steed,
And himself on a dapple grey,
With a bugelet horn hung down by his side,
And lightly they rode away.

Lord William lookit o'er his left shoulder,
To see what he could see,
And there he spy'd her seven brethren bold,
Come riding over the lee.

'Light down, light down, Lady Marg'ret,' he said,
'And hold my steed in your hand,
Until that against your seven brethren bold,
And your father, I mak a stand.'

She held his steed in her milk-white hand,
And never shed one tear,
Until that she saw her seven brethren fa',
And her father hard fighting, who lov'd her so dear.

'O hold your hand, Lord William!' she said,
'For your strokes they are wond'rous sair;
True lovers I can get many a ane,
But a father I can never get mair.'

O she's ta'en out her handkerchief,
It was o' the holland sae fine,
And aye she dighted▲ her father's bloody wounds, *dressed*
That were redder than the wine.

'O chuse, O chuse, Lady Marg'ret,' he said,
'O whether will ye gang or bide?'
'I'll gang, I'll gang, Lord William,' she said,
'For ye have left me no other guide.'

He's lifted her on a milk-white steed,
And himself on a dapple grey,
With a bugelet horn hung down by his side,
And slowly they baith rade away.

O they rade on, and on they rade,
And a' by the light of the moon,
Until they came to yon wan water,
And there they lighted down.

They lighted down to tak a drink
Of the spring that ran sae clear;
And down the stream ran his gude heart's blood,
And sair she gan to fear.

'Hold up, hold up, Lord William,' she says,
'For I fear that you are slain!'
reflection ''Tis naething but the shadow▲ of my scarlet cloak,
That shines in the water sae plain.'

O they rade on, and on they rade,
And a' by the light of the moon,
Until they cam to his mother's ha' door,
And there they lighted down.

'Get up, get up, lady mother,' he says,
'Get up, and let me in!—
Get up, get up, lady mother,' he says,
'For this night my fair lady I've win.'

'O mak my bed, lady mother,' he says,
'O mak it braid and deep!
And lay Lady Marg'ret close at my back,
And the sounder I will sleep.'

Lord William was dead lang ere midnight,
Lady Marg'ret lang ere day—
And all true lovers that go thegither,
May they have mair luck than they!

Lord William was buried in St Marie's kirk,
Lady Marg'ret in Marie's quire;
Out o' the lady's grave grew a bonny red rose,
And out o' the knight's a brier.

And they twa met, and they twa plat,
And fain they wad be near;
And a' the warld might ken right weel,
They were twa lovers dear.

But bye and rade the Black Douglas,
And wow but he was rough!
For he pull'd up the bonny brier,
And flang'd in St Mary's Loch.

EDWARD, EDWARD

'Why does your brand sae drop wi' blude,
Edward, Edward?
Why does your brand sae drop wi' blude,
And why sae sad gang ye, O?'—
'O I hae kill'd my hawk sae gude,
Mither, mither;
O I hae kill'd my hawk sae gude,
And I had nae mair but he, O'.

'Your hawk's blude was never sae red,
Edward, Edward;
Your hawk's blude was never sae red,
My dear son, I tell thee, O'.—
'O I hae kill'd my red-roan steed,
Mither, mither;
O I hae kill'd my red-roan steed,
That erst was sae fair and free, O.'

'Your steed was auld, and ye hae got mair,
Edward, Edward;
Your steed was auld, and ye hae got mair;
grief; suffer Some other dule▲ ye dree▲, O.'—
'O I hae kill'd my father dear,
Mither, mither;
O I hae kill'd my father dear,
Alas, and wae is me, O!'

'And whatten penance will ye dree for that,
Edward, Edward?
Whatten penance will ye dree for that?

My dear son, now tell me, O.'—
'I'll set my feet in yonder boat,
Mither, mither;
I'll set my feet in yonder boat,
And I'll fare over the sea, O.'

'And what will ye do wi' your tow'rs and your ha',
Edward, Edward?
And what will ye do wi' your tow'rs and your ha',
That were sae fair to see, O?'—
'I'll let them stand till they doun fa',
Mither, mither;
I'll let them stand till they doun fa',
must For here never mair maun˄ I be, O.'

'And what will ye leave to your bairns and your wife,
Edward, Edward?
And what will ye leave to your bairns and your wife,
When ye gang owre the sea, O?'—
'The warld's room: let them beg through life,
Mither, mither;
The warld's room: let them beg through life;
For them never mair will I see, O.'

'And what will ye leave to your ain mither dear,
Edward, Edward?
And what will ye leave to your ain mither dear,
My dear son, now tell me, O?'—
'The curse of hell frae me sall ye bear,
Mither, mither;
The curse of hell frae me sall ye bear:
Sic counsels ye gave to me, O!'

THE THREE RAVENS

There were three ravens sat on a tree,
Downe a downe, hay down, hay downe
There were three ravens sat on a tree,
With a downe

There were three ravens sat on a tree,
They were as blacke as they might be.
With a downe derrie, derrie, derrie, downe, downe.

The one of them said to his mate,
'Where shall we our breakfast take?'

'Downe in yonder greene field,
There lies a knight slain under his shield.

'His hounds they lie downe at his feete,
So well they can their master keepe.

'His haukes they flie so eagerly,
bird There's no fowle▲ dare him come nie.'

Downe there comes a fallow doe,
As great with yong as she might goe.

She lift up his bloudy hed,
And kist his wounds that were so red.

She got him up upon her backe,
shroud, grave, of earth And carried him to earthen lake▲.

first hour, sunrise She buried him before the prime▲,
She was dead herselfe e're even-song time.

God send every gentleman,
lover Such haukes, such hounds, and such a leman▲.

THE TWA CORBIES

As I was walking all alane,
two crows; moan I heard twa corbies▲ making a mane▲;
one The tane▲ unto the t'other say,
'Where sall we gang and dine to-day?'

turf 'In behint yon auld fail▲ dyke,
knew I wot▲ there lies a new-slain knight;
And nae body kens that he lies there,
But his hawk, his hound, and lady fair.

'His hound is to the hunting gane,
His hawk to fetch the wild-fowl hame,
His lady's ta'en another mate,
So we may make our dinner sweet.

neck bone 'Ye'll sit on his white hause bane▲,
And I'll pike out his bonny blue een:
Wi' ae lock o' his gowden hair,
thatch We'll theek▲ our nest when it grows bare.

'Mony a one for him makes mane,
But nane sall ken whare he is gane:
O'er his white banes, when they are bare,
The wind sall blaw for evermair.'

SIR PATRICK SPENS

(FIRST VERSION)

The king sits in Dumferling toune,
Drinking the blude-reid wine:
'O whar will I get guid sailor,
To sail this schip of mine?'

Up and spak an eldern knicht,
Sat at the kings richt kne:
'Sir Patrick Spens is the best sailor
That sails upon the se.'

long The king has written a braid▲ letter,
And signed it wi his hand,
And sent it to Sir Patrick Spens,
Was walking on the sand.

The first line that Sir Patrick red,
laugh A loud lauch▲ lauchèd he;
The next line that Sir Patrick red,
The teir blinder his ee.

'O wha is this has don this deid,
This ill deid don to me,
To send me out this time o' the yeir,
To sail upon the se!

'Mak hast, mak hast, my mirry men all,
Our guid schip sails the morne.'
'O say na sae, my master deir,
For I feir a deadlie storme.

'Late, late yestreen I saw the new moone,
Wi the auld moone in hir arme,
And I feir, I feir, my dier master,
That we will cum to harme.'

O our Scots nobles wer richt laith
To weet their cork-heild schoone;
Bot lang owre a' the play wer playd,
Thair hats they swam aboone.

O lang, lang may their ladies sit,
Wi thair fans into their hand,
Or eir they se Sir Patrick Spens
Cum sailing to the land.

O lang, lang may the ladies stand,
combs Wi thair gold kems▲ in their hair,
Waiting for thair ain deir lords,
For they'll see thame na mair.

half over Haf owre▲, haf owre to Aberdour,
It's fiftie fadom deip,
And thair lies guid Sir Patrick Spens,
Wi the Scots lords at his feit.

SIR PATRICK SPENS

(SECOND VERSION)

I. THE SAILING

The king sits in Dunfermline town
Drinking the blude-red wine;
skilful 'O whare will I get a skeely▲ skipper
To sail this new ship o' mine?'

O up and spak an eldern knight,
Sat at the king's right knee:
'Sir Patrick Spens is the best sailor
That ever sail'd the sea.'

Our king has written a braid letter,
And seal'd it with his hand
And sent it to Sir Patrick Spens,
Was walking on the strand.

'To Noroway, to Noroway,
foam To Noroway o'er the faem▲;
The king's daughter o' Noroway,
'Tis thou must bring her hame.'

The first word that Sir Patrick read
So loud, loud laugh'd he;
The neist word that Sir Patrick read
The tear blinded his e'e.

'O wha is this has done this deed
And tauld the king o' me,
To send us out, at this time o' year,
To sail upon the sea?

'Be it wind, be it weet, be it hail, be it sleet,
Our ship must sail the faem;
The king's daughter o' Noroway,
'Tis we must fetch her hame.'

They hoysed their sails on Monenday morn
Wi' a' the speed they may;
They hae landed in Noroway
Upon a Wodensday.

II. THE RETURN

'Mak ready, mak ready, My merry men a'!
Our gude ship sails the morn.'—
'Now ever alack, my master dear,
I fear a deadly storm.

'I saw the new moon late yestreen
Wi' the auld moon in her arm;
And if we gang to sea, master,
I fear we'll come to harm.'

They hadna sail'd a league, a league,
A league but barely three,
sky When the lift▲ grew dark, and the wind blew loud,
rough And gurly▲ grew the sea.

leaped Tha ankers brak, and the topmast lap▲,
It was sic a deadly storm:
And the waves cam owre the broken ship
Till a' her sides were torn.

'O where will I get a gude sailor
To tak' my helm in hand,
Till I get up to the tall topmast
To see if I can spy land?'

'O here am I, a sailor gude,
To tak' the helm in hand,
Till you go up to the tall topmast,
But I fear you'll ne'er spy land.'

He hadna gane a step, a step,
A step but barely ane,
When a bolt flew out of our goodly ship,
And the saut sea it came in.

'Go fetch a web o' the silken claith,
Another o' the twine,
And wap* them into our ship's side, *wrap
And let nae the sea come in.'

They fetch'd a web o' the silken claith,
Another o' the twine,
And they wapp'd them round that gude ship's side
But still the sea came in.

O laith, laith were our gude Scots lords
To wet their cork-heel'd shoon;
But lang or a' the play was play'd
They wat their hats aboon.

And mony was the feather bed
That flatter'd on the faem;
And money was the gude lord's son
That never mair cam hame.

O lang, lang may the ladies sit,
Wi' their fans into their hand,
Before they see Sir Patrick Spens
Come sailing to the strand!

And lang, lang may the maidens sit
Wi' their gowd kames in their hair,
A-waiting for their ain dear loves!
For them they'll see nae mair.

Half-owre, half-owre to Aberdour,
'Tis fifty fathoms deep;
And there lies gude Sir Patrick Spens,
Wi' the Scots lords at his feet!

THE UNQUIET GRAVE

'The wind doth blow today, my love,
And a few small drops of rain;
I never had but one true-love;
In cold grave she was lain.

'I'll do as much for my true-love
As any young man may;
I'll sit and mourn all at her grave
For a twelvemonth and a day.'

The twelvemonth and a day being up,
The dead began to speak:
'Oh who sits weeping on my grave,
And will not let me sleep?'

''Tis I, my love, sits on your grave,
And will not let you sleep;
For I crave one kiss of your clay-cold lips.
And that is all I seek.'

'You crave one kiss of my clay-cold lips;
But my breath smells earthy strong;
If you have one kiss of my clay-cold lips;
Your time will not be long.

''Tis down in yonder garden green,
Love, where we used to walk,
The finest flower that ere was seen
Is withered to a stalk.

'The stalk is withered dry, my love,
So will our hearts decay;
So make yourself content, my love,
Till God calls you away.'

SIR **T**HOMAS **W**YATT
(1503–1542)

Born Kent, England. He was a courtier and a diplomat in Henry VIII's court.

They flee from me that sometime did me seek,
With naked foot stalking in my chamber:
I have seen them gentle, tame, and meek,
That now are wild, and do not remember
That some time they put themselves in danger
To take bread at my hand; and now they range
Busily seeking with a continual change.

Thankt be Fortune, it hath been otherwise
Twenty times better; but once in speciall,
style In thin array, after a pleasant guise▲,
When her loose gown from her shoulders did fall,
And she me caught in her arms long and small,
Therewith all sweetly did me kiss,
And softly said, 'Dear heart, how like you this?'

It was no dream; I lay broad waking:
But all is turn'd, thorough my gentleness,
Into a strange fashion of forsaking;
And I have leave to go of her goodness;
And she also to use new-fangleness.
But since that I so kindely am servèd,
I would fain know what *she* hath deservèd.

1. Poems that have no title are preceded by the above image. Such poems are usually referred to by their first line.

SIR THOMAS WYATT

Whoso list to hunt: I know where is an hind.
But as for me, alas I may no more:
The vain travail hath wearied me so sore,
I am of them that farthest cometh behind.
Yet may I by no means my wearied mind
Draw from the deer, but as she fleeth afore
Fainting I follow. I leave off therefore,
Sithens in a net I seek to hold the wind.
Who list her hunt, I put him out of doubt,
As well as I may spend his time in vain,
And graven with diamonds in letters plain
There is written her fair neck round about:
'*Noli me tangere*, for Caesar's I am,
And wild for to hold, though I seem tame.'

Divers doth use, as I have heard and know,
When that to change their ladies do begin,
cease To mourn and wail and never for to lin▲,
Hoping thereby to 'pease their painful woe.
And some there be that when it chanceth so
That women change and hate where love hath been,
They call them false, and think with words to win
The hearts of them which otherwise doth grow.
But as for me, though that by chance indeed
Change hath outworn the favour that I had,
I will not wail, lament, nor yet be sad,
Nor call her false that falsely did me feed,
But let it pass, and think it is of kind
That often change doth please a woman's mind.

WHOSO LIST TO HUNT: This poem is thought to be Wyatt's response to the taking of his lover, Ann Boleyn, by the king, Henry VIII. Ann is the hind, the doe. Henry is Caesar.
13. Do not touch me, said by Christ to Mary Magdalene after his resurrection.

OF HIS LOVE CALLED ANNA

What word is that, that changeth not
Though it be turned and made in twain?
It is mine answer, God it wot,
And eke the causer of my pain.
A love rewardeth with disdain,
Yet is it loved. What would ye more?
It is my health eke and my sore.

Madame, withouten many words,
Once, I am sure, ye will or no:
mockery And if ye will, then leave your bourds▲,
be sensible And use your wit▲, and show it so.

And with a beck ye shall me call,
And if of one that burneth alway
Ye have any pity at all,
Answer him fair with yea or nay.

If it be yea, I shall be fain;
If it be nay, friends as before:
Ye shall another man obtain,
And I mine own, and yours no more.

OF HIS LOVE CALLED ANNA: Wyatt did not provide titles for his poems. This title, and others in this selection, were provided by the first editor of his poems, Tottel, fifteen years after Wyatt's death. In this case, the title provides an answer to the riddle set in the poem: Anna, Ann Boleyn.

55

THE LOVER TO HIS BED, WITH DESCRIBING OF HIS UNQUIET STATE

The restful place, reviver of my smart,
The labours' salve, increasing my sorrow;
The body's ease, and troubler of my heart;
Quieter of mind, and my unquiet foe;
Forgetter of pain, remembering my woe;
The place of sleep wherein I do but wake,
sprinkled Besprent▲ with tears, my bed, I thee forsake!

The frosty snows may not redress my heat,
Nor yet no heat abate my fervent cold.
measure I know nothing to ease my pains mete▲:
Each cure causeth increase by twenty fold,
Renewing cares upon my sorrows old.
opposite(?) Such overthwart▲ effects they do me make
Besprent with tears my bed for to forsake.

Yet helpeth it not: I find no better ease
In bed or out: this most causeth my pain.
Where I do seek how best that I may please,
My lost labour, alas, is all in vain.
Yet that I gave I cannot call again;
No place from me my grief away can take;
Wherefore with tears, my bed, I thee forsake.

Help me to seek, for I lost it there,
And if that ye have found it, ye that be here,
And seek to convey it secretly,
Handle it soft, and treat it tenderly,
complain; pine away Or else it will plain▲ and then appair▲.
But rather restore it mannerly,
Since that I do ask it thus honestly.
For to lose it, it sitteth me too near:
    Help me to seek.

Alas, and is there no remedy,
But have I thus lost it wilfully?
Iwis it was a thing all too dear
To be bestowed and wist not where:
It was mine heart—I pray you heartily
 Help me to seek.

Tangled I was in love's snare,
tormented with grief Oppressed with pain, torment with care▲,
Of grief right sure, of joy full bare,
Clean in despair by cruelty:
But ha, ha, ha, full well is me,
For I am now at liberty.

The woeful days so full of pain,
The weary night all spent in vain,
The labour lost for so small gain,
To write them all it will not be:
But ha, ha, ha, full well is me,
For I am now at liberty.

Everything that fair doth show,
When proof is made it proveth not so,
But turneth mirth to bitter woe,
Which in this case full well I see:
But ha, ha, ha, full well is me,
For I am now at liberty.

Too great desire was my guide,
And wanton will went by my side;
Hope ruled still, and made me bide
Of love's craft the extremity:
But ha, ha, ha, full well is me,
For I am now at liberty.

With feigned words, which were but wind,
To long delays I was assigned;
Her wily looks my wits did blind,
Thus as she would, I did agree:
But ha, ha, ha, full well is me,
For I am now at liberty.

Was never bird tangled in lime
That broke away in better time
Than I that rotten boughs did climb
And had no hurt, but 'scaped free:
Now ha, ha, ha, full well is me,
For I am now at liberty.

Hate whom ye list, for I care not.
Love whom ye list, and spare not.
Do what ye list, and dread not.
Think what ye list, I fear not.
For as for me I am not
But even as one that recks not
Whether ye hate or hate not,
For in your love I dote not.
Wherefore I pray you forget not,
But love whom ye list, for I care not.

My lute awake! Perform the last
Labour that thou and I shall waste,
And end that I have now begun;
For when this song is sung and past,
My lute be still, for I have done.

As to be heard where ear is none,
As lead to grave in marble stone,
My song may pierce her heart as soon.
Should we then sigh or sing or moan?
No, no, my lute, for I have done.

The rocks do not so cruelly
Repulse the waves continually
As she my suit and affection,
So that I am past remedy,
Whereby my lute and I have done.

Proud of the spoil that thou has got
Of simple hearts thorough Love's shot,
By whom, unkind, thou hast them won,
Think not he hath his bow forgot,
Although my lute and I have done.

Vengeance shall fall on thy disdain
That makest but game on earnest pain!
Think not alone under the sun
Unquit to cause thy lovers plain,
Although my lute and I have done.

Perchance thee lie withered and old
The winter night that are so cold,
Plaining in vain unto the moon:
Thy wishes then dare not be told.
Care then who list, for I have done.

And then may chance thee to repent
The time that thou hast lost and spent
To cause thy lovers sigh and swoon.
Then shalt thou know beauty but lent,
And wish and want as I have done.

Now cease, my lute: this is the last
Labour that thou and I shall waste,
And ended is that we begun.
Now is this song both sun and past:
My lute, be still, for I have done.

WILLIAM **S**HAKESPEARE
(1564–1616)

Born Stratford-on-Avon. He lived most of his life in London, writing, performing, and producing plays. Most of the sonnets were written during the 1590s, before his greatest plays.

from SONNETS

18

Shall I compare thee to a Sommers day?
Thou art more lovely and more temperate:
Rough windes do shake the darling buds of Maie,
And Sommers lease hath all too short a date:
Sometime too hot the eye of heaven shines,
And often is his gold complexion dimm'd,
And every faire from faire some-time declines,
divested of ornament By chance, or natures changing course untrim'd▲:
But thy eternall Sommer shall not fade,
lose; ownest Nor loose▲ possession of that faire thou ow'st▲,
Nor shall death brag thou wandr'st in his shade,
When in eternall lines to time thou grow'st,
  So long as men can breath or eyes can see,
  So long lives this, and this gives life to thee.

29

When in disgrace with Fortune and mens eyes,
I all alone beweepe my out-cast state,
useless And trouble deafe heaven with my bootlesse▲ cries,
And looke upon my selfe and curse my fate,
Wishing me like to one more rich in hope,
Featur'd like him, like him with friends possest,
Desiring this mans art, and that mans skope,
With what I most injoy contented least,
Yet in these thoughts my selfe almost despising,
Haplye I thinke on thee, and then my state,
(Like to the Larke at breake of day arising)
From sullen earth sings himns at Heavens gate,
  For thy sweet love remembred such welth brings,
  That then I skorne to change my state with Kings.

30

When to the Sessions of sweet silent thought,
I sommon up remembrance of things past,
I sigh the lacke of many a thing I sought,
And with old woes new waile my deare times waste:
Then can I drowne an eye (un-us'd to flow)
For precious friends hid in deaths dateles night,
And weepe a fresh loves long since canceld woe,
And mone th'expence of many a vannisht sight.
Then can I greeve at greevances fore-gon,
count And heavily from woe to woe tell▲ ore
The sad account of fore-bemoned mone,
Which I new pay as if not payd before.
  But if the while I thinke on thee (deare friend)
  All losses are restord, and sorrowes end.

60

pebbled Like as the waves make towards the pibled▲ shore,
So do our minuites hasten to their end,
Each changing place with that which goes before,
In sequent toile all forwards do contend.
newborn child; Nativity▲ once in the maine of light▲,
sphere of heaven Crawles to maturity, wherewith being crown'd,
Crooked eclipses gainst his glory fight,
And time that gave, doth now his gift confound.
destroy; bloom Time doth transfixe▲ the florish▲ set on youth,
And delves the paralels in beauties brow,
Feedes on the rarities of natures truth,
scythe And nothing stands but for his sieth▲ to mow.
  And yet to times in hope, my verse shall stand
  Praising thy worth, dispight his cruell hand.

65

Since brasse, nor stone, nor earth, nor boundlesse sea,
But sad mortallity ore-swaies their power,
How with this rage shall beautie hold a plea,
Whose action is no stronger then a flower?
O how shall summers hunny breath hold out,
Against the wrackfull siedge of battring dayes,
When rocks impregnable are not so stoute,
Nor gates of steele so strong but time decayes?
O fearefull meditation, where alack,
Shall times best Jewell from times chest lie hid?
Or what strong hand can hold his swift foote back,
Or who his spoile of beautie can forbid?
  O none, unlesse this miracle have might,
  That in black inck my love may still shine bright.

73

That time of yeeare thou maist in me behold,
When yellow leaves, or none, or few doe hange
cold Upon those boughes which shake against the could▲,
Bare ruin'd quiers, where late the sweet birds sang.
In me thou seest the twi-light of such day,
As after Sun-set fadeth in the West,
Which by and by blacke night doth take away,
Deaths second selfe that seals up all in rest.
In me thou seest the glowing of such fire,
That on the ashes of his youth doth lye,
As the death bed, whereon it must expire,
Consum'd with that which it was nurrisht by.
This thou percev'st, which makes thy love more strong,
To love that well, which thou must leave ere long.

94

They that have powre to hurt, and will doe none,
That doe not do the thing, they most do showe,
Who moving others, are themselves as stone,
Unmooved, could, and to temptation slow:
They rightly do inherrit heavens graces,
And husband natures ritches from expence,
They are the Lords and owners of their faces,
Others, but stewards of their excellence:
The sommers flowre is to the sommer sweet,
Though to it selfe, it onely live and die,
But if that flowre with base infection meete,
The basest weed out-braves his dignity:
For sweetest things turne sowrest by their deedes,
Lillies that fester, smell far worse than weeds.

63

WILLIAM SHAKESPEARE

106

When in the Chronicle of wasted time,
I see discriptions of the fairest wights,
And beautie making beautifull old rime,
In praise of Ladies dead, and lovely Knights,
Then in the blazon of sweet beauties best,
Of hand, of foote, of lip, of eye, of brow,
I see their antique Pen would have exprest,
possess Even such a beauty as you maister▲ now.
So all their praises are but prophesies
Of this our time, all you prefiguring,
because And for they look'd but▲ with devining eyes,
They had not still enough your worth to sing:
  For we which now behold these present dayes,
  Have eyes to wonder, but lack toungs to praise.

116

Let me not to the marriage of true mindes
Admit impediments, love is not love
Which alters when it alteration findes,
Or bends with the remover to remove.
O no, it is an ever fixed marke
That lookes on tempests and is never shaken;
It is the star to every wandring barke,
Whose worths unknowne, although his higth be taken.
Lov's not Times foole, though rosie lips and cheeks
Within his bending sickles compasse come,
Love alters not with his breefe houres and weekes,
But beares it out even to the edge of doome:
  If this be error and upon me proved,
  I never writ, nor no man ever loved.

129

Th'expence of Spirit in a waste of shame
Is lust in action, and till action, lust
lying Is perjurd▲, murdrous, blouddy full of blame,
Savage, extreame, rude, cruell, not to trust,
Injoyd no sooner but dispised straight,
Past reason hunted, and no sooner had
Past reason hated as a swollowed bayt,
On purpose layd to make the taker mad.
Mad in pursut and in possession so,
Had, having, and in quest, to have extreame,
A blisse in proofe and prov'd a very wo,
Before a joy proposd behind a dreame,
  All this the world well knowes yet none knowes well,
  To shun the heaven that leads men to this hell.

130

My Mistres eyes are nothing like the Sunne,
Currall is farre more red, then her lips red,
If snow be white, why then her brests are dun:
If haires be wiers, black wiers grow on her head:
I have seene Roses damaskt, red and white,
But no such Roses see I in her cheekes,
And in some perfumes is there more delight,
is exhaled Then in the breath that from my Mistres reekes▲.
I love to heare her speake, yet well I know,
That Musicke hath a farre more pleasing sound:
I graunt I never saw a goddesse goe,
My Mistres when shee walkes treads on the ground.
  And yet by heaven I thinke my love as rare,
  As any she beli'd with false compare.

138

When my love sweares that she is made of truth,
I do beleeve her though I know she lyes,
That she might thinke me some untuterd youth,
Unlearned in the worlds false subtilties.
Thus vainely thinking that she thinkes me young,
Although she knowes my dayes are past the best,
Simply I credit her false speaking tongue,
On both sides thus is simple truth suppress:
But wherefore sayes she not she is unjust?
And wherefore say not I that I am old?
O loves best habit is in seeming trust,
And age in love, loves not t'have yeares told.
  Therefore I lye with her, and she with me,
  And in our faults by lyes we flattered be.

146

Poore soule the center of my sinfull earth,
Gull'd by these rebbell powres that thee array,
Why dost thou pine within and suffer dearth
Painting thy outward walls so costlie gay?
Why so large cost having so short a lease,
Dost thou upon thy fading mansion spend?
Shall wormes inheritors of this excesse
Eate up thy charge? is this thy bodies end?
Then soule live thou upon thy servants losse,
increase And let that pine to aggravat▴ thy store;
Buy tearmes divine in selling houres of drosse:
Within be fed, without be rich no more,
  So shalt thou feed on death, that feeds on men,
  And death once dead, ther's no more dying then.

JOHN DONNE
(1572–1631)

Born London, son of a merchant. A political career was cut short when Donne secretly married his patron's niece. He was educated as a Catholic but later joined the Church of England and became Dean of St Paul's in London in 1621.

from SONGS AND SONETS
THE GOOD-MORROW

I wonder by my troth, what thou, and I
Did, till we lov'd? were we not wean'd till then?
But suck'd on countrey pleasures, childishly?
Or snorted we in the seaven sleepers den?
beside T'was so; But^ this, all pleasures fancies bee.
If ever any beauty I did see,
Which I desir'd, and got, t'was but a dreame of thee.

And now good morrow to our waking soules,
Which watch not one another out of feare;
For love, all love of other sights controules,
And makes one little roome, an every where.
Let sea-discoverers to new worlds have gone,
Let Maps to other, worlds on worlds have showne,
Let us possesse one world, each hath one, and is one.

4. Christian youths of Ephesus hid in a cave as a refuge from persecution, and slept there for over a century.

My face in thine eye, thine in mine appeares,
And true plaine hearts doe in the faces rest,
Where can we finde two better hemispheares
Without sharpe North, without declining West?
What ever dyes, was not mixt equally;
If our two loves be one, or, thou and I
Love so alike, that none doe slacken, none can die.

THE SUNNE RISING

Busie old foole, unruly Sunne,
Why dost thou thus,
Through windowes, and through curtaines call on us?
Must to thy motions lovers seasons run?
Sawcy pedantique wretch, goe chide
Late schoole boyes and sowre prentices,
Goe tell Court-huntsmen, that the King will ride,
Call countrey ants to harvest offices;
Love, all alike, no season knowes, nor clyme,
Nor houres, dayes, moneths, which are the rags of time.

Thy beames, so reverend, and strong
Why shouldst thou thinke?
I could eclipse and cloud them with a winke,
But that I would not lose her sight so long:
If her eyes have not blinded thine,
Looke, and to morrow late, tell mee,
Whether both the 'India's of spice and Myne
Be where thou leftst them, or lie here with mee.
Aske for those Kings whom thou saw'st yesterday,
And thou shalt heare, All here in one bed lay.

19. THE GOOD-MORROW In Galen's medicine, disease and death arose from an imbalance in one's constituent elements.

17. THE SUNNE RISING both the 'India's: the East Indies, known for spice, and the West Indies, known for gold.

She'is all States, and all Princes, I,
Nothing else is.
Princes doe but play us; compar'd to this,
All honor's mimique▲; All wealth alchimie.
Thou sunne art halfe as happy'as wee,
In that the world's contracted thus;
Thine age askes ease, and since thy duties bee
To warme the world, that's done in warming us.
Shine here to us, and thou art every where;
This bed thy center is, these walls thy spheare.

a glittering pretence

A VALEDICTION: FORBIDDING MOURNING

As virtuous men passe mildly away,
And whisper to their soules, to goe,
Whilst some of their sad friends doe say,
The breath goes now, and some say, no:

So let us melt, and make no noise,
No teare-floods, nor sigh-tempests move,
T'were prophanation of our joyes
To tell the layetie our love.

Moving of th'earth brings harmes and feares,
Men reckon what it did and meant,
But trepidation of the spheares,
Though greater farre, is innocent.

Dull sublunary lovers love
(Whose soule is sense) cannot admit
Absence, because it doth remove
Those things which elemented it.

11–12. In Ptolemaic astronomy the stars moved in concentric spheres around the earth. Their trembling was said to account for otherwise unexplained movements of stars.

But we by a love, so much refin'd,
    That our selves know not what it is,
Inter-assured of the mind,
    Care lesse, eyes, lips, and hands to misse.

Our two soules therefore, which are one,
    Though I must goe, endure not yet
A breach, but an expansion,
    Like gold to ayery thinnesse beate.

If they be two, they are two so
    As stiffe twin compasses are two,
Thy soule the fixt foot, makes no show
    To move, but doth, if the'other doe.

And though it in the center sit,
    Yet when the other far doth rome,
It leanes, and hearkens after it,
    And growes erect, as that comes home.

Such wilt thou be to mee, who must
    Like th'other foot, obliquely runne;
Thy firmnes drawes my circle just,
    And makes me end, where I begunne.

A VALEDICTION: OF WEEPING

        Let me pour forth
My tears before thy face, whilst I stay here,
For thy face coins them, and thy stamp they bear,
And by this mintage they are something worth,
        For thus they be
        Pregnant of thee;
Fruits of much grief they are, emblems of more,
When a tear falls, that thou falls which it bore,
So thou and I are nothing then, when on a divers shore.

On a round ball
A workman that hath copies by, can lay
An Europe, Afric, and an Asia,
And quickly make that, which was nothing, all,
So doth each tear,
Which thee doth wear,
A globe, yea world by that impression grow,
Till thy tears mixed with mine do overflow
This world, by waters sent from thee, my heaven dissolved so.

O more than moon,
Draw not up seas to drown me in thy sphere,
Weep me not dead, in thine arms, but forbear
To teach the sea, what it may do too soon;
Let not the wind
Example find,
To do me more harm, than it purposeth;
Since thou and I sigh one another's breath,
Whoe'er sighs most, is cruellest, and hastes the other's death.

THE RELIQUE

When my grave is broke up againe
Some second ghest to entertaine,
(For graves have learn'd that woman-head▲ *womanhood*
To be to more than one a Bed)
And he that digs it, spies
A bracelet of bright haire about the bone,
Will he not let'us alone,
And thinke that there a loving couple lies,
Who thought that this device might be some way
To make their soules, at the last busie day▲, *Judgement Day*
Meet at this grave, and make a little stay?

15. Her face is reflected from the surface of each of his tears.

If this fall in a time, or land,
Where mis-devotion doth command,
Then, he that digges us up, will bring
Us, to the Bishop, and the King,
To make us Reliques; then
Thou shalt be a Mary Magdalen, and I
A something else thereby;
All women shall adore us, and some men;
And since at such time, miracles are sought,
I would have that age by this paper taught
What miracles wee harmeless lovers▲ wrought.
loving without blame

First, we lov'd well and faithfully,
Yet knew not what wee lov'd, nor why,
Difference of sex no more wee knew▲,
ngels have no sexual nature
Than our Guardian Angells doe;
Comming and going▲, wee
meeting and departing from each other
Perchance might kisse, but not between those meales;
Our hands ne'r toucht the seales,
Which nature, injur'd by late law, sets free:
These miracles wee did; but not alas,
All measure, and all language, I should passe,
Should I tell what a miracle shee was.

17. Mary Magdalen was said to have long golden hair.

29–30. Laws setting restrictions upon love are contrasted with the original untrammelled state of Nature.

A NOCTURNAL UPON S. LUCY'S DAY, BEING THE SHORTEST DAY

'Tis the year's midnight, and it is the day's,
Lucy's who scarce seven hours herself unmasks,
stars The sun is spent, and now his flasks▴
Send forth light squibs, no constant rays;
The world's whole sap is sunk:
immoderately thirsty The general balm th'hydroptic▴ earth hath drunk,
Whither, as to the bed's-feet, life is shrunk,
Dead and interred; yet all these seem to laugh,
Compared with me, who am their epitaph.

Study me then, you who shall lovers be
At the next world, that is, at the next spring:
For I am every dead thing,
In whom love wrought new alchemy.
For his art did express
A quintessence even from nothingness,
From dull privations, and lean emptiness
He ruined me, and I am re-begot
Of absence, darkness, death; things which are not.

All others, from all things, draw all that's good,
Life, soul, form, spirit, whence they being have;
I, by love's limbeck, am the grave
Of all, that's nothing. Oft a flood
Have we two wept, and so
Drowned the whole world, us two; oft did we grow
To be two chaoses, when we did show
Care to aught else; and often absences
Withdrew our souls, and made us carcases.

TITLE: December 12, thought to be the winter solstice.
S. Lucy: patron saint of light.
13. Instead of making something precious from something base, in this case the process is reversed.
14. Distil by crushing out.
21. Alembic: distilling apparatus.
25. Chaos is a state in which everything is separate, acting independently of everything else. They, in their mutual absorption, have ignored the rest of the world.

But I am by her death (which word wrongs her)
Of the first nothing, the elixir grown;
Were I a man, that I were one,
I needs must know; I should prefer,
If I were any beast,
Some ends, some means; yea plants, yea stones detest,
And love; all, all some properties invest;
If I an ordinary nothing were,
As shadow, a light, and body must be here.

But I am none; nor will my sun renew.
You lovers, for whose sake, the lesser sun
At this time to the Goat is run
To fetch new lust, and give it you,
Enjoy your summer all;
Since she enjoys her long night's festival,
Let me prepare towards her, and let me call
This hour her vigil, and her eve, since this
Both the year's, and the day's deep midnight is.

from the ELEGIES
5 HIS PICTURE

a miniature portrait
Here take my Picture▲; though I bid farewell,
Thine, in my heart, where my soule dwels, shall dwell.
'Tis like me now, but I dead, 'twill be more
the picture and the ghost of the speaker
When wee are shadowes both▲, than 'twas before.
When weather-beaten I come backe; my hand,
Perhaps with rude oares torne, or Sun beams tann'd,
My face and brest of hairecloth, and my head
With cares rash sodaine stormes, being o'rspread,
My body'a sack of bones, broken within,
gunpowders
And powders▲ blew staines scatter'd on my skinne;
If rivall fooles taxe thee to'have lov'd a man,
So foule, and course, as, Oh, I may seeme then,

38. The sun. His greater sun, the lady, is dead.

This shall say what I was: and thou shalt say,
Doe his hurts reach mee? doth my worth decay?
Or doe they reach his judging minde, that hee
Should now love lesse, what hee did love to see?
That which in him was faire and delicate,
Was but the milke, which in loves childish state
nourish Did nurse▲ it: who now is growne strong enough
unaccustomed To feed on that, which to disus'd▲ tasts seemes tough.

19 TO HIS MISTRIS GOING TO BED

Come, Madam, come, all rest my powers defie,
Until I labour, I in labour lie.
The foe oft-times having the foe in sight,
Is tir'd with standing though they never fight.
Off with that girdle, like heavens Zone glistering,
But a far fairer world incompassing.
Unpin that spangled breastplate which you wear
That th'eyes of busie fooles may be stopt there.
Unlace your self, for that harmonious chyme,
Tells me from you, that now 'tis your bed time.
corset Off with that happy busk▲, whom I envie,
That still can be, and still can stand so nigh.
Your gowne's going off, such beautious state reveals,
As when from flowery meads th'hills shadow steales.
Off with your wyerie Coronet and shew
The haiery Diademe which on you doth grow:
Off with those shooes, and then safely tread
In this loves hallow'd temple, this soft bed.
In such white robes, heaven's Angels us'd to be
Receav'd by men; Thou Angel bringst with thee
a heaven of sensual delight A heaven like Mahomets Paradise▲; and though
Ill spirits walk in white, we easily know,
By this these Angels from an evil sprite,
They set our hairs, but these the flesh upright.

Licence my roaving hands, and let them go,
Behind, before, above, between, below.
O my America! my new-found-land,
My kingdome, safeliest when with one man man'd,
My Myne of precious stones, My Emperie,
How blest am I in this discovering thee!
To enter into these bonds, is to be free;
Then where my hand is set, my seal shall be.
Full nakedness! All joyes are due to thee,
As souls unbodied, bodies uncloth'd must be,
To taste whole joyes. Gems which you women use
Are as Atlanta's balls, cast in mens views,
That when a fools eye lighteth on a Gem,
His earthly soul may covet theirs, not them.
Like pictures, or like books gay coverings made
For lay-men, are all women thus array'd;
Themselves are mystick books, which onely wee
(Whom their imputed grace will dignifie)
Must see reveal'd. Then since I may know;
As liberally, as to a Midwife, shew
Thy self: cast all, yea, this white lynnen hence,
Here is no pennance, much lesse innocence.
To teach thee, I am naked first: why then
What needst thou have more covering than a man.

36. Atlanta's balls: Atlanta would marry only someone who could beat her in a foot race. Nobody could until Hippomenes defeated her by throwing down three golden balls as he ran, to distract her. Donne reverses the idea to make the woman the distracter.

from the DIVINE POEMS
HOLY SONNETS

7

At the round earths imagin'd corners, blow
Your trumpets, Angells, and arise, arise
From death, you numberlesse infinities
Of soules, and to your scattred bodies▲ goe,
All whom the flood did, and fire shall o'erthrow,
All whom warre, dearth, age, agues, tyrannies,
Despaire, law, chance, hath slaine, and you whose eyes,
Shall behold God, and never tast deaths woe.
But let them sleepe, Lord, and mee mourne a space,
For, if above all these, my sinnes abound,
'Tis late to aske abundance of thy grace,
When wee are there; here on this lowly ground,
Teach mee how to repent; for that's as good
As if thou'hadst seal'd my pardon, with thy blood.

dispersed about the earth as dust and bones

10

Death be not proud, though some have called thee
Mighty and dreadfull, for, thou art not soe,
For, those, whom thou think'st, thou dost overthrow,
Die not, poore death, not yet canst thou kill mee.
From rest and sleepe, which but thy pictures bee,
Much pleasure, then from thee, much more must flow,
And soonest our best men with thee doe goe,
Rest of their bones, and soules deliverie.
Thou art slave to Fate, Chance, kings,
and desperate men,
And dost with poyson, warre, and sicknesse dwell,
And poppie▲, or charmes can make us sleepe as well,
And better than thy stroake; why swell'st▲ thou then?
One short sleepe past, wee wake eternally,
And death shall be no more; death, thou shalt die.

opiates

puff yourself with pride

A HYMNE TO GOD THE FATHER

original sin

Wilt thou forgive that sinne▲ where I begunne,
Which is my sin, though it were done before?
Wilt thou forgive those sinnes through which I runne,
And doe them still: though still I doe deplore?
When thou hast done, thou hast not done,
For, I have more.

Wilt thou forgive that sinne by which I wonne
Others to sinne? and, made my sinne their doore?
Wilt thou forgive that sinne which I did shunne
A yeare, or two: but wallowed in, a score?
When thou hast done, thou hast not done,
For, I have more.

I have a sinne of feare, that when I have spunne
My last thred, I shall perish on the shore;
Sweare by thy selfe, that at my death thy Sunne
Shall shine as it shines now, and heretofore;
And, having done that, Thou hast done,
I have no more.

HYMNE TO GOD MY GOD, IN MY SICKNESSE

heaven

Since I am comming to that Holy roome▲,
Where, with thy Quire of Saints for evermore,
I shall be made thy Musique; As I come
I tune the Instrument now at the dore,
And what I must doe then, thinke now before.

ers of maps of heaven and earth

Whilst my Physitians by their love are growne
Cosmographers▲, and I their Mapp, who lie
Flat on this bed, that by them may be showne
That this is my South-west discoverie
Per fretum febris▲, by these streights to die,

gh the straits of fever

9. HYMNE TO GOD MY GOD, IN MY SICKNESSE South-west discoverie: South is an area of heat and fever; west is an area of decline.

I joy, that in these straits, I see my West;
For, though theire currants yeeld return to none,
What shall my West hurt me? As West and East
In all flatt Maps (and I am one) are one,
So death doth touch the Resurrection.

Is the Pacifique Sea my home? Or are
The Easterne riches? Is *Jerusalem*?
Anyan, and *Magellan*, and *Gibraltare*,
All streights, and none but streights, are wayes to them.
Whether where *Japhet* dwelt, or *Cham*, or *Sem*.

We think that *Paradise* and *Calvarie*,
Christs Crosse, and *Adams* tree, stood in one place;
Christ is the second Adam
Looke Lord, and finde both *Adams*▲ met in me;
As the first *Adams* sweat surrounds my face,
May the last *Adams* blood my soule embrace.

So, in his purple wrapp'd receive mee Lord,
By these his thornes give me his other Crowne;
And as to others soules I preach'd thy word,
Be this my Text, my Sermon to mine owne,
Therfore that he may raise the Lord throws down.

18. Anyan: thought to be a strait between America and Asia.
20. Japhet, Cham, Sem: sons of Noah between whom the world was divided.

BEN JONSON
(1573–1637)

Born London, England. He was a poet and dramatist influenced by classical authors.

ON MY FIRST SONNE

Farewell, thou child of my right hand, and joy;
　　My sin was too much hope of thee, loved boy.
Seven years thou wert lent to me, and I thee pay,
　　Exacted by thy fate, on the just day.
O, could I lose all father now! For why
　　Will man lament the state he should envy?
To have so soon 'scaped world's and flesh's rage,
　　And, if no other misery, yet age?
Rest in soft peace, and, asked, say here doth lie
　　Ben Jonson, his best piece of poetry.
For whose sake, henceforth, all his vows be such
　　As what he loves may never like too much.

INVITING A FRIEND TO SUPPER

To night, grave sir, both my poore house, and I
Doe equally desire your companie:
Not that we thinke us worthy such a ghest,
But that your worth will dignifie our feast,
With those that come; whose grace may make that seeme
Something, which, else, could hope for no esteeme.
It is the faire acceptance, Sir, creates
food The entertaynment perfect: not the cates▲.
Yet shall you have, to rectifie your palate,
An olive, capers, or some better sallade
Ushring the mutton; with a short-leg'd hen,
If we can get her, full of egs, and then,
rabbit Limons, and wine for sauce: to these, a coney▲
Is not to be despair'd of, for our money;
scholars And, though fowle, now, be scarce, yet there are clarkes▲,
The skie not falling, thinke we may have larkes.
Ile tell you more, and lye, so you will come:
Of patrich, pheasant, wood-cock, of which some
May yet be there; and godwit, if we can:
Knat, raile, and ruffe too. How so ere, my man
Shall reade a piece of *Virgil, Tacitus,*
Livie, or of some better booke to us,
Of which wee'll speake our minds, amidst our meate;
And Ile professe no verses to repeate:
To this, if ought appeare, which I not know of,
That will the pastrie, not my paper, show of.
Digestive cheese, and fruit there sure will bee;
But that, which most doth take my Muse, and mee,
Is a pure cup of rich Canary-wine,
the tavern Which is the Mermaids▲, now, but shall be mine:
Of which had *Horace*, or *Anacreon* tasted,
Their lives, as doe their lines, till now had lasted.
Tabacco, Nectar, or the Thespian spring,
Are all but *Luthers* beere, to this I sing.

19–20. Wading birds
34. German beer, weaker than English.

Of this we will sup free, but moderately,
notorious government informers And we will have no Pooly', or Parrot▲ by;
Nor shall our cups make any guiltie men:
But, at our parting, we will be, as when
We innocently met. No simple word,
That shall be utter'd at our mirthfull boord,
Shall make us sad next morning: or affright
The libertie, that wee'll enjoy to night.

TO PENSHURST

Thou art not, *Penshurst*, built to envious show,
black marble Of touch▲, or marble; nor canst boast a row
Of polish'd pillars, or a roofe of gold:
skylight Thou has no lantherne▲, whereof tales are told;
Or stayre, or courts; but stand'st an ancient pile,
And these grudg'd at, art reverenc'd the while.
Thou joy'st in better markes, of soyle, of ayre,
Of wood, of water: therein thou art faire.
Thou hast thy walkes for health, as well as sport:
Thy Mount, to which the Dryads doe resort,
Where *Pan*, and *Bacchus* their high feasts have made,
Beneath the broad beech, and the chest-nut shade;
That taller tree, which of a nut was set,
Sir Philip Sidney's At his▲ great birth, where all the Muses met.
There, in the writhed barke, are cut the names
semi-deity of the woods Of many a *Sylvane*▲, taken with his flames.
And thence, the ruddy Satyres oft provoke
The lighter Faunes, to reach thy Ladies oke.
Thy copp's, too, nam'd of *Gamage*, thou hast there,
That never failes to serve thee season'd deere,
When thou would'st feast, or exercise thy friends.
The lower land, that to the river bends,

TITLE: Estate of the Sidney family, in Kent.
18–19. Barbara Gamage, the then current Lady of Penshurst, was said to have begun labour under 'thy Ladies oke'.

cows Thy sheepe, thy bullocks, kine▲, and calves doe feed:
The middle grounds thy mares, and horses breed.
rabbits Each banke doth yeeld thee coneyes▲; and the topps
Fertile of wood, *Ashore*, and *Sydney's* copp's,
To crowne thy open table, doth provide
The purpled pheasant, with the speckled side:
The painted partrich lyes in every field,
And, for thy messe, is willing to be kill'd.
And if the high swolne Medway faile thy dish,
Thou hast thy ponds, that pay thee tribute fish,
Fat, aged carps, that runne into thy net.
And pikes, now weary their owne kinde to eat,
As loth, the second draught, or cast to stay,
Officiously, at first, themselves betray.
Bright eeles, that emulate them, and leape on land,
Before the fisher, or into his hand.
Then hath thy orchard fruit, thy garden flowers,
Fresh as the ayre, and new as are the houres.
The earely cherry, with the later plum,
Fig, grape, and quince, each in his time doth come:
The blushing apricot, and woolly peach
Hang on thy walls, that every child may reach.
And though thy walls be of the countrey stone,
They'are rear'd with no mans ruine, no mans grone,
There's none, that dwell about them, wish them downe;
countryman But all come in, the farmer, and the clowne▲:
And no one empty-handed, to salute
petition, obligation Thy lord, and lady, though they have no sute▲.
Some bring a capon, some a rurall cake,
Some nuts, some apples; some that thinke they make
The better cheeses, bring 'hem; or else send
By their ripe daughters, whom they would commend
This way to husbands; and whose baskets beare
An embleme of themselves, in plum, or peare.
But what can this (more then expresse their love)
Adde to thy free provisions, farre above
The neede of such? whose liberall boord doth flow,
With all, that hospitalitie doth know!

Where comes no guest, but is allow'd to eate,
Without his feare, and of the lords owne meate:
Where the same beere, and bread, and self-same wine,
That is his Lordships, shall be also mine.
And I not faine to sit (as some, this day,
At great mens tables) and yet dine away.
Here no man tells my cups; nor, standing by,
A waiter, doth my gluttony envy:
But gives me what I call, and lets me eate,
He knowes, below, he shall finde plentie of meate,
Thy tables hoord not up for the next day,
Nor, when I take my lodging, need I pray
service For fire, or lights, or livorie▲: all is there;
As if thou, then, wert mine, or I reign'd here:
There's nothing I can wish, for which I stay.
That found King *James*, when hunting late, this way,
With his brave sonne, the Prince, they saw thy fires
Shine bright on every harth as the desires
Roman household gods Of thy Penates▲ had beene set on flame,
To entertayne them; or the countrey came,
With all their zeale, to warme their welcome here.
What (great, I will not say, but) sodayne cheare
Did'st thou, then, make 'hem! and what praise was heap'd
On thy good lady, then! who, therein reap'd
The just reward of her high huswifery,
To have her linnen, plate, and all things nigh,
When shee was farre: and not a roome, but drest,
As if it had expected such a guest!
These, *Penshurst*, are thy praise, and yet not all.
Thy lady's noble, fruitfull, chaste withall.
His children thy great lord may call his owne:
A fortune, in this age, but rarely knowne.
They are, and have beene taught religion: Thence
Their gentler spirits have suck'd innocence.
Each morne, and even, they are taught to pray,
With the whole houshold, and may, every day,
Reade, in their vertuous parents noble parts,
The mysteries of manners, armes, and arts.

compare Now, *Penshurst*, they that will proportion▲ thee
With other edifices, when they see
Those proud, ambitious heaps, and nothing else,
May say, their lords have built, but thy lord dwells.

SONG – TO CELIA

Come my *Celia*, let us prove,
While we may, the sports of love;
Time will not be ours, for ever:
He, at length, our good will sever.
Spend not then his guifts in vaine.
Sunnes, that set, may rise againe:
lose But if once we loose▲ this light,
'Tis, with us, perpetuall night.
Why should we deferre our joyes?
Fame, and rumor are but toyes.
Cannot we delude the eyes
Of a few poore houshold spyes?
Or his easier eares beguile,
So removed by our wile?
'Tis no sinne, loves fruit to steale,
But the sweet theft to reveale:
To be taken, to be seene,
These have crimes accounted beene.

SONG: TO CELIA

Drinke to me onely, with thine eyes,
  And I will pledge with mine;
Or leave a kisse but in the cup,
  And Ile not looke for wine.
The thirst, that from the soule doth rise,
  Doth aske a drinke divine:
But might I of *Jove's* Nectar sup,
  I would not change for thine.

I sent thee, late, a rosie wreath,
Not so much honoring thee,
As giving it hope, that there
It could not withered bee.
But thou thereon did'st onely breath,
And sent'st it backe to mee:
Since when it growes, and smells, I sweare,
Not of it selfe, but thee.

For Loves-sake, kisse me once againe,
I long, and should not beg in vaine,
Here's none to spie, or see;
Why doe you doubt, or stay?
I'le taste as lightly as the Bee,
That doth but touch his flower, and flies away.
Once more, and (faith) I will be gone.
Can he that loves, aske lesse then one?
Nay, you may erre in this,
And all your bountie wrong:

This could be call'd but halfe a kisse.
What w'are but once to doe, we should doe long.
I will but mend the last, and tell
Where, how it would have relish'd well;
Joyne lip to lip, and try:
Each suck others breath.
And whilst our tongues perplexed lie,
Let who will thinke us dead, or wish our death.

MY PICTURE LEFT IN SCOTLAND

I now thinke, *Love* is rather deafe, then blind,
For else it could not be,
That she,
Whom I adore so much, should so slight me,
And cast my love behind:
I'm sure my language to her, was as sweet,
And every close did meet
In sentence, of as subtile feet,
As hath the youngest Hee,
That sits in shadow of *Apollo's* tree.
Oh, but my conscious feares,
That flie my thoughts betweene,
Tell me that she hath seene
My hundreds of gray haires,
Told seven and fortie yeares,
Read so much wast, as she cannot imbrace
My mountaine belly, and my rockie face,
And all these through her eyes, have stopt her eares.

Still to be neat, still to be drest,
As, you were going to a feast;
Still to be pou'dred, still perfum'd:
Lady, it is to be presum'd,
Though arts hid causes are not found,
All is not sweet, all is not sound.

Give me a looke, give me a face,
That makes simplicitie a grace;
Robes loosely flowing, haire as free:
Such sweet neglect more taketh me,
Then all th'adulteries of art.
They strike mine eyes, but not my heart.

Though I am young, and cannot tell,
Either what Death, or Love is well,
Yet I have heard, they both beare darts,
And both doe ayme at humane hearts:
And then againe, I have beene told,
Love wounds with heat, as Death with cold;
So that I feare, they doe but bring
Extreames to touch, and meane one thing.

As in a ruine, we it call
One thing to be blowne up, or fall;
Or to our end, like way may have,
By a flash of lightning, or a wave:
So Loves inflamed shaft, or brand,
May kill as soone as Deaths cold hand;
Except Loves fires the vertue have
To fright the frost out of the grave.

ANDREW MARVELL
(1621–1678)

Born Hull, son of a Calvinist preacher. In youth he was briefly a Catholic, but reverted to the puritan cause and worked for Cromwell. In later life, 1659–1678, he was a member of parliament, defending political liberty and freedom of conscience.

TO HIS COY MISTRESS

Had we but World enough, and Time,
This coyness Lady were no crime.
We would sit down, and think which way
To walk, and pass our long Loves Day.
Thou by the *Indian Ganges* side
Should'st rubies find: I by the Tide
Of *Humber* would complain. I would
Love you ten years before the Flood:
And you should if you please refuse
Till the Conversion of the *Jews*▲. [*till Judgment Day*]
My vegetable Love should grow▲ [*grows slowly, without intent*]
Vaster then Empires, and more slow.
An hundred years should go to praise
Thine Eyes, and on thy Forehead Gaze.
Two hundred to adore each Breast:
But thirty thousand to the rest.
An Age at least to every part,
And the last Age should show your Heart.
For Lady you deserve this State;
Nor would I love at lower rate.

But at my back I alwaies hear
Times winged Charriot hurrying near:
And yonder all before us lye
Desarts of vast Eternity.
Thy Beauty shall no more be found,
Nor, in thy marble Vault, shall sound
My ecchoing Song: then Worms shall try
That long preserv'd Virginity:
And your quaint Honour turn to dust;
And into ashes all my Lust.
The Grave's a fine and private place,
But none I think do there embrace.
Now therefore, while the youthful hew
Sits on thy skin like morning dew,
And while thy willing Soul transpires
At every pore with instant Fires,
Now let us sport us while we may;
And now, like am'rous birds of prey,
Rather at once our Time devour,
Than languish in his slow-chapt pow'r▴.
Let us roll all our Strength, and all
Our sweetness, up into one Ball:
And tear our Pleasures with rough strife,
Thorough the Iron gates of Life.
Thus, though we cannot make our Sun
Stand still, yet we will make him run.

power of his slowly devouring jaws

THE DEFINITION OF LOVE

I

My Love is of a birth as rare
As 'tis for object strange and high:
It was begotten by despair
Upon Impossibility.

II

Magnanimous Despair alone
Could show me so divine a thing,
Where feeble Hope could ne'r have flown
But vainly flapt its Tinsel Wing.

III

And yet I quickly might arrive
Where my extended Soul is fixt,
But Fate does Iron wedges drive,
And alwaies crouds it self betwixt.

IV

For Fate with jealous Eye does see
unite Two perfect Loves; nor lets them close▲:
Their union would her ruine be,
And her Tyrannick pow'r depose.

V

And therefore her Decrees of Steel
Us as the distant Poles have plac'd
(Though Loves whole World on us doth wheel)
by each other Not by themselves▲ to be embrac'd.

VI

Unless the giddy Heaven fall,
And Earth some new Convulsion tear;
And, us to joyn, the World should all
Be cramp'd into a *Planisphere*▲.

a flat projection of the world with the two poles together

VII

As Lines so Loves *oblique* may well
Themselves in every Angle greet:
But ours so truly *Paralel*,
Though infinite can never meet.

VIII

Therefore the Love which us doth bind,
But Fate so enviously debarrs,
Is the Conjunction of the Mind,
And Opposition of the Stars.

THE GARDEN

I

How vainly men themselves amaze
To win the Palm, the Oke, or Bayes▲;
And their uncessant Labours see
Crown'd from some single Herb or Tree,
Whose short and narrow verged Shade
Does prudently their Toyles upbraid;
While all Flow'rs and all Trees do close
To weave the Garlands of repose.

symbols of military, civic and poetic success

II

Fair quiet, have I found thee here,
And Innocence thy Sister dear!
Mistaken long, I sought you then
In busie Companies of Men.
Your sacred Plants, if here below,
Only among the Plants will grow.
Society is all but rude,
To this delicious Solitude.

III

representative of feminine beauty

No white nor red▲ was ever seen
So am'rous as this lovely green.
Fond Lovers, cruel as their Flame,
Cut in these Trees their Mistress name.
Little, Alas, they know, or heed,
How far these Beauties Hers exceed!
Fair Trees! where s'eer your barkes I wound,
No Name shall but your own be found.

IV

When we have run our Passions heat,
Love hither makes his best retreat.
The *Gods*, that mortal Beauty chase.
Still in a Tree did end their race.
Apollo hunted *Daphne* so,
Only that She might Laurel grow.
And *Pan* did after *Syrinx* speed,
Not as a Nymph, but for a Reed.

29. Daphne was turned into a laurel tree to protect her from amorous pursuit by Apollo.
31. Syrinx, pursued by Pan, was changed into a reed, of which he made a flute.

V

What wond'rous Life in this I lead!
Ripe Apples drop about my head;
The Luscious Clusters of the Vine
Upon my Mouth do crush their Wine;
exquisite The Nectaren, and curious▲ Peach,
Into my hands themselves do reach;
Stumbling on Melons, as I pass,
Insnar'd with Flow'rs, I fall on Grass.

VI

Mean while the Mind, from pleasure less,
Withdraws into its happiness:
The Mind, that Ocean where each kind
Does streight its own resemblance find;
Yet it creates, transcending these,
Far other Worlds, and other Seas;
Annihilating all that's made
To a green Thought in a green Shade.

VII

Here at the Fountains sliding foot,
Or at some Fruit-trees mossy root,
vestment, garment Casting the Bodies Vest▲ aside,
My Soul into the boughs does glide:
There like a Bird it sits, and sings,
preens Then whets, and combs▲ its silver Wings;
And, till prepar'd for longer flight,
Waves in its Plumes the various Light.

43–44. Each land animal was said to have an equivalent in the sea.

VIII

Such was that happy Garden-state,
While Man there walk'd without a Mate:
After a Place so pure, and sweet,
a play on 'Helpmate' What other Help could yet be meet▲!
But 'twas beyond a Mortal's share
To wander solitary there:
Two Paradises 'twere in one
To live in Paradise alone.

IX

How well the skilful Gardner drew
sundial Of flow'rs and herbes this Dial▲ new;
Where from above the milder Sun
Does through a fragrant Zodiack run;
And, as it works, th'industrious Bee
Computes its time as well as we.
How could such sweet and wholsome Hours
Be reckon'd but with herbs and flow'rs!

AN HORATIAN ODE UPON CROMWEL'S RETURN FROM IRELAND

The forward Youth that would appear
Must now forsake his *Muses* dear,
  Nor in the Shadows sing
  His Numbers languishing.
'Tis time to leave the Books in dust,
And oyl th' unused Armours rust,
  Removing from the Wall
  The Corslet of the Hall.

TITLE: Cromwell returned in May, 1650.

So restless *Cromwel* could not cease
In the inglorious Arts of Peace,
    But through adventrous War
    Urged his active Star.
And, like the three fork'd Lightning, first
Breaking the Clouds where it was nurst,
    Did thorough his own Side
    His fiery way divide.
For 'tis all one to Courage high
The Emulous or Enemy;
    And with such to inclose
    Is more then to oppose.
Then burning through the Air he went,
And Pallaces and Temples rent:
    And *Caesars*▲ head at last
    Did through his Laurels blast.
'Tis Madness to resist or blame
The force of angry Heavens flame:
    And, if we would speak true,
    Much to the Man is due.
Who, from his private Gardens, where
He liv'd reserved and austere,
    As if his highest plot
    To plant the Bergamot▲,
Could by industrious Valour climbe
To ruine the great Work of Time,
    And cast the Kingdome old
    Into another Mold.
Though justice against Fate complain,
And plead the antient Rights in vain:
    But those do hold or break
    As Men are strong or weak.
Nature that hateth emptiness,
Allows of penetration▲ less:
    And therefore must make room
    Where greater spirits come.

Charles I, beheaded in 1649

a choice variety of pear

two things in one space

15. side: cloud and party. Cromwell left the Parliamentary side and became leader of the new-model army.

24. Laurels: these were thought to be proof against lightning.

What Field of all the Civil Wars,
Where his were not the deepest Scars?
And *Hampton* shows what part
He had of wiser Art.
Where, twining subtile fears with hope,
He wove a Net of such a scope,
That *Charles* himself might chase
To *Caresbrooks*▲ narrow case.

Carisbrooke, on the Isle of Wight

That thence the *Royal Actor* born
The *Tragick Scaffold* might adorn:
While round the armed Bands
Did clap their bloody hands.
He nothing common did or mean
Upon that memorable Scene:
But with his keener Eye
The Axes edge did try:
Nor call'd the *Gods* with vulgar spight
To vindicate his helpless Right,
But bow'd his comely Head,
Down as upon a Bed.
This was that memorable Hour
Which first assur'd the forced Pow'r.
So when they did design
The *Capitols* first Line,
A bleeding Head where they begun,
Did fright the Architects to run;
And yet in that the *State*
Foresaw it's happy Fate.
And now the *Irish* are asham'd
To see themselves in one Year tam'd:
So much one Man can do,
That does both act and know.
They can affirm his Praises best,
And have, though overcome, confest
How good he is, how just,
And fit for highest Trust:

47. Hampton: Marvell accepts the view that Charles escaped from Hampton Court with Cromwell's connivance.

Nor yet grown stiffer with Command,
But still in the *Republick*'s hand:
How fit he is to sway
That can so well obey.
He to the *Commons Feet* presents
A *Kingdome*, for his first years rents:
And, what he may, forbears
His Fame to make it theirs:
And has his Sword and Spoyls ungirt,
To lay them at the *Publick*'s skirt.
So when the Falcon high
Falls heavy from the Sky,
She, having kill'd, no more does search.
But on the next green Bow to pearch;
Where, when he first does lure,
The Falckner has her sure.
What may not then our *Isle* presume
While Victory his Crest does plume!
What may not other fear
If thus he crown each Year!
A *Caesar* he ere long to *Gaul*,
To *Italy* an *Hannibal*,
And to all States not free
critical, making an epoch Shall *Clymacterick*▲ be.
The *Pict* no shelter now shall find
Within his party-colour'd Mind;
severe But from this Valour sad▲
retreat Shrink▲ underneath the Plad:
Happy if in the tufted brake
The *English Hunter* him mistake;
Nor lay his Hounds in near
The *Caledonian* Deer.
But thou the Wars and Fortunes Son
March indefatigably on:
And for the last effect
Still keep thy Sword erect;

105. Pict: an old name of some Scots is Picts, because of their painted bodies.
106. party colour'd: variously coloured. The Scots were regarded as fickle and treacherous.

Besides the force it has to fright
The Spirits of the shady Night,
 The same *Arts* that did *gain*
 A *Pow'r* must it *maintain*.

BERMUDAS

Where the remote Bermudas ride
In the ocean's bosom unespied,
From a small boat, that rowed along,
The listening winds received this song.
 'What should we do but sing his praise
That led us through the watery maze,
Unto an isle so long unknown
And yet far kinder than our own?
Where he the huge sea-monsters wracks,
That lift the deep upon their backs.
He lands us on a grassy stage,
Safe from the storms' and prelates' rage.
He gave us this eternal.spring,
Which here enamels everything;
And sends the fowls to us in care,
On daily visits through the air.
He hangs in shades the orange bright,
Like golden lamps in a green night,
And does in the pomegranates close
Jewels more rich than Ormus▲ shows.
Persian island exporting jewels
He makes the figs our mouths to meet,
And throws the melons at our feet;
But apples plants of such a price
No tree could ever bear them twice.
With cedars, chosen by his hand,
From Lebanon, he stores the land;
And makes the hollow seas that roar
Proclaim the ambergris▲ on shore.
secretion of whales used in perfumes

He cast (of which we rather boast)
The Gospel's pearl upon our coast,
And in these rocks for us did frame
A temple, where to sound his Name.
Oh let our voice his praise exalt,
Till it arrive at heaven's vault,
Which thence, perhaps, rebounding may
Echo beyond the Mexique Bay.'
  Thus sung they, in the English boat,
An holy and a cheerful note,
And all the way, to guide their chime,
With falling oars they kept the time.

ALEXANDER POPE
(1688–1744)

Born London, of Catholic parents. For much of his life he was at the centre of literary life in London, attracting intense literary and political loyalties and enmities.

EPISTLE TO MISS BLOUNT

ON HER LEAVING THE TOWN AFTER THE CORONATION

As some fond virgin, whom her mother's care
Drags from the town to wholesome country air,
Just when she learns to roll a melting eye,
And hear a spark, yet think no danger nigh;
From the dear man unwilling she must sever,
Yet takes one kiss before she parts for ever:
Teresa Blount Thus from the world fair Zephalinda▲ flew,
Saw others happy, and with sighs withdrew;
Not that their pleasures caused her discontent,
She sighed not that they stayed, but that she went.
She went, to plain-work, and to purling brooks;
Old-fashioned halls, dull aunts, and croaking rooks;
She went from op'ra, park, assembly, play,
To morning walks, and pray'rs three hours a day;
black China tea To pass her time 'twixt reading and bohea▲,
To muse, and spill her solitary tea,
Or o'er cold coffee trifle with the spoon,
Count the slow clock, and dine exact at noon;

SUBTITLE: the Coronation of George I, 1715.

Divert her eyes with pictures in the fire,
Hum half a tune, tell stories to the squire;
Up to her godly garret after sev'n,
There starve and pray, for that's the way to Heav'n.
Some squire, perhaps, you take delight to rack;
whist; rough red wine Whose game is whisk▲, whose treat a toast in sack▲,
Who visits with a gun, presents you birds,
kiss Then gives a smacking buss▲, and cries,—No words!
Or with his hound comes hollowing from the stable,
Makes love with nods and knees beneath a table;
Whose laughs are hearty, though his jests are coarse,
And loves you best of all things—but his horse.
In some fair ev'ning, on your elbow laid,
You dream of triumphs in the rural shade;
In pensive thought recall the fancied scene,
See coronations rise on ev'ry green;
Before you pass th' imaginary sights
Of lords, and earls, and dukes, and gartered knights;
While the spread fan o'ershades your closing eyes;
a flick of the fan Then give one flirt▲, and all the vision flies.
Thus vanish sceptres, coronets, and balls,
And leave you in lone woods, or empty walls.
So when your slave, at some dear, idle time,
(Not plagued with headaches, or the want of rhyme)
Stands in the streets, abstracted from the crew,
And while he seems to study, thinks of you:
Just when his fancy points your sprightly eyes,
Teresa's sister, Martha Or sees the blush of soft Parthenia▲ rise,
playwright, John Gay Gay▲ pats my shoulder, and you vanish quite;
conceited showy person Streets, chairs, and coxcombs▲ rush upon my sight;
Vexed to be still in town, I knit my brow,
Look sour, and hum a tune—as you may now.

AN EPISTLE TO DR ARBUTHNOT

Pope's servant, John Serle

P. Shut, shut the door, good John▲! fatigued, I said,
Tie up the knocker, say I'm sick, I'm dead.
The Dog Star rages! nay 'tis past a doubt,

asylum; Muses' home

All Bedlam▲, or Parnassus▲, is let out:
Fire in each eye, and papers in each hand,
They rave, recite, and madden round the land.
What walls can guard me, or what shades can hide?
They pierce my thickets, through my Grot they glide;
By land, by water, they renew the charge;
They stop the chariot, and they board the barge.
No place is sacred, not the Church is free;
Even Sunday shines no Sabbath day to me:
Then from the Mint walks forth the Man of rhyme,
Happy! to catch me just at Dinner time.
Is there a Parson, much bemused in beer,
A maudlin Poetess, a rhyming Peer,
A Clerk, foredoomed his father's soul to cross,

prepare legal documents

Who pens a Stanza, when he should *engross*▲?
Is there, who, locked from ink and paper, scrawls
With desperate charcoal round his darkened walls?
All fly to TWITNAM, and in humble strain
Apply to me, to keep them mad or vain.
Arthur, whose giddy son neglects the Laws,
Imputes to me and my damned works the cause:
Poor Cornus sees his frantic wife elope,
And curses Wit, and Poetry, and Pope.
Friend to my life! (which did not you prolong,
The world had wanted many an idle song)
What *Drop* or *Nostrum* can this plague remove?
Or which must end me, a Fool's wrath or love?

TITLE: Dr Arbuthnot was Pope's physician and friend. He had advised Pope to moderate his attacks upon his enemies, and this poem is Pope's reply.

3. Dog Star: Sirius appeared in late summer, a time when dogs are said to go mad, and in Ancient Rome it was also a time of public readings of verse.

13. Mint: a sanctuary for insolvent debtors. On Sundays they could walk free anywhere.

23. Arthur: Arthur Moore, father of James Moore Smythe, a playwright who plagiarised some lines of Pope.

25. Cornus: from Latin: cornu-horn. The name labels a man a cuckold.

A dire dilemma! either way I'm sped,
If foes, they write, if friends, they read me dead.
Seized and tied down to judge, how wretched I!
Who can't be silent, and who will not lie:
To laugh, were want of goodness and of grace,
And to be grave, exceeds all Power of face.
I sit with sad civility, I read
With honest anguish, and an aching head;
And drop at last, but in unwilling ears,
This saving counsel, 'Keep your piece nine years.'
in a garret in the theatre district
'Nine years!' cries he, who high in Drury Lane▲,
Lulled by soft Zephyrs through the broken pane,
Rhymes ere he wakes, and prints before *Term* ends,
Obliged by hunger, and request of friends:
'The piece, you think, is incorrect? why, take it,
I'm all submission, what you'd have it, make it.'
Three things another's modest wishes bound,
My Friendship, and a Prologue, and ten pound.
Pitholeon sends to me: 'You knew his Grace,
I want a Patron; ask him for a Place.'
Pitholeon libelled me—'but here's a letter
Informs you, Sir, 'twas when he knew no better.
Edward Curll, an unscrupulous publisher
Dare you refuse him? Curll▲ invites to dine,
He'll write a *Journal*, or he'll turn Divine.'
Bless me! a packet.—''Tis a stranger sues,
A Virgin Tragedy, an Orphan Muse.'
If I dislike it, 'Furies, death and rage!'
If I approve, 'Commend it to the Stage.'
There (thank my stars) my whole commission ends,
The Players and I are, luckily, no friends.
playhouse
Fired that the house▲ reject him, ''Sdeath I'll print it,
published Pope's early work
And shame the fools—Your Interest, Sir, with Lintot▲.'
Lintot, dull rogue! will think your price too much:
'Not, Sir, if you revise it, and retouch.'
All my demurs but double his attacks;
shares
At last he whispers, 'Do; and we go snacks▲.'
Glad of a quarrel, straight I clap the door,
'Sir, let me see your works and you no more.'

'Tis sung, when Midas' Ears began to spring,
(Midas, a sacred person and a King)
His very Minister who spied them first,
(Some say his Queen) was forced to speak, or burst.
And is not mine, my friend, a sorer case,
When every coxcomb perks them in my face?
A. Good friend, forbear! you deal in dangerous things.
I'd never name Queens, Ministers, or Kings;
Keep close to Ears, and those let asses prick;
'Tis nothing—P. Nothing? if they bite and kick?
Out with it, DUNCIAD▲! let the secret pass, *satirical work by Pope*
That secret to each fool, that he's an Ass:
The truth once told (and wherefore should we lie?)
The Queen of Midas slept, and so may I.
You think this cruel? take it for a rule,
No creature smarts so little as a fool.
Let peals of laughter, Codrus▲! round thee break, *poet mocked by Virgil*
Thou unconcerned canst hear the mighty crack:
Pit, Box, and gallery in convulsions hurled,
Thou standst unshook amidst a bursting world..,
Who shames a Scribbler? break one cobweb through,
He spins the slight, self-pleasing thread anew:
Destroy his fib or sophistry, in vain,
The creature's at his dirty work again,
Throned in the centre of his thin designs,
Proud of a vast extent of flimsy lines!
Whom have I hurt? has Poet yet, or Peer,
Lost the arched eyebrow, or Parnassian sneer?
And has not Colley▲ still his Lord, and whore? *Colley Cibber, poet laureate*
His butchers Henley, his Freemasons Moore?
Does not one table Bavius still admit?
Still to one Bishop Philips seem a wit?
Still Sappho—A. Hold! for God's sake—you'll offend,
No Names—be calm—learn prudence of a friend:
I too could write, and I am twice as tall;

69. Midas: Apollo gave King Midas ass's ears for preferring Pan's music to his own.
98–101. John Henley was an independent preacher with a mass following. James Moore Smythe was a member of the Masonic order. Bavins is a bad poet referred to by Virgil. The Bishop of Armagh employed Ambrose Philips as his secretary. Sappho: Lady Mary Wartley Montagu.

But foes like these—P. One Flatterer's worse than all.
Of all mad creatures, if the learned are right,
It is the slaver kills, and not the bite.
A fool quite angry is quite innocent:
Alas! 'tis ten times worse when they *repent*.
One dedicates in high heroic prose,
And ridicules beyond a hundred foes:
haunt of hack writers One from all Grubstreet▲ will my fame defend,
And, more abusive, calls himself my friend.
This prints my *Letters*, that expects a bribe,
pay for copies before publication And others roar aloud, 'Subscribe, subscribe▲.'
There are, who to my person pay their court:
I cough like *Horace*, and, though lean, am short,
Alexander the Great *Ammon's* great son▲ one shoulder had too high,
Such *Ovid's* nose, and 'Sir! you have an Eye'—
Go on, obliging creatures, make me see
All that disgraced my Betters, met in me.
Say for my comfort, languishing in bed,
Virgil 'Just so immortal *Maro*▲ held his head:'
And when I die, be sure you let me know
Great *Homer* died three thousand years ago.
Why did I write? what sin to me unknown
Dipped me in ink, my parents', or my own?
As yet a child, nor yet a fool to fame,
I lisped in numbers, for the numbers came.
I left no calling for this idle trade,
No duty broke, no father disobeyed.
The Muse but served to ease some friend, not Wife,
To help me through this long disease, my Life,
To second, ARBUTHNOT! thy Art and Care,
life And teach the Being you preserved, to bear▲.
But why then publish? *Granville* the polite,
And knowing *Walsh*, would tell me I could write;
Well-natured *Garth* inflamed with early praise;
And *Congreve* loved, and *Swift* endured my lays;
The courtly *Talbot*, *Somers*, *Sheffield* read,
Even mitred *Rochester* would nod the head,

113. prints my letters: as Curll had done without permission.
135 *ff*. Granville et al.: older writers who encouraged Pope in his early years.

And *St John's* self (great *Dryden's* friends before)
With open arms received one Poet more.
Happy my studies, when by these approved!
Happier their author, when by these beloved!
From these the world will judge of men and books,
critics of Pope's work
Not from the *Burnets*, *Oldmixons*, and *Cookes*▲.
    Soft were my numbers; who could take offence
While pure Description held the place of Sense?
Lord Hervey, Sporus of lines 305 ff.
Like gentle *Fanny's*▲ was my flowery theme,
A painted mistress, or a purling stream.
Yet then did *Gildon* draw his venal quill;
I wished the man a dinner, and sat still.
Yet then did *Dennis* rave in furious fret;
I never answered—I was not in debt.
If want provoked, or madness made them print,
I waged no war with *Bedlam* or the *Mint*.
    Did some more sober Critic come abroad;
If wrong, I smiled; if right, I kissed the rod.
Pains, reading, study, are their just pretence,
And all they want is spirit, taste, and sense.
Commas and points they set exactly right,
And 'twere a sin to rob them of their mite.
Yet ne'er one sprig of laurel graced these ribalds,
From slashing *Bentley* down to pidling *Tibalds*:
Each wight, who reads not, and but scans and spells,
Each Word-catcher, that lives on syllables.
Even such small Critics some regard may claim,
Preserved in *Milton's* or in *Shakespeare's* name.
Pretty! in amber to observe the forms
Of hairs, or straws, or dirt, or grubs, or worms!
The things, we know, are neither rich nor rare,
But wonder how the devil they got there.
    Were others angry: I excused them too;
Well might they rage, I gave them but their due.
A man's true merit 'tis not hard to find;
But each man's secret standard in his mind,
That Casting weight pride adds to emptiness,

164 *ff*. Bentley produced an edition of Milton's *Paradise Lost*. Lewis Theobald (*Tibalds*) criticised Pope's edition of Shakespeare.

This, who can gratify? for who can *guess*?
The Bard who pilfered Pastorals renown,
Who turns a Persian tale for half a Crown,
Just writes to make his barrenness appear,
And strains, from hard-bound brains, eight lines a year;
He, who still wanting, though he lives on theft,
Steals much, spends little, yet has nothing left:
And He, who now to sense, now nonsense leaning,
Means not, but blunders round about a meaning:
bombast
And He, whose fustian's▲ so sublimely bad,
It is not Poetry, but prose run mad:
All these, my modest Satire bade *translate*,
Nahum Tate, poet laureate
And owned that nine such Poets made a *Tate*▲.
How did they fume, and stamp, and roar, and chafe!
And swear, not ADDISON himself was safe.
    Peace to all such! but were there One whose fires
True Genius kindles, and fair Fame inspires;
Blest with each talent and each art to please,
And born to write, converse, and live with ease:
Should such a man, too fond to rule alone,
Bear, like the Turk, no brother near the throne,
View him with scornful, yet with jealous eyes,
And hate for arts that caused himself to rise;
Damn with faint praise, assent with civil leer,
And without sneering, teach the rest to sneer;
Willing to wound, and yet afraid to strike,
Just hint a fault, and hesitate dislike;
Alike reserved to blame, or to commend,
A timorous foe, and a suspicious friend;
Dreading even fools, by Flatterers besieged,
And so obliging, that he ne'er obliged;
Addison, author of Cato
Like *Cato*▲, give his little Senate laws,
And sit attentive to his own applause;
law students of The Temple, in London
While Wits and Templars▲ every sentence raise,
And wonder with a foolish face of praise—
Who but must laugh, if such a man there be?

198. The Ottoman Turk rulers were thought to protect themselves, on ascending the throne, by killing their closest relatives as potential rivals.

Addison Who would not weep, if ATTICUS▲ were he?
in red posters What though my Name stood rubric▲ on the walls,
Or plastered posts, with claps, in capitals?
Or smoking forth, a hundred hawkers' load,
On wings of wind came flying all abroad?
I sought no homage from the Race that write;
I kept, like *Asian* Monarchs, from their sight:
Poems I heeded (now berhymed so long)
No more than thou, great GEORGE! a birthday song.
I ne'er with wits or witlings passed my days,
To spread about the itch of verse and praise;
Nor like a puppy, daggled through the town,
To fetch and carry singsong up and down;
Nor at Rehearsals sweat, and mouthed, and cried,
With handkerchief and orange at my side;
But sick of fops, and poetry, and prate,
the field of letters To *Bufo* left the whole *Castalian* state▲.
the twin peaks of Parnassus Proud as *Apollo* on his forked hill▲,
Sat full-blown *Bufo*, puffed by every quill;
Fed with soft Dedication all day long
Horace and he went hand in hand in song.
His Library (where busts of Poets dead
And a true *Pindar* stood without a head)
Received of wits an undistinguished race,
Who first his judgment asked, and then a place:
estate Much they extolled his pictures, much his seat▲,
And flattered every day, and some days eat:
Till grown more frugal in his riper days,
He paid some bards with port, and some with praise;
without performance To some a dry rehearsal▲ was assigned,
And others (harder still) he paid in kind.
Dryden alone (what wonder?) came not nigh,
Dryden alone escaped this judging eye:
But still the *Great* have kindness in reserve,
He helped to bury whom he helped to starve.
May some choice patron bless each grey goose quill!
May every *Bavius* have his *Bufo* still!
So, when a Statesman wants a day's defence,
Or Envy holds a whole week's war with Sense,

Or simple pride for flattery makes demands,
May dunce by dunce be whistled off my hands!
Blest be the *Great*! for those they take away,
And those they left me; for they left me GAY*;
Left me to see neglected Genius bloom,
Neglected die, and tell it on his tomb:
Of all thy blameless life the sole return,
My Verse, and QUEENSBURY weeping o'er thy urn!
Oh let me live my own, and die so too!
(To live and die is all I have to do:)
Maintain a Poet's dignity and ease,
And see what friends, and read what books I please:
Above a Patron, though I condescend
Sometimes to call a Minister my friend.
I was not born for Courts or great affairs;
I pay my debts, believe, and say my prayers;
Can sleep without a Poem in my head,
Nor know, if *Dennis* be alive or dead.
Why am I asked what next shall see the light?
Heavens! was I born for nothing but to write?
Has Life no joys for me? or, (to be grave)
Have I no friend to serve, no soul to save?
'I found him close with *Swift*'—'Indeed? no doubt,'
(Cries prating *Balbus*) 'something will come out.'
'Tis all in vain, deny it as I will.
'No, such a Genius never can lie still;'
And then for mine obligingly mistakes
The first Lampoon Sir *Will*. or *Bubo* makes.
Poor guiltless I! and can I choose but smile,
When every Coxcomb knows me by my *Style*?
Cursed be the verse, how well soe'er it flow,
That tends to make one worthy man my foe,
Give Virtue scandal, Innocence a fear,
Or from the soft-eyed Virgin steal a tear!
But he who hurts a harmless neighbour's peace,
Insults fallen worth, or Beauty in distress,
Who loves a Lie, lame slander helps about,
Who writes a Libel, or who copies out:
That Fop, whose pride affects a patron's name,

John Gay, author of The Beggar's Opera

Yet absent, wounds an author's honest fame:
Who can *your* merit *selfishly* approve,
And show the sense of it without the *love*;
Who has the vanity to call you friend,
Yet wants the honour, injured, to defend;
Who tells whate'er you think, whate'er you say,
And, if he lie not, must at least betray:
Who to the *Dean*, and *silver bell* can swear,
And sees at *Canons* what was never there;
Who reads, but with a lust to misapply,
Make Satire a Lampoon, and Fiction, Lie.
A lash like mine no honest man shall dread,
But all such babbling blockheads in his stead.
    Let *Sporus*▲ tremble—A. What? that thing of silk, (*Lord Hervey*)
Sporus, that mere white curd of Ass's milk▲? (*drunk by those of delicate constitution*)
Satire or sense, alas! can *Sporus* feel?
Who breaks a butterfly upon a wheel?
P. Yet let me flap this bug with gilded wings,
This painted child of dirt, that stinks and stings;
Whose buzz▲ the witty and the fair annoys, (*annoying insect-like talk*)
Yet wit ne'er tastes, and beauty ne'er enjoys:
So well-bred spaniels civilly delight
In mumbling of the game they dare not bite.
Eternal smiles his emptiness betray,
As shallow streams run dimpling all the way.
Whether in florid impotence he speaks,
And, as the prompter breathes, the puppet squeaks;
Or at the ear of *Eve*▲, familiar Toad, (*Queen Caroline, with Sporus her Satan*)
Half froth, half venom, spits himself abroad.
In puns, or politics, or tales, or lies,
Or spite, or smut, or rhymes, or blasphemies.
His wit all seesaw, between *that* and *this*,
Now high, now low, now master up, now miss,
And he himself one vile Antithesis.
Amphibious thing! that acting either part,
The trifling head, or the corrupted heart,
Fop at the toilet, flatterer at the board,

299–300. Enemies of Pope perversely identified Timon's villa, its dean and its chapel bell, in *Epistle to Burlington*, with Pope's friend Chandos (Cannon).

Now trips a Lady, and now struts a Lord.
Hebrew scholars *Eve's* tempter thus the Rabbins▲ have exprest,
A Cherub's face, a reptile all the rest;
abilities Beauty that shocks you, parts▲ that none will trust,
Wit that can creep, and pride that licks the dust.
Not Fortune's worshipper, nor Fashion's fool,
Money's Not Lucre's▲ madman, nor Ambition's tool,
Not proud, nor servile; Be one Poet's praise,
That, if he pleased, he pleased by manly ways:
That Flattery, even to Kings, he held a shame,
And thought a Lie in verse or prose the same.
That not in Fancy's maze he wandered long,
But stooped to Truth and moralized his song:
That not for Fame, but Virtue's better end,
He stood the furious foe, the timid friend,
The damning critic, half approving wit,
The coxcomb hit, or fearing to be hit;
Laughed at the loss of friends he never had,
The dull, the proud, the wicked, and the mad;
The distant threats of vengeance on his head,
The blow unfelt, the tear he never shed;
The tale revived, the lie so oft o'erthrown,
Th' imputed trash, and dulness not his own;
The morals blackened when the writings 'scape,
The libeled person, and the pictured shape;
Abuse, on all he loved, or loved him, spread,
A friend in exile, or a father, dead;
The whisper, that to greatness still too near,
Perhaps, yet vibrates on his SOVEREIGN'S ear—
Welcome for thee, fair *Virtue*! all the past:
For thee, fair Virtue! welcome even the *last*!
A. But why insult the poor, affront the great?
P. A knave's a knave, to me, in every state:
Alike my scorn, if he succeed or fail,
Sporus at court, or *Japhet* in a jail,
A hireling scribbler, or a hireling peer,
paid for false evidence Knight of the post corrupt▲, or of the shire;

363, 366–367: Japhet: a forger, was pilloried and had his ears cut off.

If on a Pillory, or near a Throne,
He gain his Prince's ear, or lose his own.
  Yet soft by nature, more a dupe than wit,
Sappho can tell you how this man was bit▲: *deceived*
This dreaded Satirist *Dennis* will confess
Foe to his pride, but friend to his distress:
So humble, he has knocked at *Tibbald's* door,
Has drunk with *Cibber*, nay, has rhymed for *Moore*.
Full ten years slandered, did he once reply?
Three thousand suns went down on *Welsted's* lie.
To please a Mistress one aspersed his life;
He lashed him not, but let her be his wife:
Let *Budgel* charge low *Grubstreet* on his quill,
And write whate'er he pleased, except his Will;
Let the two *Curlls* of Town and Court, abuse
His father, mother, body, soul, and muse.
Yet why? that Father held it for a rule,
It was a sin to call our neighbour fool:
That harmless Mother thought no wife a whore:
Hear this, and spare his family, *James Moore*!
Unspotted names, and memorable long!
If there be force in Virtue, or in Song.
  Of gentle blood (part shed in Honour's cause,
While yet in *Britain* Honour had applause)
Each parent sprung—A. What fortune pray?—
    P. Their own,
And better got, than *Bestia's* from the throne.
Born to no Pride, inheriting no Strife,
Nor marrying Discord in a noble wife,
Stranger to civil and religious rage,
The good man walked innoxious through his age.
No Courts he saw, no suits would ever try,
Nor dared an Oath, nor hazarded a Lie.
Unlearned, he knew no schoolman's subtle art,
No language, but the language of the heart.
By Nature honest, by Experience wise,
Healthy by temperance, and by exercise;
His life, though long, to sickness past unknown,
His death was instant, and without a groan.

O grant me, thus to live, and thus to die!
Who sprung from Kings shall know less joy than I.
  O Friend! may each domestic bliss be thine!
Be no unpleasing Melancholy mine:
Me, let the tender office long engage,
To rock the cradle of reposing Age,
With lenient arts extend a Mother's breath,
Make Languor smile, and smooth the bed of Death,
Explore the thought, explain the asking eye,
And keep a while one parent from the sky!
On cares like these if length of days attend,
May Heaven, to bless those days, preserve my friend,
Preserve him social, cheerful, and serene,
Queen Anne
And just as rich as when he served a QUEEN.
A. Whether that blessing be denied or given,
Thus far was right, the rest belongs to Heaven.

WILLIAM BLAKE
(1757–1827)

Born London, was a printer and engraver. He illustrated and printed his own poetry. Poor all his life, Blake was a religious and political visionary, following his own very individualistic Christianity, and defending the French Revolution against the monarchy.

from SONGS OF INNOCENCE

THE ECHOING GREEN

The Sun does arise,
And make happy the skies;
The merry bells ring
To welcome the Spring;
The skylark and thrush,
The birds of the bush,
Sing louder around
To the bells' cheerful sound,
While our sports shall be seen
On the Echoing Green.

Old John, with white hair,
Does laugh away care,
Sitting under the oak
Among the old folk.
They laugh at our play,

And soon they all say:
'Such, such were the joys
When we all, girls and boys,
In our youth time were seen
On the Echoing Green.'

Till the little ones, weary,
No more can be merry;
The sun does descend,
And our sports have an end.
Round the laps of their mothers
Many sisters and brothers,
Like birds in their nest,
Are ready for rest,
And sport no more seen
On the darkening Green.

THE LAMB

Little Lamb, who made thee?
Dost thou know who made thee?
Gave thee life, and bid thee feed
By the stream and o'er the mead;
Gave thee clothing of delight,
Softest clothing, woolly, bright;
Gave thee such a tender voice,
Making all the vales rejoice?
  Little Lamb, who made thee?
  Dost thou know who made thee?

  Little Lamb, I'll tell thee,
  Little Lamb, I'll tell thee:
He is callèd by thy name,
For he calls himself a Lamb.
He is meek, and he is mild;
He became a little child.

I a child, and thou a lamb,
We are callèd by his name.
    Little Lamb, God bless thee!
    Little Lamb, God bless thee!

HOLY THURSDAY

'Twas on a Holy Thursday, their innocent faces clean,
The children▴ walking two and two, in red and blue and green, — *of charity schools*
Grey-headed beadles▴ walked before, with wands as white as snow, — *ushers, to keep order*
Till into the high dome of Paul's they like Thames' waters flow.

O what a multitude they seemed, these flowers of London town!
Seated in companies they sit with radiance all their own.
The hum of multitudes was there, but multitudes of lambs,
Thousands of little boys and girls raising their innocent hands.

Now like a mighty wind they raise to Heaven the voice of song,
Or like harmonious thunderings the seats of Heaven among.
Beneath them sit the agèd men, wise guardians of the poor;
Then cherish pity, lest you drive an angel from your door.

from SONGS OF EXPERIENCE

THE TIGER

Tiger! Tiger! burning bright
In the forests of the night,
What immortal hand or eye
Could frame thy fearful symmetry?

In what distant deeps or skies
Burnt the fire of thine eyes?
On what wings dare he aspire?
What the hand dare seize the fire?

And what shoulder, and what art,
Could twist the sinews of thy heart?
And when thy heart began to beat,
What dread hand? and what dread feet?

What the hammer? what the chain?
In what furnace was thy brain?
What the anvil? what dread grasp
Dare its deadly terrors clasp?

When the stars threw down their spears,
And watered heaven with their tears,
Did he smile his work to see?
Did he who made the Lamb make thee?

Tiger! Tiger! burning bright
In the forests of the night,
What immortal hand or eye
Dare frame thy fearful symmetry?

A POISON TREE

I was angry with my friend:
I told my wrath, my wrath did end.
I was angry with my foe:
I told it not, my wrath did grow.

And I watered it in fears,
Night and morning with my tears;
And I sunnèd it with smiles,
And with soft deceitful wiles.

And it grew both day and night,
Till it bore an apple bright;
And my foe beheld it shine,
And he knew that it was mine,

And into my garden stole,
When the night had veiled the pole:
In the morning glad I see
My foe outstretched beneath the tree.

THE SICK ROSE

O Rose, thou art sick!
The invisible worm
That flies in the night,
In the howling storm,

Has found out thy bed
Of crimson joy:
And his dark secret love
Does thy life destroy.

THE CLOD AND THE PEBBLE

'Love seeketh not Itself to please,
Nor for itself hath any care,
But for another gives its ease,
And builds a Heaven in Hell's despair.'

So sang a little Clod of Clay
Trodden with the cattle's feet,
But a Pebble of the brook
Warbled out these metres meet:

'Love seeketh only Self to please,
To bind another to Its delight,
Joys in another's loss of ease,
And builds a Hell in Heaven's despite.'

THE GARDEN OF LOVE

I went to the Garden of Love,
And saw what I never had seen:
A Chapel was built in the midst,
Where I used to play on the green.

And the gates of this Chapel were shut,
And 'Thou shalt not' writ over the door;
So I turn'd to the Garden of Love
That so many sweet flowers bore;

And I saw it was filled with graves,
And tomb-stones where flowers should be;
And Priests in black gowns were walking their rounds,
And binding with briars my joys and desires.

INFANT SORROW

My mother groaned, my father wept,
Into the dangerous world I leapt;
Helpless, naked, piping loud,
Like a fiend hid in a cloud.

Struggling in my father's hands,
Striving against my swaddling-bands,
Bound and weary, I thought best
To sulk upon my mother's breast.

LONDON

I wander thro' each chartered street,
Near where the chartered Thames does flow,
And mark in every face I meet
Marks of weakness, marks of woe.

In every cry of every Man,
In every Infant's cry of fear,
In every voice, in every ban,
The mind-forged manacles I hear.

How the Chimney-sweeper's cry
Every black'ning Church appals;
And the hapless Soldier's sigh
Runs in blood down Palace walls.

But most thro' midnight streets I hear
How the youthful Harlot's curse
Blasts the new-born Infant's tear,
And blights with plagues the Marriage hearse.

1. LONDON chartered: mapped out; legally defined; constricted; hired.
7. LONDON ban: legal command, insisting or forbidding.

NEVER SEEK TO TELL THY LOVE

Never seek to tell thy love,
Love that never told can be;
For the gentle wind does move
Silently, invisibly.

I told my love, I told my love,
I told her all my heart;
Trembling, cold, in ghastly fears,
Ah! she doth depart.

Soon as she was gone from me,
A traveller came by,
Silently, invisibly:
He took her with a sigh.

THE HUMAN ABSTRACT

Pity would be no more
If we did not make somebody poor;
And Mercy no more could be
If all were as happy as we.

And mutual fear brings peace,
Till the selfish loves increase:
Then Cruelty knits a snare,
And spreads his baits with care.

He sits down with holy fears,
And waters the ground with tears;
Then Humility takes its root
Underneath his foot.

Soon spreads the dismal shade
Of Mystery over his head;
And the caterpillar and fly
Feed on the Mystery.

And it bears the fruit of Deceit,
Ruddy and sweet to eat;
And the raven his nest has made
In its thickest shade.

The Gods of the earth and sea
Sought thro' Nature to find this tree;
But their search was all in vain:
There grows one in the human brain.

from **AUGURIES OF INNOCENCE**

To see a World in a grain of sand,
And a Heaven in a wild flower,
Hold Infinity in the palm of your hand,
And Eternity in an hour.
A robin redbreast in a cage
Puts all Heaven in a rage.
A dove-house filled with doves and pigeons
Shudders Hell thro' all its regions,
A dog starv'd at his master's gate
Predicts the ruin of the State.
harmed A horse misused▲ upon the road
Calls to Heaven for human blood.
Each outcry of the hunted hare
A fibre from the brain does tear.
A skylark wounded in the wing,
A cherubim does cease to sing.
The game-cock clipt and armed for fight
Does the rising sun affright.

Every wolf's and lion's howl
Raises from Hell a Human soul.
The wild deer, wandering here and there,
Keeps the Human soul from care.
The lamb misused breeds public strife,
And yet forgives the butcher's knife.
The bat that flits at close of eve
Has left the brain that won't believe.
The owl that calls upon the night
Speaks the unbeliever's fright.

from **MILTON**

feet: of Christ

And did those feet▲ in ancient time,
Walk upon England's mountains green:
And was the holy Lamb of God
On England's pleasant pastures seen!

And did the Countenance Divine,
Shine forth upon our clouded hills?
And was Jerusalem builded here,
Among these dark Satanic Mills▲?

factories

Bring me my Bow of burning gold:
Bring me my Arrows of desire:
Bring me my Spear: O clouds unfold:
Bring me my Chariot of fire:

I will not cease from Mental Fight,
Nor shall my Sword sleep in my hand:
Till we have built Jerusalem,
In England's green & pleasant Land.

WILLIAM WORDSWORTH
(1770–1850)

Born Lake District, England. In rejecting the artifice of late eighteenth-century poetry, Wordsworth saw himself writing in 'language really used', in scenes from 'humble and rustic life', to present 'the essential passions of the heart'.

COMPOSED UPON WESTMINSTER BRIDGE

SEPTEMBER 3, 1802

Earth has not anything to show more fair:
Dull would he be of soul who could pass by
A sight so touching in its majesty:
This City now doth, like a garment, wear
The beauty of the morning; silent, bare,
Ships, towers, domes, theatres, and temples lie
Open unto the fields, and to the sky;
All bright and glittering in the smokeless air.
Never did sun more beautifully steep
In his first splendour, valley, rock, or hill;
Ne'er saw I, never felt, a calm so deep!
The river glideth at his own sweet will:
Dear God! the very houses seem asleep;
And all that mighty heart is lying still!

A SLUMBER DID MY SPIRIT SEAL

A slumber did my spirit seal;
I had no human fears:
She seemed a thing that could not feel
The touch of earthly years.

No motion has she now, no force;
She neither hears nor sees;
Rolled round in earth's diurnal course,
With rocks, and stones, and trees.

SURPRISED BY JOY

Surprised by joy—impatient as the Wind
I turned to share the transport—Oh! with whom
But Thee, deep buried in the silent tomb,
That spot which no vicissitude can find?
Love, faithful love, recalled thee to my mind—
But how could I forget thee? Through what power,
Even for the least division of an hour,
Have I been so beguiled as to be blind
To my most grievous loss!—That thought's return
Was the worst pang that sorrow ever bore,
Save one, one only, when I stood forlorn,
Knowing my heart's best treasure was no more;
That neither present time, nor years unborn
Could to my sight that heavenly face restore.

THE SOLITARY REAPER

Behold her, single in the field,
Yon solitary Highland Lass!
Reaping and singing by herself;
Stop here, or gently pass!

Alone she cuts and binds the grain,
And sings a melancholy strain;
O listen! for the Vale profound
Is overflowing with the sound.

No Nightingale did ever chaunt
More welcome notes to weary bands
Of travellers in some shady haunt,
Among Arabian sands:
A voice so thrilling ne'er was heard
In spring-time from the Cuckoo-bird,
Breaking the silence of the seas
Among the farthest Hebrides.

Will no one tell me what she sings?—
Perhaps the plaintive numbers flow
For old, unhappy, far-off things,
And battles long ago:
Or is it some more humble lay,
Familiar matter of to-day?
Some natural sorrow, loss, or pain,
That has been, and may be again?

Whate'er the theme, the Maiden sang
As if her song could have no ending;
I saw her singing at her work,
And o'er the sickle bending:—
I listened, motionless and still;
And, as I mounted up the hill,
The music in my heart I bore,
Long after it was heard no more.

from THE PRELUDE

from BOOK ONE

Oh, many a time have I, a five years' child,
In a small mill-race severed from his stream,
Made one long bathing of a summer's day;
Basked in the sun, and plunged and basked again
Alternate, all a summer's day, or scoured
The sandy fields, leaping through flowery groves
Of yellow ragwort; or when rock and hill,
The woods, and distant Skiddaw's lofty height,
Were bronzed with deepest radiance, stood alone
Beneath the sky, as if I had been born
On Indian plains, and from my mother's hut
Had run abroad in wantonness, to sport,
A naked savage, in the thunder shower.

Fair seed-time had my soul, and I grew up
Fostered alike by beauty and by fear:
Much favoured in my birthplace, and no less
In that beloved Vale to which erelong
We were transplanted—there were we let loose
For sports of wider range. Ere I had told
Ten birth-days, when among the mountain-slopes
Frost, and the breath of frosty wind, had snapped
The last autumnal crocus, 'twas my joy
With store of springes▲ o'er my shoulder hung *(snares)*
To range the open heights where wood-cocks run
Among the smooth green turf. Through half the night,
Scudding away from snare to snare, I plied
That anxious visitation;—moon and stars
Were shining o'er my head. I was alone,
And seemed to be a trouble to the peace
That dwelt among them. Sometimes it befell
In these night wanderings, that a strong desire
O'erpowered my better reason, and the bird
Which was the captive of another's toil
Became my prey; and when the deed was done
I heard among the solitary hills

Low breathings coming after me, and sounds
Of undistinguishable motion, steps
Almost as silent as the turf they trod.

cultivated Nor less when spring had warmed the cultured▲ Vale,
Roved we as plunderers where the mother-bird
Had in high places built her lodge; though mean
Our object and inglorious, yet the end
Was not ignoble. Oh! when I have hung
Above the raven's nest, by knots of grass
And half-inch fissures in the slippery rock
But ill sustained, and almost (so it seemed)
Suspended by the blast that blew amain,
Shouldering the naked crag, oh, at that time
While on the perilous ridge I hung alone,
With what strange utterance did the loud dry wind
Blow through my ear! the sky seemed not a sky
Of earth—and with what motion moved the clouds!

Dust as we are, the immortal spirit grows
Like harmony in music; there is a dark
Inscrutable workmanship that reconciles
Discordant elements, makes them cling together
In one society. How strange that all
The terrors, pains, and early miseries,
Regrets, vexations, lassitudes interfused
Within my mind, should e'er have borne a part,
And that a needful part, in making up
The calm existence that is mine when I
Am worthy of myself! Praise to the end!
Thanks to the means which Nature deigned to employ;
Whether her fearless visitings, or those
That came with soft alarm, like hurtless light
Opening the peaceful clouds; or she may use
Severer interventions, ministry
More palpable, as best might suit her aim.

One summer evening (led by her) I found
A little boat tied to a willow tree

Within a rocky cave, its usual home.
Straight I unloosed her chain, and stepping in
Pushed from the shore. It was an act of stealth
And troubled pleasure, nor without the voice
Of mountain-echoes did my boat move on;
Leaving behind her still, on either side,
Small circles glittering idly in the moon,
Until they melted all into one track
Of sparkling light. But now, like one who rows,
Proud of his skill, to reach a chosen point
With an unswerving line, I fixed my view
Upon the summit of a craggy ridge,
The horizon's utmost boundary; for above
Was nothing but the stars and the grey sky.
She was an elfin pinnace; lustily
I dipped my oars into the silent lake,
And, as I rose upon the stroke, my boat
Went heaving through the water like a swan;
When, from behind that craggy steep till then
The horizon's bound, a huge peak, black and huge,
As if with voluntary power instinct
Upreared its head. I struck and struck again,
And growing still in stature the grim shape
Towered up between me and the stars, and still,
For so it seemed, with purpose of its own
And measured motion like a living thing,
Strode after me. With trembling oars I turned,
And through the silent water stole my way
Back to the covert of the willow tree;
There in her mooring-place I left my bark,—
And through the meadows homeward went, in grave
And serious mood; but after I had seen
That spectacle, for many days, my brain
Worked with a dim and undetermined sense
Of unknown modes of being; o'er my thoughts
There hung a darkness, call it solitude
Or blank desertion. No familiar shapes
Remained, no pleasant images of trees,
Of sea or sky, no colours of green fields;

But huge and mighty forms, that do not live
Like living men, moved slowly through the mind
By day, and were a trouble to my dreams.

Wisdom and Spirit of the universe!
Thou Soul that art the eternity of thought,
That givest to forms and images a breath
And everlasting motion, not in vain
By day or star-light thus from my first dawn
Of childhood didst thou intertwine for me
The passions that build up our human soul;
Not with the mean and vulgar works of man,
But with high objects, with enduring things—
With life and nature—purifying thus
The elements of feeling and of thought.
And sanctifying, by such discipline,
Both pain and fear, until we recognise
A grandeur in the beatings of the heart.
Nor was this fellowship vouchsafed to me
With stinted kindness. In November days,
When vapours rolling down the valley made
A lonely scene more lonesome, among woods,
At noon and 'mid the calm of summer nights,
When, by the margin of the trembling lake,
Beneath the gloomy hills homeward I went,
In solitude, such intercourse was mine;
Mine was it in the fields both day and night,
And by the waters, all the summer long.

And in the frosty season, when the sun
Was set, and visible for many a mile
The cottage windows blazed through twilight gloom,
I heeded not their summons; happy time
It was indeed for all of us—for me
It was a time of rapture! Clear and loud
The village clock tolled six,—I wheeled about,
Proud and exulting like an untired horse
That cares not for his home. All shod with steel,
We hissed along the polished ice in games

Confederate, imitative of the chase
And woodland pleasures,—the resounding horn,
The pack loud chiming, and the hunted hare.
So through the darkness and the cold we flew,
And not a voice was idle; with the din
Smitten, the precipices rang aloud;
The leafless trees and every icy crag
Tinkled like iron; while far distant hills
Into the tumult sent an alien sound
Of melancholy not unnoticed, while the stars
Eastward were sparkling clear, and in the west
The orange sky of evening died away.
Not seldom from the uproar I retired
Into a silent bay, or sportively
Glanced sideway, leaving the tumultuous throng,
reflection To cut across the reflex▲ of a star
That fled, and, flying still before me, gleamed
Upon the glassy plain; and oftentimes,
When we had given our bodies to the wind,
And all the shadowy banks on either side
Came sweeping through the darkness, spinning still
The rapid line of motion, then at once
Have I, reclining back upon my heels,
Stopped short; yet still the solitary cliffs
Wheeled by me—even as if the earth had rolled
With visible motion her diurnal round!
Behind me did they stretch in solemn train,
Feebler and feebler, and I stood and watched
Till all was tranquil as a dreamless sleep.

JOHN KEATS
(1795–1821)

Born London. Keats studied, in turn, medicine and pharmacy, before giving up both to devote himself to poetry. He wrote most of his major poems during nine months of 1819. He died of tuberculosis at the age of twenty-six.

ON FIRST LOOKING INTO CHAPMAN'S HOMER

Much have I travell'd in the realms of gold,
And many goodly states and kingdoms seen;
Round many western islands have I been
Which bards in fealty to Apollo hold.
Oft of one wide expanse had I been told
That deep-brow'd Homer ruled as his demesne;
Yet did I never breathe its pure serene
Till I heard Chapman speak out loud and bold:
Then felt I like some watcher of the skies
When a new planet swims into his ken;
Or like stout Cortez when with eagle eyes
He star'd at the Pacific—and all his men
Look'd at each other with a wild surmise—
Silent, upon a peak in Darien.

TITLE: George Chapman's translation of Homer's *Iliad*, 1616.

4. Apollo: God of poetic inspiration.

11. Cortez: Spanish conqueror of Mexico. In fact, Balboa was the first European to see the Pacific, from Darien, in Panama.

ODE TO A NIGHTINGALE

My heart aches, and a drowsy numbness pains
poisonous sedative herb
My sense, as though of hemlock▴ I had drunk,
Or emptied some dull opiate to the drains
One minute past, and Lethe-wards had sunk:
'Tis not through envy of thy happy lot,
But being too happy in thine happiness,—
wood nymph
That thou, light-wingèd Dryad▴ of the trees,
In some melodious plot
Of beechen green, and shadows numberless,
Singest of summer in full-throated ease.

O, for a draught of vintage! that hath been
Cooled a long age in the deep-delvèd earth,
Roman goddess of flowers
Tasting of Flora▴ and the country green,
Dance, and Provençal song, and sunburnt mirth!
O for a beaker full of the warm South,
Full of the true, the blushful Hippocrene,
With beaded bubbles winking at the brim,
And purple-stained mouth;
That I might drink, and leave the world unseen,
And with thee fade away into the forest dim:

Fade far away, dissolve, and quite forget
What thou among the leaves hast never known,
The weariness, the fever, and the fret
Here, where men sit and hear each other groan;
Where palsy shakes a few, sad, last gray hairs,
Where youth grows pale, and spectre-thin, and dies;
Where but to think is to be full of sorrow
And leaden-eyed despairs,
Where beauty cannot keep her lustrous eyes,
Or new Love pine at them beyond to-morrow.

4. Lethe-wards: towards Lethe: Lethe was a river in Hades bringing on the forgetfulness of death.

16. Hippocrene: fountain of the Muses on Mt Helicon whose waters induced poetic inspiration.

Away! away! for I will fly to thee,
god of wine; leopards Not charioted by Bacchus▲ and his pards▲,
invisible But on the viewless▲ wings of Poesy,
Though the dull brain perplexes and retards:
Already with thee! tender is the night,
And haply the Queen-Moon is on her throne,
fairies Clustered around by all her starry Fays▲;
But here there is no light,
Save what from heaven is with the breezes blown
Through verdurous glooms and winding mossy ways.

I cannot see what flowers are at my feet,
Nor what soft incense hangs upon the boughs,
But, in embalmed darkness, guess each sweet
Wherewith the seasonable month endows
The grass, the thicket, and the fruit-tree wild;
White hawthorn, and the pastoral eglantine;
Fast fading violets covered up in leaves;
And mid-May's eldest child,
The coming musk-rose, full of dewy wine,
The murmorous haunt of flies on summer eves.

Darkling I listen; and, for many a time
I have been half in love with easeful Death,
Called him soft names in many a musèd rhyme,
To take into the air my quiet breath;
Now more than ever seems it rich to die,
To cease upon the midnight with no pain,
While thou art pouring forth thy soul abroad
In such an ecstasy!
Still wouldst thou sing, and I have ears in vain—
To thy high requiem become a sod.

Thou wast not born for death, immortal Bird!
No hungry generations tread thee down;
The voice I hear this passing night was heard
In ancient days by emperor and clown:
Perhaps the self-same song that found a path
in the Old Testament, an exile Through the sad heart of Ruth▲, when, sick for home,

She stood in tears amid the alien corn;
The same that oft-times hath
Charmed magic casements, opening on the foam
Of perilous seas, in faery lands forlorn.

Forlorn! the very word is like a bell
To toll me back from thee to my sole self!
Adieu! the fancy cannot cheat so well
As she is famed to do, deceiving elf.
Adieu! adieu! thy plaintive anthem fades
Past the near meadows, over the still stream,
Up the hill-side; and now 'tis buried deep
In the next valley-glades:
Was it a vision, or a waking dream?
Fled is that music:—Do I wake or sleep?

ODE ON MELANCHOLY

No, no, go not to Lethe, neither twist
Wolf's-bane, tight-rooted, for its poisonous wine;
Nor suffer thy pale forehead to be kiss'd
Queen of Hades By nightshade, ruby grape of Proserpine▲;
Make not your rosary of yew-berries,
Nor let the beetle, nor the death-moth be
Your mournful Psyche, nor the downy owl
A partner in your sorrow's mysteries;
For shade to shade will come too drowsily,
And drown the wakeful anguish of the soul.

But when the melancholy fit shall fall
Sudden from heaven like a weeping cloud,
That fosters the droop-headed flowers all,
And hides the green hill in an April shroud;

1. Lethe: river in Hades whose waters bring forgetfulness to the dead.
2 and 4. Wolf's bane and nightshade: poisonous plants.
5. yew-berries: from yew trees, symbols of mourning, often planted in cemeteries.
6–7. beetle, moth, owl: all associated with darkness, death and burial; Psyche: soul, symbolised by a moth or butterfly.

Then glut thy sorrow on a morning rose,
Or on the rainbow of the salt sand-wave,
Or on the wealth of the globed peonies;
Or if thy mistress some rich anger shows,
Emprison her soft hand, and let her rave,
And feed deep, deep upon her peerless eyes.

She dwells with Beauty—Beauty that must die;
And Joy, whose hand is ever at his lips
Bidding adieu; and aching Pleasure nigh,
Turning to poison while the bee-mouth sips:
Ay, in the very temple of Delight
Veil'd Melancholy has her sovereign shrine,
Though seen of none save him whose strenuous tongue
Can burst Joy's grape against his palate fine;
His soul shall taste the sadness of her might,
And be among her cloudy trophies hung.

ODE ON A GRECIAN URN

Thou still unravished bride of quietness,
Thou foster-child of silence and slow time,
Sylvan historian, who canst thus express
A flowery tale more sweetly than our rhyme:
What leaf-fringed legend haunts about thy shape
Of deities or mortals, or of both,
In Tempe or the dales of Arcady?
What men or gods are these? What maidens loth?
What mad pursuit? What struggle to escape?
What pipes and timbrels? What wild ecstasy?

Heard melodies are sweet, but those unheard
Are sweeter; therefore, ye soft pipes, play on;
Not to the sensual ear, but, more endeared,
Pipe to the spirit ditties of no tone:

Fair youth, beneath the trees, thou canst not leave
Thy song, nor ever can those trees be bare;
Bold Lover, never, never canst thou kiss,
Though winning near the goal—yet, do not grieve;
She cannot fade, though thou hast not thy bliss,
For ever wilt thou love, and she be fair!

Ah, happy, happy boughs! that cannot shed
Your leaves, nor ever bid the Spring adieu;
And, happy melodist, unwearièd,
For ever piping songs for ever new;
More happy love! more happy, happy love!
For ever warm and still to be enjoyed,
For ever panting, and for ever young;
All breathing human passion far above,
That leaves a heart high-sorrowful and cloyed,
A burning forehead, and a parching tongue.

Who are these coming to the sacrifice?
To what green altar, O mysterious priest,
Lead'st thou that heifer lowing at the skies,
And all her silken flanks with garlands drest?
What little town by river or sea shore,
Or mountain-built with peaceful citadel,
Is emptied of its folk, this pious morn?
And, little town, thy streets for evermore
Will silent be; and not a soul to tell
Why thou art desolate, can e'er return.

Athenian, Greek O Attic▲ shape! Fair attitude! with brede
embroidered Of marble men and maidens overwrought▲,
With forest branches and the trodden weed;
Thou, silent form, dost tease us out of thought
As doth eternity: Cold Pastoral!
When old age shall this generation waste,
Thou shalt remain, in midst of other woe
Than ours, a friend to man, to whom thou say'st,
'Beauty is truth, truth beauty,'—that is all
Ye know on earth, and all ye need to know.

TO AUTUMN

Season of mists and mellow fruitfulness,
Close bosom-friend of the maturing sun;
Conspiring with him how to load and bless
With fruit the vines that round the thatch-eaves run;
To bend with apples the mossed cottage-trees,
And fill all fruit with ripeness to the core;
marrow, melon To swell the gourd▲, and plump the hazel shells
With a sweet kernel; to set budding more,
And still more, later flowers for the bees,
Until they think warm days will never cease,
For Summer has o'er-brimmed their clammy cells.

Who hath not seen thee oft amid thy store?
Sometimes whoever seeks abroad may find
Thee sitting careless on a granary floor,
separating grain from chaff Thy hair soft-lifted by the winnowing▲ wind;
Or on a half-reaped furrow sound asleep,
Drowsed with the fume of poppies, while thy hook
Spares the next swath and all its twinèd flowers:
And sometimes like a gleaner thou dost keep
Steady thy laden head across a brook;
Or by a cyder-press, with patient look,
Thou watchest the last oozings hours by hours.

Where are the songs of Spring? Ay, where are they?
Think not of them, thou hast music too,—
While barrèd clouds bloom the soft-dying day,
And touch the stubble-plains with rosy hue;
Then in a wailful choir the small gnats mourn
low-growing willows Among the river sallows▲, borne aloft
Or sinking as the light wind lives or dies;
field And full-grown lambs loud bleat from hilly bourn▲;
Hedge-crickets sing; and now with treble soft
small field near house The red-breast whistles from a garden-croft▲;
And gathering swallows twitter in the skies.

LA BELLE DAME SANS MERCI

A BALLAD

O what can ail thee, knight-at-arms,
Alone and palely loitering?
The sedge has withered from the lake,
And no birds sing.

O what can ail thee, knight-at-arms!
So haggard and so woe-begone?
The squirrel's granary is full,
And the harvest's done.

I see a lily on thy brow,
With anguish moist and fever dew,
And on thy cheeks a fading rose
Fast withereth too.

meadows I met a lady in the meads▲,
Full beautiful—a faery's child,
Her hair was long, her foot was light,
And her eyes were wild.

I made a garland for her head,
girdle And bracelets too, and fragrant zone▲;
She looked at me as she did love,
And made sweet moan.

I set her on my pacing steed,
And nothing else saw all day long;
For sidelong would she bend, and sing
A faery's song.

She found me roots of relish sweet,
And honey wild, and manna dew,
And sure in language strange she said—
'I love thee true'.

TITLE: The Beautiful Lady Without Pity.

grotto She took me to her elfin grot▲,
And there she wept, and sighed full sore,
And there I shut her wild wild eyes
With kisses four.

And there she lullèd me asleep,
And there I dreamed—Ah! woe betide!
last The latest▲ dream I ever dreamed
On the cold hill side.

I saw pale kings, and princes too,
Pale warriors, death-pale were they all;
They cried—'La Belle Dame sans Merci
Hath thee in thrall!'

I saw their starved lips in the gloam,
With horrid warning gapèd wide,
And I awoke and found me here,
On the cold hill's side.

And this is why I sojourn here
Alone and palely loitering,
Though the sedge has withered from the lake,
And no birds sing.

ALFRED, LORD TENNYSON
(1809–1892)

Born Lincolnshire, England. Much of his finest verse is in In Memoriam, *to his friend Arthur Hallam. Many of his poems present versions of the Greek and the Arthurian legends. He wrote many patriotic occasional poems, particularly after he became Poet Laureate in 1850.*

ULYSSES

It little profits that an idle king,
By this still hearth, among these barren crags,
Matched with an aged wife, I mete and dole
Unequal laws unto a savage race,
That hoard, and sleep, and feed, and know not me.
I cannot rest from travel: I will drink
Life to the lees: all times I have enjoyed
Greatly, have suffered greatly, both with those
That loved me, and alone; on shore, and when
Thro' scudding drifts the rainy Hyades
Vext the dim sea: I am become a name;
For always roaming with a hungry heart
Much have I seen and known; cities of men
And manners, climates, councils, governments,
Myself not least, but honoured of them all;

TITLE: Ulysses is the Roman name for the Greek hero Odysseus.
10. Hyades: seven stars in the constellation of Taurus, portending rain if they appeared near sunrise.

And drunk delight of battle with my peers,
Far on the ringing plains of windy Troy.
I am a part of all that I have met;
Yet all experience is an arch wherethro'
Gleams that untravelled world, whose margin fades
For ever and for ever when I move.
How dull it is to pause, to make an end,
To rust unburnished, not to shine in use!
As tho' to breathe were life. Life piled on life
Were all too little, and of one to me
Little remains: but every hour is saved
From that eternal silence, something more,
A bringer of new things; and vile it were
For some three suns▲ to store and hoard myself,

three years

And this gray spirit yearning in desire
To follow knowledge, like a sinking star,
Beyond the utmost bound of human thought.
This is my son, mine own Telemachus,
To whom I leave the sceptre and the isle—
Well-loved of me, discerning to fulfil
This labour, by slow prudence to make mild
A rugged people, and thro' soft degrees
Subdue them to the useful and the good.
Most blameless is he, centred in the sphere
Of common duties, decent not to fail
In offices of tenderness, and pay
Meet adoration to my household gods,
When I am gone. He works his work, I mine.
There lies the port; the vessel puffs her sail:
There gloom the dark broad seas. My mariners,
Souls that have toiled, and wrought, and thought
with me—
That ever with a frolic welcome took
The thunder and the sunshine, and opposed
Free hearts, free foreheads—you and I are old;
Old age hath yet his honour and his toil;
Death closes all: but something ere the end,
Some work of noble note, may yet be done,
Not unbecoming men that strove with Gods.

The lights begin to twinkle from the rocks:
The long day wanes: the slow moon climbs: the deep
Moans round with many voices. Come, my friends,
'Tis not too late to seek a newer world.
Push off, and sitting well in order smite
The sounding furrows; for my purpose holds
To sail beyond the sunset, and the baths
Of all the western stars, until I die.
It may be that the gulfs will wash us down:
It may be we shall touch the Happy Isles▲,
And see the great Achilles▲, whom we knew.
Tho' much is taken, much abides; and tho'
We are not now that strength which in old days
Moved earth and heaven; that which we are, we are;
One equal temper of heroic hearts,
Made weak by time and fate, but strong in will
To strive, to seek, to find, and not to yield.

the Hesperides, earthly paradise

Greek hero of siege of Troy

SONG OF THE LOTOS-EATERS

There is sweet music here that softer falls
Than petals from blown roses on the grass,
Or night-dews on still waters between walls
Of shadowy granite, in a gleaming pass;
Music that gentlier on the spirit lies,
Than tired eyelids upon tired eyes;
Music that brings sweet sleep down from the blissful skies.
Here are cool mosses deep,
And through the moss the ivies creep,
And in the stream the long-leaved flowers weep,
And from the craggy ledge the poppy hangs in sleep.

TITLE: One of Odysseus' (Ulysses') adventures on the way home from the Trojan War was to visit the land of the lotus eaters. Some of his crewmen ate the lotus fruit which made them forget home and desire to stay in Lotus Land forever. Odysseus had to take them back to his ships by force. See *The Odyssey*, Book 9.

Why are we weighed upon with heaviness,
And utterly consumed with sharp distress,
While all things else have rest from weariness?
All things have rest: why should we toil alone,
We only toil, who are the first of things,
And make perpetual moan,
Still from one sorrow to another thrown:
Nor ever fold our wings,
And cease from wanderings,
Nor steep our brows in slumber's holy balm;
Nor harken what the inner spirit sings,
'There is no joy but calm!'
Why should we only toil, the roof and crown of things?

Lo! in the middle of the wood,
The folded leaf is wooed from out the bud
With winds upon the branch, and there
Grows green and broad, and takes no care,
Sun-steeped at noon, and in the moon
Nightly dew-fed; and turning yellow
Falls, and floats adown the air.
Lo! sweetened with the summer light,
The full-juiced apple, waxing over-mellow,
Drops in a silent autumn night.
All its allotted length of days,
The flower ripens in its place,
Ripens and fades, and falls, and hath no toil,
Fast-rooted in the fruitful soil.

Hateful is the dark-blue sky,
Vaulted o'er the dark-blue sea.
Death is the end of life; ah, why
Should life all labour be?
Let us alone. Time driveth onward fast,
And in a little while our lips are dumb.
Let us alone. What is it that will last?
All things are taken from us, and become
Portions and parcels of the dreadful Past.
Let us alone. What pleasure can we have

To war with evil? Is there any peace
In ever climbing up the climbing wave?
All things have rest, and ripen toward the grave
In silence; ripen, fall and cease:
Give us long rest or death, dark death, or dreamful ease.

How sweet it were, hearing the downward stream,
With half-shut eyes ever to seem
Falling asleep in a half-dream!
To dream and dream, like yonder amber light,
Which will not leave the myrrh-bush on the height;
To hear each other's whispered speech;
Eating the Lotos day by day,
To watch the crisping ripples on the beach,
And tender curving lines of creamy spray;
To lend our hearts and spirits wholly
To the influence of mild-minded melancholy;
To muse and brood and live again in memory,
With those old faces of our infancy
Heaped over with a mound of grass,
Two handfuls of white dust, shut in an urn of brass!

Dear is the memory of our wedded lives,
And dear the last embraces of our wives
And their warm tears: but all hath suffered change:
For surely now our household hearths are cold:
Our sons inherit us: our looks are strange:
And we should come like ghosts to trouble joy.
Or else the island princes over-bold
Have eat our substance, and the minstrel sings
Before them of the ten years' war in Troy,
And our great deeds, as half-forgotten things.
Is there confusion in the little isle?
Let what is broken so remain.
The Gods are hard to reconcile:
'Tis hard to settle order once again.
There *is* confusion worse than death,
Trouble on trouble, pain on pain,
Long labour unto agèd breath,

Sore tasks to hearts worn out by many wars
And eyes grown dim with gazing on the pilot-stars.
But, propt on beds of amaranth and moly,
How sweet (while warm airs lull us, blowing lowly)
With half-dropt eyelid still,
Beneath a heaven dark and holy,
To watch the long bright river drawing slowly
His waters from the purple hill—
To hear the dewy echoes calling
From cave to cave through the thick-twinèd vine—
To watch the emerald-coloured water falling
decorative vine Through many a woven acanthus▲-wreath divine!
Only to hear and see the far-off sparkling brine,
Only to hear were sweet, stretched out beneath the pine.

The Lotos blooms below the barren peak:
The Lotos blows by every winding creek:
All day the wind breathes low with mellower tone:
Through every hollow cave and alley lone
Round and round the spicy downs the yellow Lotos-dust
  is blown.
We have had enough of action, and of motion we,
Rolled to starboard, rolled to larboard, when the surge was
  seething free,
Where the wallowing monster spouted his foam-fountains
  in the sea.

Let us swear an oath, and keep it with an equal mind,
In the hollow Lotos-land to live and lie reclined
On the hills like Gods together, careless of mankind.
For they lie beside their nectar, and the bolts are hurled
Far below them in the valleys, and the clouds are lightly
  curled
Round their golden houses, girdled with the gleaming
  world:

88. amaranth: flowers that never fade. Moly: magical flowers that protected Odysseus from the sorceress Circe.

106. larboard: port side of a vessel, the left hand side as one faces toward the prow, the front.

Where they smile in secret, looking over wasted lands,
Blight and famine, plague and earthquake, roaring deeps
and fiery sands,
Clanging fights, and flaming towns, and sinking ships, and
praying hands.
But they smile, they find a music centred in a doleful song
Steaming up, a lamentation and an ancient tale of wrong,
Like a tale of little meaning though the words are strong;
Chanted from an ill-used race of men that cleave the soil,
Sow the seed, and reap the harvest with enduring toil,
Storing yearly little dues of wheat, and wine and oil;
Till they perish and they suffer—some, 'tis whispered—
down in hell
Suffer endless anguish, others in Elysian valleys dwell,
Resting weary limbs at last on beds of asphodel.
Surely, surely, slumber is more sweet than toil, the shore
Than labour in the deep mid-ocean, wind and wave and oar;
Oh rest ye, brother mariners, we will not wander more.

from **THE PRINCESS**
NOW SLEEPS THE CRIMSON PETAL

Now sleeps the crimson petal, now the white,
Nor waves the cypress in the palace walk;
Nor winks the gold fin in the porphyry font.
The fire-fly wakens; waken thou with me.

Now droops the milk-white peacock like a ghost,
And like a ghost she glimmers on to me.

Now lies the Earth all Danaë to the stars,
And all thy heart lies open unto me.
Now slides the silent meteor on, and leaves
A shining furrow, as thy thoughts in me.

124. Elysium: home of the blessed, after death.
125. asphodel: daffodil, immortal flower abounding in Elysium.
7. THE PRINCESS Danaë: as Danaë slept she was visited by Zeus in the form of a shower of gold.

Now folds the lily all her sweetness up,
And slips into the bosom of the lake.
So fold thyself, my dearest, thou, and slip
Into my bosom and be lost in me.

BREAK, BREAK, BREAK

Break, break, break,
On thy cold gray stones, O Sea!
And I would that my tongue could utter
The thoughts that arise in me.

O well for the fisherman's boy,
That he shouts with his sister at play!
O well for the sailor lad,
That he sings in his boat on the bay!

And the stately ships go on
To their haven under the hill;
But O for the touch of a vanished hand,
And the sound of a voice that is still!

Break, break, break,
At the foot of thy crags, O Sea!
But the tender grace of a day that is dead
Will never come back to me.

from IN MEMORIAM A.H.H.

2

Old yew, which graspest at the stones
That name the underlying dead,
Thy fibres net the dreamless head,
Thy roots are wrapt about the bones.

The seasons bring the flower again,
And bring the firstling to the flock;
And in the dusk of thee the clock
Beats out the little lives of men.

O, not for thee the glow, the bloom,
Who changest not in any gale,
Nor branding summer suns avail
To touch thy thousand years of gloom;

And gazing on thee, sullen tree,
Sick for thy stubborn hardihood,
I seem to fail from out my blood
And grow incorporate into thee.

15

To-night the winds begin to rise
And roar from yonder dropping day:
The last red leaf is whirled away,
The rooks are blown about the skies;

The forest cracked, the waters curled,
The cattle huddled on the lea;
And wildly dashed on tower and tree
The sunbeam strikes along the world:

assert, affirm And but for fancies, which aver▲
That all thy motions gently pass
Athwart a plane of molten glass,
I scarce could brook the strain and stir

TITLE: Arthur Henry Hallam (1811–1833), a close friend of Tennyson.

That makes the barren branches loud;
And but for fear it is not so,
The wild unrest that lives in woe
Would dote and pore on yonder cloud

That rises upward always higher,
And onward drags a labouring breast,
And topples round the dreary west,
A looming bastion fringed with fire.

115

Now fades the last long streak of snow,
Now burgeons every maze of quick
About the flowering squares, and thick
By ashen roots the violets blow.

Now rings the woodland loud and long,
The distance takes a lovelier hue,
And drowned in yonder living blue
The lark becomes a sightless song.

open grassland

Now dance the lights on lawn and lea▲,
The flocks are whiter down the vale,
And milkier every milky sail
On winding stream or distant sea;

Where now the seamew pipes, or dives
In yonder greening gleam, and fly
The happy birds, that change their sky
To build and brood; that live their lives

From land to land; and in my breast
Spring wakens too; and my regret
Becomes an April violet,
And buds and blossoms like the rest.

ROBERT BROWNING
(1812–1889)

Born London, lived many years in Italy. Some of his best poems are dramatic monologues set in Renaissance Italy.

MY LAST DUCHESS
FERRARA

That's my last Duchess painted on the wall,
Looking as if she were alive. I call
That piece a wonder, now: Frà Pandolf's hands
Worked busily a day, and there she stands.
Will't please you sit and look at her? I said
'Frà Pandolf' by design, for never read
Strangers like you that pictured countenance,
The depth and passion of its earnest glance,
But to myself they turned (since none puts by
The curtain I have drawn for you, but I)
And seemed as they would ask me, if they durst,
How such a glance came there; so, not the first
Are you to turn and ask thus. Sir, 'twas not
Her husband's presence only, called that spot
Of joy into the Duchess' cheek: perhaps
Frà Pandolf chanced to say 'Her mantle laps
Over my lady's wrist too much,' or 'Paint
Must never hope to reproduce the faint
Half-flush that dies along her throat:' such stuff
Was courtesy, she thought, and cause enough

Ferrara: The speaker in the poem is the Duke of Ferrara.
6–9. The word order is difficult: 'For strangers like you never read that pictured countenance ... without turning to me.'

For calling up that spot of joy. She had
A heart—how shall I say?—too soon made glad,
Too easily impressed; she liked whate'er
She looked on, and her looks went everywhere.
Sir, 'twas all one! My favour at her breast,
The dropping of the daylight in the West,
The bough of cherries some officious fool
Broke in the orchard for her, the white mule
She rode with round the terrace—all and each
Would draw from her alike the approving speech,
Or blush, at least. She thanked men,—good! but thanked
Somehow—I know not how—as if she ranked
My gift of a nine-hundred-years-old name
With anybody's gift. Who'd stoop to blame
This sort of trifling? Even had you skill
In speech—(which I have not)—to make your will
Quite clear to such an one, and say, 'Just this
Or that in you disgusts me; here you miss,
Or there exceed the mark'—and if she let
Herself be lessoned so, nor plainly set
Her wits to yours, forsooth, and made excuse,
—E'en then would be some stooping; and I choose
Never to stoop. Oh sir, she smiled, no doubt,
Whene'er I passed her; but who passed without
Much the same smile? This grew; I gave commands;
Then all smiles stopped together. There she stands
As if alive. Will't please you rise? We'll meet
The company below, then. I repeat,
The Count your master's known munificence
Is ample warrant that no just pretence
Of mine for dowry will be disallowed;
Though his fair daughter's self, as I avowed
At starting, is my object. Nay, we'll go
Together down, sir. Notice Neptune, though,
Taming a sea-horse, thought a rarity,
Which Claus of Innsbruck cast in bronze for me!

PORPHYRIA'S LOVER

The rain set early in to-night,
   The sullen wind was soon awake,
It tore the elm-tops down for spite,
   And did its worst to vex the lake:
   I listened with heart fit to break.
When glided in Porphyria; straight
   She shut the cold out and the storm,
And kneeled and made the cheerless grate
   Blaze up, and all the cottage warm;
   Which done, she rose, and from her form
Withdrew the dripping cloak and shawl,
   And laid her soiled gloves by, untied
Her hat and let the damp hair fall,
   And, last, she sat down by my side
   And called me. When no voice replied,
She put my arm about her waist,
   And made her smooth white shoulder bare,
And all her yellow hair displaced,
   And, stooping, made my cheek lie there,
   And spread, o'er all, her yellow hair,
Murmuring how she loved me—she
   Too weak, for all her heart's endeavour,
To set its struggling passion free
   From pride, and vainer ties dissever,
   And give herself to me forever.
But passion sometimes would prevail,
   Nor could to-night's gay feast restrain
A sudden thought of one so pale
   For love of her, and all in vain:
   So, she was come through wind and rain.
Be sure I looked up at her eyes
   Happy and proud; at last I knew
Porphyria worshipped me: surprise
   Made my heart swell, and still it grew
   While I debated what to do.
That moment she was mine, mine, fair,
   Perfectly pure and good: I found

A thing to do, and all her hair
In one long yellow string I wound
Three times her little throat around,
And strangled her. No pain felt she;
I am quite sure she felt no pain.
As a shut bud that holds a bee,
I warily oped her lids: again
Laughed the blue eyes without a stain.
And I untightened next the tress
About her neck; her cheek once more
Blushed bright beneath my burning kiss:
I propped her head up as before,
Only, this time my shoulder bore
Her head, which droops upon it still:
The smiling rosy little head,
So glad it has its utmost will,
That all it scorned at once is fled,
And I, its love, am gained instead!
Porphyria's love: she guessed not how
Her darling one wish would be heard.
And thus we sit together now,
And all night long we have not stirred,
And yet God has not said a word!

THE BISHOP ORDERS HIS TOMB AT ST PRAXED'S CHURCH

ROME, 15–

cf. Ecclesiastes I: 2

Vanity, saith the preacher, vanity▲!
Draw round my bed: is Anselm keeping back?
Nephews—sons mine . . . ah God, I know not! Well—
She, men would have to be your mother once,
Old Gandolf envied me, so fair she was!
What's done is done, and she is dead beside,
Dead long ago, and I am Bishop since,

5. The 16th-century bishop who speaks here is fictional, as is his predecessor, Gandolf.

And as she died so must we die ourselves,
And thence ye may perceive the world's a dream.
Life, how and what is it? As here I lie
In this state-chamber, dying by degrees,
Hours and long hours in the dead night, I ask
'Do I live, am I dead?' Peace, peace seems all.
Saint Praxed's ever was the church for peace;
And so, about this tomb of mine. I fought
With tooth and nail to save my niche, ye know:
cheated
—Old Gandolf cozened▲ me, despite my care;
Shrewd was that snatch from out the corner South
He graced his carrion with, God curse the same!
Yet still my niche is not so cramped but thence
from which New Testament Epistles were read
One sees the pulpit o' the epistle-side▲,
And somewhat of the choir, those silent seats,
And up into the aery dome where live
The angels, and a sunbeam's sure to lurk:
And I shall fill my slab of basalt there,
canopy over his tomb
And 'neath my tabernacle▲ take my rest,
With those nine columns round me, two and two,
The odd one at my feet where Anselm stands:
Peach-blossom marble all, the rare, the ripe
As fresh-poured red wine of a mighty pulse.
an inferior marble
—Old Gandolf with his paltry onion-stone▲,
Put me where I may look at him! True peach,
Rosy and flawless: how I earned the prize!
Draw close: that conflagration of my church
—What then? So much was saved if aught were missed!
My sons, ye would not be my death? Go dig
The white-grape vineyard where the oil-press stood,
Drop water gently till the surface sink,
And if ye find . . . Ah God, I know not, I! . . .
Bedded in store of rotten fig-leaves soft,
olive basket
And corded up in a tight olive-frail▲,
precious bright blue stone
Some lump, ah God, of *lapis lazuli*▲,
Big as a Jew's head cut off at the nape,
Blue as a vein o'er the Madonna's breast . . .
Sons, all have I bequeathed you, villas, all,
That brave Frascati villa with its bath,

So, let the blue lump poise between my knees,
Like God the Father's globe on both his hands
Ye worship in the Jesu Church so gay,
For Gandolf shall not choose but see and burst!
Swift as a weaver's shuttle fleet our years:
Man goeth to the grave, and where is he?
Did I say basalt for my slab, sons? Black—
'Twas ever antique-black I meant! How else
Shall ye contrast my frieze to come beneath?
The bas-relief in bronze ye promised me,
Those Pans and Nymphs ye wot of, and perchance
Some tripod, thyrsus▲, with a vase or so, *staff used in Bacchic rites*
The Saviour at his sermon on the mount,
Saint Praxed in a glory▲, and one Pan *saintly golden aura*
Ready to twitch the Nymph's last garment off,
And Moses with the tables . . . but I know
Ye mark me not! What do they whisper thee,
Child of my bowels, Anselm? Ah, ye hope
To revel down my villas while I gasp
Bricked o'er with beggar's mouldy travertine▲ *an inexpensive limestone*
Which Gandolf from his tomb-top chuckles at!
Nay, boys, ye love me—all of jasper, then!
'Tis jasper ye stand pledged to, lest I grieve.
My bath must needs be left behind, alas!
One block, pure green as a pistachio-nut,
There's plenty jasper somewhere in the world—
And have I not Saint Praxed's ear to pray
Horses for ye, and brown Greek manuscripts,
And mistresses with great smooth marbly limbs?
—That's if ye carve my epitaph aright,
Choice Latin, picked phrase, Tully's▲ every word, *Cicero*
No gaudy ware like Gandolf's second line—
Tully, my masters? Ulpian serves his need!
And then how I shall lie through centuries,
And hear the blessed mutter of the mass,
And see God made and eaten all day long,

49. Jesu church: Jesuit church in Rome, housing a globe of the largest known block of lapis lazuli.

And feel the steady candle-flame, and taste
Good strong thick stupefying incense-smoke!
For as I lie here, hours of the dead night,
Dying in state and by such slow degrees,
bishop's crozier, like a shepherd's crook
I fold my arms as if they clasped a crook▲,
And stretch my feet forth straight as stone can point,
pall draped over a coffin
And let the bedclothes, for a mortcloth▲, drop
Into great laps and folds of sculptor's-work:
And as yon tapers dwindle, and strange thoughts
Grow, with a certain humming in my ears,
About the life before I lived this life,
And this life too, popes, cardinals and priests,
Saint Praxed at his sermon on the mount,
Your tall pale mother with her talking eyes,
And new-found agate urns as fresh as day,
And marble's language, Latin pure, discreet.
to shine forth
—Aha, ELUCESCEBAT▲ quoth our friend?
No Tully, said I, Ulpian at the best!
Evil and brief hath been my pilgrimage.
brilliant blue semi-precious stone
All *lapis*▲, all, sons! Else I give the Pope
My villas! Will ye ever eat my heart?
Ever your eyes were as a lizard's quick,
They glitter like your mother's for my soul,
Or ye would heighten my impoverished frieze,
Piece out its starved design, and fill my vase
a mask; a bust on a pillar
With grapes, and add a vizor▲ and a Term▲,
of cat family
And to the tripod ye would tie a lynx▲
That in his struggle throws the thyrsus down,
To comfort me on my entablature
Whereon I am to lie till I must ask
'Do I live, am I dead?' There, leave me, there!
For ye have stabbed me with ingratitude
To death—ye wish it—God, ye wish it! Stone—
Gritstone, a-crumble! Clammy squares which sweat
As if the corpse they keep were oozing through—
And no more *lapis* to delight the world!

99. elucescebat: Cicero might have used the superior form 'elucebat' of the word.

Well go! I bless ye. Fewer tapers there,
But in a row: and, going, turn your backs
—Ay, like departing altar-ministrants,
And leave me in my church, the church for peace,
That I may watch at leisure if he leers—
Old Gandolf, at me, from his onion-stone,
And still he envied me, so fair she was!

ANDREA DEL SARTO

(CALLED THE FAULTLESS PAINTER)

But do not let us quarrel any more,
No, my Lucrezia; bear with me for once:
Sit down and all shall happen as you wish.
You turn your face, but does it bring your heart?
I'll work then for your friend's friend, never fear,
Treat his own subject after his own way,
Fix his own time, accept too his own price,
And shut the money into this small hand
When next it takes mine. Will it? tenderly?
Oh, I'll content him,—but to-morrow, Love!
I often am much wearier than you think,
This evening more than usual, and it seems
As if—forgive now—should you let me sit
Here by the window with your hand in mine
And look a half hour forth on Fiesole▲,
Both of one mind, as married people use,
Quietly, quietly, the evening through,
I might get up to-morrow to my work
Cheerful and fresh as ever. Let us try.
To-morrow how you shall be glad for this!
Your soft hand is a woman of itself,
And mine the man's bared breast she curls inside.
Don't count the time lost, either; you must serve

hill town overlooking Florence

TITLE: Florentine painter (1486–1531).

For each of the five pictures we require—
It saves a model. So! keep looking so—
My serpentining beauty, rounds on rounds!
—How could you ever prick those perfect ears,
Even to put the pearl there! oh, so sweet—
My face, my moon, my everybody's moon,
Which everybody looks on and calls his,
And, I suppose, is looked on by in turn,
While she looks—no one's: very dear, no less!
You smile? why, there's my picture ready made,
There's what we painters call our harmony!
A common greyness silvers everything,—
All in a twilight, you and I alike
—You, at the point of your first pride in me
(That's gone you know),—but I, at every point;
My youth, my hope, my art, being all toned down
To yonder sober pleasant Fiesole.
There's the bell clinking from the chapel-top;
That length of convent-wall across the way
Holds the trees safer, huddled more inside;
The last monk leaves the garden; days decrease
And autumn grows, autumn in everything.
Eh? the whole seems to fall into a shape
As if I saw alike my work and self
And all that I was born to be and do,
A twilight-piece. Love, we are in God's hand.
How strange now, looks the life He makes us lead!
So free we seem, so fettered fast we are!
I feel He laid the fetter: let it lie!
This chamber for example—turn your head—
All that's behind us! you don't understand
Nor care to understand about my art,
But you can hear at least when people speak;
And that cartoon, the second from the door
—It is the thing, Love! so such things should be—
Behold Madonna! I am bold to say.
I can do with my pencil what I know,
What I see, what at bottom of my heart
I wish for, if I ever wish so deep—

Do easily, too—when I say perfectly
I do not boast, perhaps: yourself are judge
Who listened to the Legate's▲ talk last week, *ambassador from the Pope*
And just as much they used to say in France.
At any rate 'tis easy, all of it,
No sketches first, no studies, that's long past—
I do what many dream of all their lives
—Dream? strive to do, and agonise to do,
And fail in doing. I could count twenty such
On twice your fingers, and not leave this town,
Who strive—you don't know how the others strive
To paint a little thing like that you smeared
Carelessly passing with your robes afloat,—
Yet do much less, so much less, Someone says,
(I know his name, no matter)—so much less!
Well, less is more, Lucrezia! I am judged.
There burns a truer light of God in them,
In their vexed, beating, stuffed and stopped-up brain,
Heart, or whate'er else, than goes on to prompt
This low-pulsed forthright craftsman's hand of mine.
Their works drop groundward, but themselves, I know,
Reach many a time a heaven that's shut to me,
Enter and take their place there sure enough,
Though they come back and cannot tell the world.
My works are nearer heaven, but I sit here.
The sudden blood of these men! at a word—
Praise them, it boils, or blame them, it boils too.
I, painting from myself and to myself,
Know what I do, am unmoved by men's blame
Or their praise either. Somebody remarks
Morello's▲ outline there is wrongly traced, *mountain in the Apennines*
His hue mistaken—what of that? or else,
Rightly traced and well ordered—what of that?
Speak as they please, what does the mountain care?
Ah, but a man's reach should exceed his grasp,
Or what's a Heaven for? all is silver-grey
Placid and perfect with my art—the worse!
I know both what I want and what might gain—
And yet how profitless to know, to sigh

'Had I been two, another and myself,
Our head would have o'erlooked the world!' No doubt.
Yonder's a work, now, of that famous youth
The Urbinate▲ who died five years ago.
('Tis copied, George Vasari sent it me.)
Well, I can fancy how he did it all,
Pouring his soul, with kings and popes to see,
Reaching, that Heaven might so replenish him,
Above and through his art—for it gives way;
That arm is wrongly put—and there again—
A fault to pardon in the drawing's lines,
Its body, so to speak: its soul is right,
He means right—that, a child may understand.
Still, what an arm! and I could alter it.
But all the play, the insight and the stretch—
Out of me! out of me! And wherefore out?
Had you enjoined them on me, given me soul,
We might have risen to Rafael, I and you.
Nay, Love, and you did give all I asked, I think—
More than I merit, yes, by many times.
But had you—oh, with the same perfect brow,
And perfect eyes, and more than perfect mouth,
And the low voice my soul hears, as a bird
The fowler's pipe, and follows to the snare—
Had you, with these the same, but brought a mind!
Some women do so. Had the mouth there urged
'God and the glory! never care for gain.
The Present by the Future, what is that?
Live for fame, side by side with Angelo▲—
Rafael is waiting. Up to God all three!'
I might have done it for you. So it seems—
Perhaps not. All is as God over-rules.
Beside, incentives come from the soul's self;
The rest avail not. Why do I need you?
What wife had Rafael, or has Angelo?
In this world, who can do a thing, will not—
And who would do it, cannot, I perceive:
Yet the will's somewhat—somewhat, too, the power—
And thus we half-men struggle. At the end,

Raphael (1483–1520) was born at Urbino

Michelangelo (1475–1564)

God, I conclude, compensates, punishes.
'Tis safer for me, if the award be strict,
That I am something underrated here,
Poor this long while, despised, to speak the truth.
I dared not, do you know, leave home all day,
For fear of chancing on the Paris lords.
The best is when they pass and look aside;
But they speak sometimes; I must bear it all.
Well may they speak! That Francis▲, that first time,
And that long festal year at Fontainebleau!

King Francis I of France

I surely then could sometimes leave the ground,
Put on the glory, Rafael's daily wear,
In that humane great monarch's golden look,—
One finger in his beard or twisted curl
Over his mouth's good mark that made the smile,
One arm about my shoulder, round my neck,
The jingle of his gold chain in my ear,
I painting proudly with his breath on me,
All his court round him, seeing with his eyes,
Such frank French eyes, and such a fire of souls
Profuse, my hand kept plying by those hearts,—
And, best of all, this, this, this face beyond,
This in the background, waiting on my work,
To crown the issue with a last reward!
A good time, was it not, my kingly days?
And had you not grown restless—but I know—
'Tis done and past; 'twas right, my instinct said;
Too live the life grew, golden and not grey,
And I'm the weak-eyed bat no sun should tempt
Out of the grange whose four walls make his world.
How could it end in any other way?
You called me, and I came home to your heart.
The triumph was, to have ended there; then if
I reached it ere the triumph, what is lost?
Let my hands frame your face in your hair's gold,
You beautiful Lucrezia that are mine!
'Rafael did this, Andrea painted that—
The Roman's is the better when you pray,
But still the other's Virgin was his wife—'

Men will excuse me. I am glad to judge
Both pictures in your presence; clearer grows
My better fortune, I resolve to think.
For, do you know, Lucrezia, as God lives,
Said one day Angelo, his very self,
To Rafael . . . I have known it all these years . . .
(When the young man was flaming out his thoughts
Upon a palace-wall for Rome to see,
Too lifted up in heart because of it)
'Friend, there's a certain sorry little scrub
Goes up and down our Florence, none cares how,
Who, were he set to plan and execute
As you are, pricked on by your popes and kings,
Would bring the sweat into that brow of yours!'
To Rafael's!—And indeed the arm is wrong.
I hardly dare—yet, only you to see,
Give the chalk here—quick, thus the line should go!
Ay, but the soul! he's Rafael! rub it out!
Still, all I care for, if he spoke the truth,
(What he? why, who but Michael Angelo?
Do you forget already words like those?)
If really there was such a chance, so lost,—
Is, whether you're—not grateful—but more pleased.
Well, let me think so. And you smile indeed!
This hour has been an hour! Another smile?
If you would sit thus by me every night
I should work better, do you comprehend?
I mean that I should earn more, give you more.
See, it is settled dusk now; there's a star;
Morello's gone, the watch-lights show the wall,
The cue-owls speak the name we call them by.
Come from the window, Love,—come in, at last,
Inside the melancholy little house
We built to be so gay with. God is just.
King Francis may forgive me. Oft at nights
When I look up from painting, eyes tired out,
The walls become illumined, brick from brick
Distinct, instead of mortar, fierce bright gold,
That gold of his I did cement them with!

Let us but love each other. Must you go?
That Cousin here again? he waits outside?
Must see you—you, and not with me? Those loans?
More gaming debts to pay? you smiled for that?
Well, let smiles buy me! have you more to spend?
While hand and eye and something of a heart
Are left me, work's my ware, and what's it worth?
I'll pay my fancy. Only let me sit
The grey remainder of the evening out,
Idle, you call it, and muse perfectly
How I could paint, were I but back in France,
One picture, just one more—the Virgin's face,
Not yours this time! I want you at my side
To hear them—that is, Michael Angelo—
Judge all I do and tell you of its worth.
Will you? To-morrow, satisfy your friend.
I take the subjects for his corridor,
Finish the portrait out of hand—there, there,
And throw him in another thing or two
If he demurs; the whole should prove enough
To pay for this same Cousin's freak. Beside,
What's better and what's all I care about,
Get you the thirteen scudi for the ruff.
Love, does that please you? Ah, but what does he,
The Cousin! what does he to please you more?
    I am grown peaceful as old age to-night.
I regret little, I would change still less.
Since there my past life lies, why alter it?
The very wrong to Francis!—it is true
I took his coin, was tempted and complied,
And built this house and sinned, and all is said.
My father and my mother died of want.
Well, had I riches of my own? you see
How one gets rich! Let each one bear his lot.
They were born poor, lived poor, and poor they died:
And I have laboured somewhat in my time
And not been paid profusely. Some good son
Paint my two hundred pictures—let him try!
No doubt, there's something strikes a balance. Yes,

You loved me quite enough, it seems to-night.
This must suffice me here. What would one have?
In Heaven, perhaps, new chances, one more chance—
Four great walls in the New Jerusalem
Meted on each side by the angel's reed,
Leonardo da Vinci For Leonard▲, Rafael, Angelo and me
To cover—the three first without a wife,
While I have mine! So—still they overcome
Because there's still Lucrezia,—as I choose.

Again the Cousin's whistle! Go, my Love.

EMILY DICKINSON
(1830–1888)

Born Amherst, Massachusetts, USA. Writing as she did, outside nineteenth-century manners and concerns, only a handful of her poems were published, anonymously, in her lifetime. She was an intensely private person and only a few friends knew of her verse. However, even they had no idea of her immense output until after her death.

I felt a Funeral, in my Brain,
And Mourners to and fro
Kept treading—treading—till it seemed
That Sense was breaking through—

And when they all were seated,
A Service, like a Drum—
Kept beating—beating—till I thought
My Mind was going numb—

And then I heard them lift a Box
And creak across my Soul
With those same Boots of Lead, again,
Then Space—began to toll,

As all the Heavens were a Bell,
And Being, but an Ear,
And I, and Silence, some strange Race
Wrecked, solitary, here—

And then a Plank in Reason, broke,
And I dropped down, and down—
And hit a World, at every plunge,
And Finished knowing—then—

I'm Nobody! Who are you?
Are you—Nobody—Too?
Then there's a pair of us!
Don't tell! they'd banish us—you know!

How dreary—to be—Somebody!
How public—like a Frog—
To tell your name—the livelong June—
To an admiring Bog!

I cannot dance upon my Toes—
No Man instructed me—
But oftentimes, among my mind,
A Glee possesseth me,

That had I Ballet knowledge—
Would put itself abroad
In Pirouette to blanch a Troupe—
Or lay a Prima, mad,

And though I had no Gown of Gauze—
No Ringlet, to my Hair,
Nor hopped to Audiences—like Birds,
One Claw upon the Air,

the down of Eider ducks

Nor tossed my shape in Eider Balls▲,
Nor rolled on wheels of snow
Till I was out of sight, in sound,
The House encore me so—

Nor any know I know the Art
I mention—easy—Here—
Nor any Placard boast me—
It's full as Opera—

After great pain, a formal feeling comes—
The Nerves sit ceremonious, like Tombs—
The stiff Heart questions was it He, that bore,
And Yesterday, or Centuries before?

The Feet, mechanical, go round—
anything or nothing Of Ground, or Air, or Ought▲—
A Wooden way
Regardless grown,
A Quartz contentment, like a stone—

This is the Hour of Lead—
Remembered, if outlived,
As Freezing persons, recollect the Snow—
First—Chill—then Stupor—then the letting go—

There's been a Death, in the Opposite House,
As lately as Today—
I know it, by the numb look
Such Houses have—alway—

The Neighbors rustle in and out—
The Doctor—drives away—
A Window opens like a Pod—
Abrupt—mechanically—

Somebody flings a Mattress out—
The Children hurry by—
They wonder if it died—on that—
I used to—when a Boy—

The Minister—goes stiffly in—
As if the House were His—
And He owned all the Mourners—now—
And little Boys—besides—

And then the Milliner—and the Man
Of the Appalling Trade—
To take the measure of the House—
There'll be that Dark Parade—

Of Tassels—and of Coaches—soon—
It's easy as a Sign—
The Intuition of the News—
In just a Country Town—

Much Madness is divinest Sense—
To a discerning Eye—
Much Sense—the starkest Madness—
'Tis the Majority
In this, as All, prevail—
Assent—and you are sane—
Demur—you're straightaway dangerous—
And handled with a Chain—

I heard a Fly buzz—when I died—
The Stillness in the Room
Was like the Stillness in the Air—
Between the Heaves of Storm—

The Eyes around—had wrung them dry—
And Breaths were gathering firm
For that last Onset—when the King
Be witnessed—in the Room—

I willed my Keepsakes—Signed away
What portion of me be
Assignable—and then it was
There interposed a Fly—

With Blue—uncertain stumbling Buzz—
Between the light—and me—
And then the Windows failed—and then
I could not see to see—

Because I could not stop for Death—
He kindly stopped for me—
The Carriage held but just Ourselves—
And Immortality.

We slowly drove—He knew no haste
And I had put away
My labor and my leisure too,
For His Civility—

We passed the School, where Children strove
playground At Recess—in the Ring▲—
We passed the Fields of Gazing Grain—
We passed the Setting Sun—

* Or rather—He passed Us—
The Dews drew quivering and chill—
For only Gossamer, my Gown—
woman's short cape My Tippet▲—only Tulle—

We paused before a House that seemed
A Swetling of the Ground—
The Roof was scarcely visible—
high ornamental border The Cornice▲—in the Ground—

* In some editions stanza 4 is omitted.

Since then—'tis Centuries—and yet
Feels shorter than the Day
I first surmised the Horses Heads
Were toward Eternity—

The last Night that She lived
It was a Common Night
Except the Dying—this to Us
Made Nature different

We noticed smallest things—
Things overlooked before
By this great light upon our Minds
Italicized—as 'twere.

As We went out and in
Between Her final Room
And Rooms where Those to be alive
Tomorrow were, a Blame

That Others could exist
While She must finish quite
A Jealousy for Her arose
So nearly infinite—

We waited while She passed—
It was a narrow time—
Too jostled were Our Souls to speak
At length the notice came.

She mentioned, and forgot—
Then lightly as a Reed
* Bent to the Water, struggled scarce—
Consented, and was dead—

* Variant: line 23 'Bent to the water, shivered scarce.'

And We—We placed the Hair—
And drew the Head erect—
And then an awful leisure was
Belief to regulate—

There came a Wind like a Bugle—
It quivered through the Grass
And a Green Chill upon the Heat
So ominous did pass
We barred the Windows and the Doors
As from an Emerald Ghost—
The Doom's electric Moccasin
That very instant passed—
On a strange Mob of panting Trees
And Fences fled away
And Rivers where the Houses ran
Those looked that lived—that Day—
The Bell within the steeple wild
The flying tidings told—
How much can come
And much can go,
And yet abide the World!

A Bird came down the Walk—
He did not know I saw—
He bit an Angleworm in halves
And ate the fellow, raw,

And then he drank a Dew
From a convenient Grass—
And then hopped sidewise to the Wall
To let a Beetle pass—

*Variant: line 28 'Our faith to regulate.'

He glanced with rapid eyes
That hurried all around—
They looked like frightened Beads, I thought—
He stirred his Velvet Head

Like one in danger, Cautious,
I offered him a Crumb
And he unrolled his feathers
And rowed him softer home—

Than Oars divide the Ocean,
Too silver for a seam—
Or Butterflies, off Banks of Noon
Leap, plashless as they swim.

They put Us far apart—
As separate as Sea
And Her unsown Peninsula—
We signified "These see"—

They took away our Eyes—
They thwarted Us with Guns—
"I see Thee" each responded straight
Through Telegraphic Signs—

With Dungeons—They devised—
But through their thickest skill—
And their opaquest Adamant—
Our Souls saw—just as well—

They summoned Us to die—
With sweet alacrity
We stood upon our stapled feet—
Condemned—but just—to see—

11. Adamant: a dense, hard stone.

Permission to recant—
Permission to forget—
We turned our backs upon the Sun
For perjury of that—

Not Either—noticed Death—
Of Paradise—aware—
Each other's Face—was all the Disc
Each other's setting—saw—

She dealt her pretty words like Blades—
How glittering they shone—
And every One unbared a Nerve
Or wantoned with a Bone—

She never deemed—she hurt—
That—is not Steel's Affair—
A vulgar grimace in the Flesh—
How ill the Creatures bear—

To Ache is human—not polite—
The Film upon the eye
Mortality's old Custom—
Just locking up—to Die.

The Soul has Bandaged moments—
When too appalled to stir—
She feels some ghastly Fright come up
And stop to look at her—

Salute her—with long fingers—
Caress her freezing hair—
Sip, Goblin, from the very lips
The Lover—hovered—o'er—

Unworthy, that a thought so mean
Accost a Theme—so—fair—

The soul has moments of Escape—
When bursting all the doors—
She dances like a Bomb, abroad,
And swings upon the Hours,

As do the Bee—delirious borne—
Long Dungeoned from his Rose—
Touch Liberty—then know no more,
But Noon, and Paradise—

The Soul's retaken moments—
When, Felon led along,
With shackles on the plumed feet,
And staples, in the Song,

The Horror welcomes her, again,
These, are not brayed of Tongue—

A narrow Fellow in the Grass
Occasionally rides—
You may have met Him—did you not
His notice sudden is—

The Grass divides as with a Comb—
A spotted shaft is seen—
And then it closes at your feet
And opens further on—

He likes a Boggy Acre
A Floor too cool for Corn—
Yet when a Boy, and Barefoot—
I more than once at Noon

Have passed, I thought, a Whip lash
Unbraiding in the Sun
When stooping to secure it
It wrinkled, and was gone—

Several of Nature's People
I know, and they know me—
I feel for them a transport
Of cordiality—

But never met this Fellow
Attended, or alone
Without a tighter breathing
And Zero at the Bone—

THOMAS HARDY
(1840–1928)

Born Dorset, England. Trained as an architect, his early literary career was as a novelist. He wrote no further novels after 1896, and his first book of poems was not published until he was almost sixty.

NEUTRAL TONES

We stood by a pond that winter day,
And the sun was white, as though chidden of God,
And a few leaves lay on the starving sod;
　—They had fallen from an ash, and were gray.

Your eyes on me were as eyes that rove
Over tedious riddles of years ago:
And some words played between us to and fro
　On which lost the more by our love.

The smile on your mouth was the deadest thing
Alive enough to have strength to die;
And a grin of bitterness swept thereby
　Like an ominous bird a-wing…

Since then, keen lessons that love deceives,
And wrings with wrong, have shaped to me
Your face, and the God-curst sun, and a tree,
　And a pond edged with grayish leaves.

TRANSFORMATIONS

Portion of this yew
Is a man my grandsire knew,
Bosomed here at its foot:
This branch may be his wife,
A ruddy human life
Now turned to a green shoot.

These grasses must be made
Of her who often prayed,
Last century, for repose;
And the fair girl long ago
Whom I often tried to know
May be entering this rose.

So, they are not underground,
But as nerves and veins abound
In the growths of upper air,
And they feel the sun and rain,
And the energy again
That made them what they were!

THE DARKLING THRUSH

a thicket grown for periodical cutting

flexible shoots of shrubs, climbing stems

I leant upon a coppice▲ gate
  When Frost was spectre-gray,
And Winter's dregs made desolate
  The weakening eye of day.
The tangled bine-stems▲ scored the sky
  Like strings of broken lyres,
And all mankind that haunted nigh
  Had sought their household fires.

The land's sharp features seemed to be
  The Century's corpse outleant,

His crypt the cloudy canopy,
    The wind his death-lament.
The ancient pulse of germ and birth
    Was shrunken and hard and dry,
And every spirit upon earth
    Seemed fervourless as I.

At once a voice arose among
    The bleak twigs overhead
In a full-hearted evensong
    Of joy illimited;
An aged thrush, frail, gaunt, and small,
    In blast-beruffled plume,
Had chosen thus to fling his soul
    Upon the growing gloom.

So little cause for carolings
    Of such ecstatic sound
Was written on terrestrial things
    Afar or nigh around,
That I could think there trembled through
    His happy good-night air
Some blessed Hope, whereof he knew
    And I was unaware.

CHANNEL FIRING

That night your great guns, unawares,
Shook all our coffins as we lay,
And broke the chancel window-squares,
We thought it was the Judgment-day

And sat upright. While drearisome
Arose the howl of wakened hounds:
The mouse let fall the altar-crumb,
The worms drew back into the mounds,

glebe: portion of land assigned to clergymen

The glebe▲ cow drooled. Till God called, 'No;
It's gunnery practice out at sea
Just as before you went below;
The world is as it used to be:

'All nations striving strong to make
Red war yet redder. Mad as hatters
They do no more for Christés sake
Than you who are helpless in such matters.

'That this is not the judgment-hour
For some of them's a blessed thing,
For if it were they'd have to scour
Hell's floor for so much threatening. . . .

'Ha, ha. It will be warmer when
I blow the trumpet (if indeed
I ever do; for you are men,
And rest eternal sorely need).'

So down we lay again. 'I wonder,
Will the world ever saner be,'
Said one, 'than when He sent us under
In our indifferent century!'

And many a skeleton shook his head.
'Instead of preaching forty year,'
My neighbour Parson Thirdly said,
'I wish I had stuck to pipes and beer.'

Again the guns disturbed the hour,
Roaring their readiness to avenge,
As far inland as Stourton Tower,
And Camelot, and starlit Stonehenge.

IN TIME OF 'THE BREAKING OF NATIONS'

I

Only a man harrowing clods
    In a slow silent walk
With an old horse that stumbles and nods
    Half asleep as they stalk.

II

Only thin smoke without flame
    From the heaps of couch-grass;
Yet this will go onward the same
    Though Dynasties pass.

III

Yonder a maid and her wight
    Come whispering by:
War's annals will cloud into night
    Ere their story die.

THE VOICE

Woman much missed, how you call to me, call to me,
Saying that now you are not as you were
When you had changed from the one who was all to me,
But as at first, when our day was fair.

TITLE: IN TIME OF 'THE BREAKING OF NATIONS': taken from Jeremiah Chap. 51.

Can it be you that I hear? Let me view you, then,
Standing as when I drew near to the town
Where you would wait for me: yes, as I knew then,
Even to the original air-blue gown!

Or is it only the breeze, in its listlessness
Traveling across the wet mead to me here,
heedlessness You being ever dissolved to wan wistlessness▲,
Heard no more again far or near?

Thus I; faltering forward,
Leaves around me falling,
Wind oozing thin through the thorn from norward,
And the woman calling.

THE SELF-UNSEEING

Here is the ancient floor,
Footworn and hollowed and thin,
Here was the former door
Where the dead feet walked in.

She sat here in her chair,
Smiling into the fire;
He who played stood there,
Bowing it higher and higher.

Childlike, I danced in a dream;
Blessings emblazoned that day;
Everything glowed with a gleam;
Yet we were looking away!

DURING WIND AND RAIN

They sing their dearest songs—
He, she, all of them—yea,
Treble and tenor and bass,
And one to play;
With the candles mooning each face...
Ah, no; the years O!
How the sick leaves reel down in throngs!

They clear the creeping moss—
Elders and juniors—aye,
Making the pathways neat
And the garden gay;
And they build a shady seat...
Ah, no; the years, the years;
See, the white storm-birds wing across.

They are blithely breakfasting all—
Men and maidens—yea,
Under the summer tree,
With a glimpse of the bay,
While pet fowl come to the knee...
Ah, no; the years O!
And the rotten rose is ript from the wall.

They change to a high new house,
He, she, all of them—aye,
Clocks and carpets and chairs
On the lawn all day,
And brightest things that are theirs...
Ah, no; the years, the years;
Down their carved names the rain-drop ploughs.

AFTER A JOURNEY

Hereto I come to view a voiceless ghost;
Wither, O wither will its whim now draw me?
Up the cliff, down, till I'm lonely, lost,
And the unseen waters' ejaculations awe me.
Where you will next be there's no knowing,
Facing round about me everywhere,
With your nut-coloured hair,
And gray eyes, and rose-flush coming and going.

Yes: I have re-entered your olden haunts at last;
Through the years, through the dead scenes I have tracked you;
What have you now found to say of our past—
Scanned across the dark space wherein I have lacked you?
Summer gave us sweets, but autumn wrought division?
Things were not lastly as firstly well
With us twain, you tell?
But all's closed now, despite Time's derision.

I see what you are doing: you are leading me on
To the spots we knew when we haunted here together,
The waterfall, above which the mist-bow shone
At the then fair hour in the then fair weather,
And the cave just under, with a voice still so hollow
That is seems to call out to me from forty years ago,
When you were all aglow,
And not the thin ghost that I now fraily follow!

Ignorant of what there is flitting here to see,
The waked birds preen and the seals flop lazily;
Soon you will have, Dear, to vanish from me,
For the stars close their shutters and the dawn whitens hazily.
Trust me, I mind not, though Life lours▲, *darkens, threatens*
The bringing me here; nay, bring me here again!
I am just the same as when
Our days were a joy, and our paths through flowers.

PENTARGAN BAY.

AT CASTLE BOTEREL

As I drive to the junction of lane and highway,
And the drizzle bedrenches the waggonette,
I look behind at the fading byway,
And see on its slope, now glistening wet,
Distinctly yet.

Myself and a girlish form benighted
In dry March weather. We climb the road
Beside a chaise. We had just alighted
To ease the sturdy pony's load
When he sighed and slowed.

What we did as we climbed, and what we talked of
Matters not much, nor to what it led,—
Something that life will not be balked of
Without rude reason till hope is dead,
And feeling fled.

It filled but a minute. But was there ever
A time of such quality, since or before,
In that hill's story? To one mind never,
Though it has been climbed, foot-swift, foot-sore,
By thousands more.

Primaeval rocks form the road's steep border,
And much have they faced there, first and last,
Of the transitory in Earth's long order;
But what they record in colour and cast
Is—that we two passed.

And to me, though Time's unflinching rigour,
In mindless rote, has ruled from sight
The substance now, one phantom figure
Remains on the slope, as when that night
Saw us alight.

I look and see it there, shrinking, shrinking,
  I look back at it amid the rain
For the very last time; for my sand is sinking,
  And I shall traverse old love's domain
    Never again.

THE RUINED MAID

"O 'Melia, my dear, this does everything crown!
Who could have supposed I should meet you in Town?
And whence such fair garments, such prosperi-ty?"—
"O didn't you know I'd been ruined?" said she.

—"You left us in tatters, without shoes or socks,
Tired of digging potatoes, and spudding up docks;
And now you've gay bracelets and bright feathers three!"—
"Yes: that's how we dress when we're ruined," said she.

farmyard —"At home in the barton▴ you said 'thee' and 'thou,'
And 'thik oon,' and 'theäs oon,' and 't'other'; but now
Your talking quite fits 'ee for high compa-ny!"—
"Some polish is gained with one's ruin," said she.

—"Your hands were like paws then, your face blue and
  bleak
But now I'm bewitched by your delicate cheek,
And your little gloves fit as on any la-dy!"—
"We never do work when we're ruined," said she.

—"You used to call home-life a hag-ridden dream,
And you'd sigh, and you'd sock; but at present you seem
To know not of megrims or melancho-ly!"—
"True. One's pretty lively when ruined," said she.

—"I wish I had feathers, a fine sweeping gown,
And a delicate face, and could strut about Town!'—
"My dear—a raw country girl, such as you be,
Cannot quite expect that. You ain't ruined," said she.

TO LIZBIE BROWNE

I

Dear Lizbie Browne,
Where are you now?
In sun, in rain?—
Or is your brow
Past joy, past pain,
Dear Lizbie Browne?

II

Sweet Lizbie Browne,
How you could smile,
How you could sing!—
How archly wile
In glance-giving,
Sweet Lizbie Browne!

III

And, Lizbie Browne,
Who else had hair
Bay-red as yours,
Or flesh so fair
Bred out of doors,
Sweet Lizbie Browne?

IV

When, Lizbie Browne,
You had just begun
To be endeared
By stealth to one,
You disappeared
My Lizbie Browne!

V

Ay, Lizbie Browne,
So swift your life,
And mine so slow,
You were a wife

Ere I could show
Love, Lizbie Browne.

VI

Still, Lizbie Browne,
You won, they said,
The best of men
When you were wed . . .
Where went you then,
O Lizbie Browne?

VII

Dear Lizbie Browne,
I should have thought,
"Girls ripen fast,"
And coaxed and caught
You ere you passed,
Dear Lizbie Browne!

VIII

But, Lizbie Browne,
I let you slip;
Shaped not a sign;
Touched never your lip
With lip of mine,
Lost Lizbie Browne!

IX

So, Lizbie Browne,
When on a day
Men speak of me
As not, you'll say,
"And who was he?"—
Yes, Lizbie Browne!

Gerard Manley Hopkins
(1844–1889)

Born London, he converted to Catholicism at Oxford, and became a Jesuit priest in 1877. His writing sat uneasily with his vocation and his verse was not published until long after his death, when it had considerable influence upon twentieth-century poets.

FELIX RANDAL

blacksmith Felix Randal the farrier▲, O is he dead then? my duty all ended,
Who have watched his mould of man, big-boned and hardy-handsome
Pining, pining, till time when reason rambled in it and some
Fatal four disorders, fleshed there, all contended?

Sickness broke him. Impatient, he cursed at first, but mended
He had been given the last rites Being anointed▲ and all; though a heavenlier heart began some
Months earlier, since I had our sweet reprieve and ransom
ways Tendered to him. Ah well, God rest him all road▲ ever he offended!

This seeing the sick endears them to us, us too it endears.
My tongue had taught thee comfort, touch had quenched thy tears,
Thy tears that touched my heart, child, Felix, poor Felix Randal;

6–8. A priest visited him to hear confession and give absolution and the last rites.

How far from then forethought of, all thy more
boisterous years,
ramshackle, temporary compared with heaven
When thou at the random▲ grim forge, powerful amidst peers,
Didst fettle for the great grey drayhorse his bright and
battering sandal!

THE WINDHOVER:

TO CHRIST OUR LORD

favourite
I caught this morning morning's minion▲, king-
dom of daylight's dauphin, dapple-dawn-drawn Falcon,
Christ
in his▲ riding
Of the rolling level underneath him steady air,
and striding
rippling
High there, how he rung upon the rein of a wimpling▲ wing
In his ecstasy! then off, off forth on swing,
As a skate's heel sweeps smooth on a bow-bend; the hurl
and gliding
Rebuffed the big wind. My heart in hiding
Stirred for a bird,—the achieve of, the mastery of the thing!

Brute beauty and valour and act, oh, air, pride, plume here
Buckle! AND the fire that breaks from thee then,
a billion
knight, champion
Times told lovelier, more dangerous, O my chevalier▲!

furrow
No wonder of it: shéer plód makes plough down sillion▲
Shine, and blue-bleak embers, ah my dear,
Fall, gall themselves, and gash gold-vermilion.

TITLE: THE WINDHOVER Kestrel falcon.

2. THE WINDHOVER dauphin: literally the eldest son of the King of France.

4. THE WINDHOVER rung upon the rein: in horsemanship, this refers to the horse circling upon a long rein, held by the trainer. 'Rung' also refers to a falcon's soaring upward in spirals.

10. Buckle: has multiple associations such as collapse, fasten, prepare for action.

GOD'S GRANDEUR

The world is charged with the grandeur of God.
It will flame out, like shining from shook foil;
It gathers to a greatness, like the ooze of oil
Crushed. Why do men then now not reck his rod?
Generations have trod, have trod, have trod;
And all is seared with trade; bleared, smeared with toil;
And wears man's smudge and shares man's smell: the soil
Is bare now, nor can foot feel, being shod.

And for all this, nature is never spent;
There lives the dearest freshness deep down things;
And though the last lights off the black West went
Oh, morning, at the brown brink eastward, springs—
Because the Holy Ghost over the bent
World broods with warm breast and with ah!
bright wings.

PIED BEAUTY

Glory be to God for dappled things—
For skies of couple-colour as a brinded cow;
For rose-moles all in stipple upon trout that swim;
Fresh-firecoal chestnut-falls; finches' wings;
Landscape plotted and pieced—fold, fallow, and plough;
And áll trádes, their gear and tackle and trim.

All things counter, original, spare, strange;
Whatever is fickle, freckled (who knows how?)
With swift, slow; sweet, sour; adazzle, dim;
He fathers-forth whose beauty is past change:
Praise him.

BINSEY POPLARS

FELLED 1879

My aspens dear, whose airy cages quelled,
Quelled or quenched in leaves the leaping sun,
All felled, felled, are all felled;
    Of a fresh and following folded rank
        Not spared, not one
        That dandled a sandalled
      Shadow that swam or sank
On meadow and river and wind-wandering weed-
    winding bank.

O if we but knew what we do
    When we delve or hew—
  Hack and rack the growing green!
    Since country is so tender
  To touch, her being so slender,
  That, like this sleek and seeing ball
  But a prick will make no eye at all,
  Where we, even where we mean
      To mend her we end her,
    When we hew or delve:
After-comers cannot guess the beauty been.
  Ten or twelve, only ten or twelve
  Strokes of havoc unselve
    The sweet especial scene,
  Rural scene, a rural scene,
  Sweet especial rural scene.

AS KINGFISHERS CATCH FIRE

As Kingfishers catch fire, dragonflies dráw fláme;
As tumbled over rim in roundy wells
Stones ring; like each tucked▲ string tells, each hung bell's *touched, plucked*
Bow swung finds tongue to fling out broad its name;
Each mortal thing does one thing and the same:
Deals out that being indoors each one dwells;
Selves—goes itself; *myself* it speaks and spells,
Crying *Whát I do is me: for that I came.*
Í say móre: the just man justices;
Kéeps gráce: thát keeps all his goings graces;
Acts in God's eye what in God's eye he is—
Chríst—for Christ plays in ten thousand places,
Lovely in limbs, and lovely in eyes not his
To the Father through the features of men's faces.

CARRION COMFORT

Not, I'll not, carrion comfort, Despair, not feast on thee;
Not untwist—slack they may be—these last strands of man
In me ór, most weary, cry *I can no more*. I can;
Can something, hope, wish day come, not choose not to be.
But ah, but O thou terrible▲, why wouldst thou rude▲ on me *God; violently, roughly*
Thy wring-world right foot rock? lay a lionlimb against me?
 scan
With darksome devouring eyes my bruisèd bones? and fan,
O in turns of tempest, me heaped there; me frantic to avoid
 thee and flee?
 Why? That my chaff might fly; my grain lie, sheer and clear.
Nay in all that toil, that coil, since (seems) I kissed *took his vows*
 the rod▲,

3–4 AS KINGFISHERS CATCH FIRE bell's bow: the interior of the cup of the bell.
TITLE: CARRION COMFORT carrion: dead, rotting flesh.

Hand rather, my heart lo! lapped strength, stole joy,
would laugh, chéer.
Cheer whom though? the hero whose heaven handling
flung me, fóot tród
Me? or me that fought him? O which one? is it each one?
That night, that year
Of now done darkness I wretch lay wrestling with (my God!)
my God.

NO WORST, THERE IS NONE

No worst, there is none. Pitched past pitch of grief,
More pangs will, schooled at forepangs, wilder wring.
Comforter, where, where is your comforting?
Mary, mother of us, where is your relief?
headlong My cries heave, herds-long▲; huddle in a main, a chief
Woe, wórld-sorrow; on an áge-old anvil wince and sing—
Then lull, then leave off. Fury had shrieked 'No ling-
fierce, deadly; of necessity ering! Let me be fell▲: force▲ I must be brief'.

O the mind, mind has mountains; cliffs of fall
Frightful, sheer, no-man-fathomed. Hold them cheap
May whó ne'er hung there. Nor does long our small
Durance deal with that steep or deep. Here! creep,
Wretch, under a comfort serves in a whirlwind: all
Life death does end and each day dies with sleep.

I WAKE AND FEEL THE FELL OF DARK

hide of an animal I wake and feel the fell▲ of dark, not day.
What hours, O what black hoürs we have spent
This night! what sights you, heart, saw; ways you went!
And more must, in yet longer light's delay.

5. NO WORST, THERE IS NONE herds-long: headlong, but also one after another like cattle in a herd following each other.
1. I WAKE AND FEEL THE FELL OF DARK 'Fell' can also refer to bitterness, rancor, and it can mean to strike down, kill. It can also mean dangerous, fierce, savage.

With witness I speak this. But where I say
Hours I mean years, mean life. And my lament
Is cries countless, cries like dead letters sent
To dearest him that lives alas! away.

I am gall, I am heartburn. God's most deep decree
Bitter would have me taste: my taste was me;
Bones built in me, flesh filled, blood brimmed
the curse.
Selfyeast of spirit a dull dough sours. I see
The lost are like this, and their scourge to be
As I am mine, their sweating selves; but worse.

HURRAHING IN HARVEST

Summer ends now; now, barbarous in beauty, the stooks arise
Around; up above, what wind-walks! what lovely behaviour
Of silk-sack clouds! has wilder, wilful-wavier
Meal-drift moulded ever and melted across skies?

I walk, I lift up, I lift up heart, eyes,
Down all that glory in the heavens to glean our Saviour;
And, éyes, heárt, what looks, what lips yet gave you a
Rapturous love's greeting of realer, of rounder replies?

And the azurous hung hills are his world-wielding shoulder
Majestic—as a stallion stalwart, very-violet-sweet!—
These things, these things were here and but the beholder
Wanting; which two when they once meet,
The heart réars wíngs bold and bolder
And hurls for him, O half hurls earth for him off under
his feet.

THE CAGED SKYLARK

As a dare-gale skylark scanted in a dull cage
Man's mounting spirit in his bone-house, mean house, dwells—
That bird beyond the remembering his free fells;
This in drudgery, day-labouring-out life's age.

Though aloft on turf or perch or poor low stage,
Both sing sometímes the sweetest, sweetest spells,
Yet both droop deadly sómetimes in their cells
Or wring their barriers in bursts of fear or rage.

Not that the sweet-fowl, song-fowl, needs no rest—
Why, hear him, hear him babble and drop down to his nest,
But his own nest, wild nest, no prison.

Man's spirit will be flesh-bound when found at best,
But uncumbered: meadow-down is not distressed
For a rainbow footing it nor he for his bónes rísen.

SPRING AND FALL:

TO A YOUNG CHILD

Márgarét, are you gríeving
Over Goldengrove unleaving?
Leáves, líke the things of man, you
With your fresh thoughts care for, can you?
Áh! ás the heart grows older
It will come to such sights colder
By and by, nor spare a sigh
pale or dim Though worlds of wanwood▲ leafmeal lie;
And yet you wíll weep and know why.
Now no matter, child, the name:
have the same origin Sórrow's spríngs áre the same▲.

THE CAGED SKYLARK: 5. Traditionally, turf was placed in a skylark's cage.

Nor mouth had, no nor mind, expressed
living spirit What heart heard of, ghost▲ guessed:
It ís the blight man was born for,
It is Margaret you mourn for.

TO WHAT SERVES MORTAL BEAUTY?

To what serves mortal beauty | —dangerous; does set danc-
ing blood—the O-seal-that-so | feature, flung prouder form
Than Purcell tune lets tread to? | See: it does this: keeps warm
Men's wits to the things that are; | what good means—
    where a glance
Master more than gaze, | gaze out of countenance.
Those lovely lads once, wet-fresh | windfalls of war's storm,
How then should Gregory, a father, | have gleanèd else from
    swarm-
ed Rome? But God to a nation | dealt that day's dear chance.
    To man, that needs would worship | block or barren stone,
Our law says: Love what are | love's worthiest, were all
    known;
World's loveliest—men's selves. Self | flashes off frame and
    face.
What do then? how meet beauty? | Merely meet it; own,
Home at heart, heaven's sweet gift; | then leave, let that alone.
Yea, wish that though, wish all, | God's better beauty, grace.

Thou art indeed just, Lord, if I contend
With thee; but, sir, so what I plead is just.
Why do sinners' ways prosper? and why must
Disappointment all I endeavour end?
    Wert thou my enemy, O thou my friend,

7. TO WHAT SERVES MORTAL BEAUTY Pope Gregory saw the Angles in the Roman slave market and sent Augustine to Britain.

How wouldst thou worse, I wonder, than thou dost
Defeat, thwart me? Oh, the sots and thralls of lust
Do in spare hours more thrive than I that spend,
Sir, life upon thy cause. See, banks and brakes
Now, leavèd how thick! lacèd they are again
aromatic herb With fretty chervil▴, look, and fresh wind shakes
Them; birds build—but not I build; no, but strain,
Time's eunuch, and not breed one work that wakes.
Mine, O thou lord of life, send my roots rain.

WILLIAM BUTLER YEATS
(1865–1939)

Born Dublin, Ireland, of an Anglo-Irish family. Yeats had an extraordinary capacity for continuing to develop, his poetry passing through many phases over the whole of his life. He was also a playwright, co-founded the Abbey Theatre, and was a senator of the Irish Free State, 1922–1928.

THE WILD SWANS AT COOLE

The trees are in their autumn beauty,
The woodland paths are dry,
Under the October twilight the water
Mirrors a still sky;
Upon the brimming water among the stones
Are nine-and-fifty swans.

The nineteenth autumn has come upon me
Since I first made my count;
I saw, before I had well finished,
All suddenly mount
And scatter wheeling in great broken rings
Upon their clamorous wings.

I have looked upon those brilliant creatures,
And now my heart is sore.
All's changed since I, hearing at twilight,
The first time on this shore,
The bell-beat of their wings above my head,
Trod with a lighter tread.

Unwearied still, lover by lover,
They paddle in the cold
Companionable streams or climb the air;
Their hearts have not grown old;
Passion or conquest, wander where they will,
Attend upon them still.

But now they drift on the still water,
Mysterious, beautiful;
Among what rushes will they build,
By what lake's edge or pool
Delight men's eyes when I awake some day
To find they have flown away?

THE SECOND COMING

Turning and turning in the widening gyre
The falcon cannot hear the falconer;
Things fall apart; the centre cannot hold;
Mere anarchy is loosed upon the world,
The blood-dimmed tide is loosed, and everywhere
The ceremony of innocence is drowned;
The best lack all conviction, while the worst
Are full of passionate intensity.

Surely some revelation is at hand;
Surely the Second Coming is at hand.
The Second Coming! Hardly are those words out
When a vast image out of *Spiritus Mundi*
Troubles my sight: somewhere in sands of the desert
A shape with lion body and the head of a man,
A gaze blank and pitiless as the sun,
Is moving its slow thighs, while all about it
Reel shadows of the indignant desert birds.

1. gyre: the spiralling upward flight of the falcon.
12. *Spiritus Mundi:* the Great Memory, collective imagination of mankind.

The darkness drops again; but now I know
That twenty centuries of stony sleep
Were vexed to nightmare by a rocking cradle,
And what rough beast, its hour come round at last,
Slouches towards Bethlehem to be born?

SAILING TO BYZANTIUM

That is no country for old men. The young
In one another's arms, birds in the trees
—Those dying generations—at their song,
The salmon-falls, the mackerel-crowded seas,
Fish, flesh, or fowl, commend all summer long
Whatever is begotten, born, and dies.
Caught in that sensual music all neglect
Monuments of unageing intellect.

An aged man is but a paltry thing,
A tattered coat upon a stick, unless
Soul clap its hands and sing, and louder sing
For every tatter in its mortal dress,
Nor is there singing school but studying
Monuments of its own magnificence;
And therefore I have sailed the seas and come
To the holy city of Byzantium.

O sages standing in God's holy fire
As in the gold mosaic of a wall,
Come from the holy fire, perne in a gyre,
And be the singing-masters of my soul.
Consume my heart away; sick with desire
And fastened to a dying animal
It knows not what it is; and gather me
Into the artifice of eternity.

19. perne in a gyre: spiral movement, like the thread on a bobbin being wound or unwound.

Once out of nature I shall never take
My bodily form from any natural thing,
But such a form as Grecian goldsmiths make
Of hammered gold and gold enamelling
To keep a drowsy Emperor awake;
Or set upon a golden bough to sing
To lords and ladies of Byzantium
Of what is past, or passing, or to come.

MEDITATIONS IN TIME OF CIVIL WAR

I

ANCESTRAL HOUSES

Surely among a rich man's flowering lawns,
Amid the rustle of his planted hills,
Life overflows without ambitious pains;
And rains down life until the basin spills,
And mounts more dizzy high the more it rains
As though to choose whatever shape it wills
And never stoop to a mechanical
Or servile shape, at other's beck and call.

Mere dreams, mere dreams! Yet Homer had not sung
Had he not found it certain beyond dreams
That out of life's own self-delight had sprung
The abounding glittering jet; though not it seems
As if some marvellous empty sea-shell flung
Out of the obscure dark of the rich streams,
And not a fountain, were the symbol which
Shadows the inherited glory of the rich.

Some violent bitter man, some powerful man
Called architect and artist in, that they,

TITLE: Civil war in Ireland, 1922.

Bitter and violent men, might rear in stone
The sweetness that all longed for night and day,
The gentleness none there had ever known;
But when the master's buried mice can play,
And maybe the great-grandson of that house,
For all its bronze and marble, 's but a mouse.

O what if gardens where the peacock strays
With delicate feet upon old terraces,
Or else all Juno▲ from an urn displays
Before the indifferent garden deities;
O what if levelled lawns and gravelled ways
Where slippered Contemplation finds his ease
And Childhood a delight for every sense,
But takes our greatness with our violence?

queen of the gods, attended by a peacock

What if the glory of escutcheoned▲ doors,
And buildings that a haughtier age designed,
The pacing to and fro on polished floors
Amid great chambers and long galleries, lined
With famous portraits of our ancestors;
What if those things the greatest of mankind
Consider most to magnify, or to bless,
But take our greatness with our bitterness?

shields with coats of arms on them

II

MY HOUSE

An ancient bridge, and a more ancient tower,
A farmhouse that is sheltered by its wall,
An acre of stony ground,
Where the symbolic rose can break in flower,
Old ragged elms, old thorns innumerable,
The sound of the rain or sound
Of every wind that blows;
The stilted water-hen

27. Juno: in Roman religion, the female equivalent of Jupiter.

Crossing stream again
Scared by the splashing of a dozen cows;

A winding stair, a chamber arched with stone,
A grey stone fireplace with an open hearth,
A candle and written page.
in Milton's poem *Il Penseroso's*▴ Platonist toiled on
In some like chamber, shadowing forth
How the daemonic rage
Imagined everything.
Benighted travellers
From markets and from fairs
Have seen his midnight candle glimmering.

Two men have founded here. A man-at-arms
Gathered a score of horse and spent his days
In this tumultuous spot,
Where through long wars and sudden night alarms
His dwindling score and he seemed castaways
Forgetting and forgot;
And I, that after me
My bodily heirs may find,
To exalt a lonely mind,
Befitting emblems of adversity.

III

MY TABLE

Two heavy trestles, and a board
Sato gave Yeats his ancestral sword Where Sato's▴ gift, a changeless sword,
By pen and paper lies,
That it may moralise
My days out of their aimlessness.
A bit of an embroidered dress
Covers its wooden sheath.
Chaucer had not drawn breath
When it was forged. In Sato's house,

Curved like new moon, moon-luminous,
It lay five hundred years.
Yet if no change appears
No moon; only an aching heart
Conceives a changeless work of art.
Our learned men have urged
That when and where 'twas forged
A marvellous accomplishment,
In painting or in pottery, went
From father unto son
And through the centuries ran
And seemed unchanging like the sword.
Soul's beauty being most adored,
Men and their business took
The soul's unchanging look;
For the most rich inheritor,
Knowing that none could pass Heaven's door
That loved inferior art,
Had such an aching heart
That he, although a country's talk
For silken clothes and stately walk,
Had waking wits; it seemed
Juno's peacock screamed.

IV

MY DESCENDANTS

Having inherited a vigorous mind
From my old fathers, I must nourish dreams
And leave a woman and a man behind
As vigorous of mind, and yet it seems
Life scarce can cast a fragrance on the wind,
Scarce spread a glory to the morning beams,
But the torn petals strew the garden plot;
And there's but common greenness after that.
And what if my descendants lose the flower
Through natural declension of the soul,

Through too much business with the passing hour,
Through too much play, or marriage with a fool?
May this laborious stair and this stark tower
Become a roofless ruin that the owl
May build in the cracked masonry and cry
Her desolation to the desolate sky.

the prime mover, initiator

The Primum Mobile▲ that fashioned us
Has made the very owls in circles move;
And I, that count myself most prosperous,
Seeing that love and friendship are enough,
For an old neighbour's friendship chose the house
And decked and altered it for a girl's love,
And know whatever flourish and decline
These stones remain their monument and mine.

V

THE ROAD AT MY DOOR

An affable Irregular,
A heavily-built Falstaffian man,
Comes cracking jokes of civil war
As though to die by gunshot were
The finest play under the sun.

A brown Lieutenant and his men,
Half dressed in national uniform,
Stand at my door, and I complain
Of the foul weather, hail and rain,
A pear-tree broken by the storm.

I count those feathered balls of soot
The moor-hen guides upon the stream,
To silence the envy in my thought;
And turn towards my chamber, caught
In the cold snows of a dream.

VI

THE STARE'S NEST BY MY WINDOW

The bees build in the crevices
Of loosening masonry, and there
The mother birds bring grubs and flies.
My wall is loosening; honey-bees,
Come build in the empty house of the stare.

We are closed in, and the key is turned
On our uncertainty; somewhere
A man is killed, or a house burned,
Yet no clear fact to be discerned:
Come build in the empty house of the stare.

A barricade of stone or of wood;
Some fourteen days of civil war;
Last night they trundled down the road
That dead young soldier in his blood:
Come build in the empty house of the stare.

We had fed the heart on fantasies,
The heart's grown brutal from the fare;
More substance in our enmities
Than in our love; O honey-bees,
Come build in the empty house of the stare.

VII

I SEE PHANTOMS OF HATRED AND OF THE HEART'S FULLNESS AND OF THE COMING EMPTINESS

I climb to the tower-top and lean upon broken stone,
A mist that is like blown snow is sweeping over all,
Valley, river, and elms, under the light of a moon
That seems unlike itself, that seems unchangeable,
A glittering sword out of the east. A puff of wind

TITLE: THE STARE'S NEST BY MY WINDOW stare: starling.

And those white glimmering fragments of the mist sweep by.
Frenzies bewilder, reveries perturb the mind;
Monstrous familiar images swim to the mind's eye.

'Vengeance upon the murderers,' the cry goes up,
'Vengeance for Jacques Molay.' In cloud-pale rags, or in lace,
The rage-driven, rage-tormented, and rage-hungry troop,
Trooper belabouring trooper, biting at arm or at face,
Plunges towards nothing, arms and fingers spreading wide
For the embrace of nothing; and I, my wits astray
Because of all that senseless tumult, all but cried
For vengeance on the murderers of Jacques Molay.

Their legs long, delicate and slender, aquamarine their eyes,
Magical unicorns bear ladies on their backs.
The ladies close their musing eyes. No prophecies,
Remembered out of Babylonian almanacs,
Have closed the ladies' eyes, their minds are but a pool
Where even longing drowns under its own excess;
Nothing but stillness can remain when hearts are full
Of their own sweetness, bodies of their loveliness.

The cloud-pale unicorns, the eyes of aquamarine,
The quivering half-closed eyelids, the rags of cloud or of lace,
Or eyes that rage has brightened, arms it has made lean,
Give place to an indifferent multitude, give place
To brazen hawks. Nor self-delighting reverie,
Nor hate of what's to come, nor pity for what's gone
Nothing but grip of claw, and the eye's complacency,
The innumerable clanging wings that have put out the moon.

171. 'A cry of vengeance because of the murder of the Grand Master of the Templars seems to me fit symbol for those who labour from hatred, and so for sterility in various kinds' (Yeats).

I turn away and shut the door, and on the stair
Wonder how many times I could have proved my worth
In something that all others understand or share;
But O! ambitious heart, had such a proof drawn forth
A company of friends, a conscience set at ease,
It had but made us pine the more. The abstract joy,
The half-read wisdom of daemonic images,
Suffice the ageing man as once the growing boy.

LONG-LEGGED FLY

That civilisation may not sink,
Its great battle lost,
Quiet the dog, tether the pony
To a distant post;
Our master Caesar is in the tent
Where the maps are spread,
His eyes fixed upon nothing,
A hand under his head.
Like a long-legged fly upon the stream
His mind moves upon silence.

That the topless towers be burnt
Helen of Troy And men recall that face▲,
Move most gently if move you must
In this lonely place.
She thinks, part woman, three parts a child,
That nobody looks; her feet
Practise a tinker shuffle
Picked up on a street.
Like a long-legged fly upon the stream
Her mind moves upon silence.

That girls at puberty may find
The first Adam in their thought,
Sistine Chapel Shut the door of the Pope's chapel▲,

23. Pope's chapel: Michelangelo painted the ceiling of the Sistine Chapel while lying on his back on a scaffold.

Keep those children out.
There on that scaffolding reclines
Michael Angelo.
With no more sound than the mice make
His hand moves to and fro.
Like a long-legged fly upon the stream
His mind moves upon silence.

AMONG SCHOOL CHILDREN

I

I walk through the long schoolroom questioning;
A kind old nun in a white hood replies;
The children learn to cipher and to sing,
To study reading-books and histories,
To cut and sew, be neat in everything
In the best modern way—the children's eyes
In momentary wonder stare upon
A sixty-year-old smiling public man.

II

I dream of a Ledaean body, bent
Above a sinking fire, a tale that she
Told of a harsh reproof, or trivial event
That changed some childish day to tragedy—
Told, and it seemed that our two natures blent
Into a sphere from youthful sympathy,
Or else, to alter Plato's parable,
Into the yolk and white of the one shell.

8. Yeats is here in his role as Irish Free State Senator.
9. Ledaean: in Greek mythology, Leda was raped by Zeus in the guise of a swan. Helen of Troy was the product of the union.
15. In Plato's parable, the two sexes were once one, like the white and yolk of an egg. They were divided by Zeus, and ever since have sought reunion.

III

And thinking of that fit of grief or rage
I look upon one child or t'other there
And wonder if she stood so at that age—
For even daughters of the swan can share
Something of every paddler's heritage—
And had that colour upon cheek or hair,
And thereupon my heart is driven wild:
She stands before me as a living child.

IV

Her present image floats into the mind—
Did Quattrocento finger fashion it
Hollow of cheek as though it drank the wind
And took a mess of shadows for its meat?
And I though never of Ledaean kind
Had pretty plumage once—enough of that,
Better to smile on all that smile, and show
There is a comfortable kind of old scarecrow.

V

What youthful mother, a shape upon her lap
Honey of generation had betrayed,
And that must sleep, shriek, struggle to escape
As recollection or the drug decide,
Would think her son, did she but see that shape
With sixty or more winters on its head,
A compensation for the pang of his birth,
Or the uncertainty of his setting forth?

19. she: his former lover, Maud Gonne.

26. Quattrocentro: the fourteen hundreds, a great period in Italian art.

VI

Plato thought nature but a spume that plays
Upon a ghostly paradigm of things;
beat Solider Aristotle played the taws▴
Upon the bottom of a king of kings;
World-famous golden-thighed Pythagoras
Fingered upon a fiddle-stick or strings
What a star sang and careless Muses heard:
Old clothes upon old sticks to scare a bird.

VII

Both nuns and mothers worship images,
But those the candles light are not as those
That animate a mother's reveries,
But keep a marble or a bronze repose.
And yet they too break hearts—O Presences
That passion, piety or affection knows,
And that all heavenly glory symbolise—
O self-born mockers of man's enterprise;

VIII

Labour is blossoming or dancing where
The body is not bruised to pleasure soul,
Nor beauty born out of its own despair,
Nor blear-eyed wisdom out of midnight oil.
O chestnut-tree, great-rooted blossomer,
Are you the leaf, the blossom or the bole?
O body swayed to music, O brightening glance,
How can we know the dancer from the dance?

41. Plato thought ordinary life was a mere shadow play of the true reality, which was perfect and permanent.

43. Aristotle was tutor to Alexander the Great.

Taws: the taws is an instrument of discipline, especially in schools. It is a long leather thong divided into narrow strips at one end.

45. Pythagoras related mathematics to musical measurement.

JOHN SHAW NEILSON
(1872–1942)

Born Penola, South Australia. The son of a Scottish immigrant labourer who became a poor farmer in Western Victoria, he lived himself in constant hardship even after his verses began to be published in the Bulletin.

THE ORANGE TREE

The young girl stood beside me. I
　Saw not what her young eyes could see:
—A light, she said, not of the sky
　Lives somewhere in the Orange Tree.

—Is it, I said, of east or west?
　The heartbeat of a luminous boy
Who with his faltering flute confessed
　Only the edges of his joy?

Was he, I said, borne to the blue
　In a mad escapade of Spring
Ere he could make a fond adieu
　To his love in the blossoming?

—Listen! the young girl said. There calls
　No voice, no music beats on me;
But it is almost sound: it falls
　This evening on the Orange Tree.

—Does he, I said, so fear the Spring
Ere the white sap too far can climb?
See in the full gold evening
All happenings of the olden time?

Is he so goaded by the green?
Does the compulsion of the dew
Make him unknowable but keen
Asking with beauty of the blue?

—Listen! the young girl said. For all
Your hapless talk you fail to see
There is a light, a step, a call
This evening on the Orange Tree.

—Is it, I said, a waste of love
Imperishably old in pain,
Moving as an affrighted dove
Under the sunlight or the rain?

Is it a fluttering heart that gave
Too willingly and was reviled?
Is it the stammering at a grave,
The last word of a little child?

—Silence! the young girl said. Oh, why,
Why will you talk to weary me?
Plague me no longer now, for I
Am listening like the Orange Tree.

THE GENTLE WATER BIRD

(FOR MARY GILMORE)

In the far days, when every day was long,
Fear was upon me and the fear was strong,
Ere I had learned the recompense of song.

In the dim days I trembled, for I knew
God was above me, always frowning through,
And God was terrible and thunder-blue.

Creeds the discoloured awed my opening mind,
Perils, perplexities—what could I find?—
All the old terror waiting on mankind.

Even the gentle flowers of white and cream,
The rainbow with its treasury of dream,
Trembled because of God's ungracious scheme.

And in the night the many stars would say
Dark things unaltered in the light of day:
Fear was upon me even in my play.

There was a lake I loved in gentle rain:
One day there fell a bird, a courtly crane:
Wisely he walked, as one who knows of pain.

Gracious he was and lofty as a king:
Silent he was, and yet he seemed to sing
Always of little children and the Spring.

God? Did he know him? It was far he flew . . .
God was not terrible and thunder-blue:
—It was a gentle water bird I knew.

Pity was in him for the weak and strong,
All who have suffered when the days were long,
And he was deep and gentle as a song.

As a calm soldier in a cloak of grey
He did commune with me for many a day
Till the dark fear was lifted far away.

Sober-apparelled, yet he caught the glow:
Always of Heaven would he speak, and low,
And he did tell me where the wishes go.

Kinsfolk of his it was who long before
Came from the mist (and no one knows the shore)
Came with the little children to the door.

Was he less wise than those birds long ago
Who flew from God (He surely willed it so)
Bearing great happiness to all below?

Long have I learned that all his speech was true:
I cannot reason it—how far he flew—
God is not terrible nor thunder-blue.

Sometimes, when watching in the white sunshine,
Someone approaches—I can half define
All the calm beauty of that friend of mine.

Nothing of hatred will about him cling:
Silent—how silent—but his heart will sing
Always of little children and the Spring.

THE CRANE IS MY NEIGHBOUR

The bird is my neighbour, a whimsical fellow and dim;
There is in the lake a nobility falling on him.

The bird is a noble, he turns to the sky for a theme,
And the ripples are thoughts coming out to the edge of a
dream.

The bird is both ancient and excellent, sober and wise,
But he never could spend all the love that is sent for his
eyes.

He bleats no instruction, he is not an arrogant drummer;
His gown is simplicity—blue as the smoke of the summer.

How patient he is as he puts out his wings for the blue!
His eyes are as old as the twilight, and calm as the dew.

The bird is my neighbour, he leaves not a claim for a sigh,
He moves as the guest of the sunlight—he roams in the sky.

The bird is a noble, he turns to the sky for a theme,
And the ripples are thoughts coming out to the edge of a
  dream.

THE MOON WAS SEVEN DAYS DOWN

'Peter!' she said, 'the clock has struck
  At one and two and three;
You sleep so sound, and the lonesome hours
  They seem so black to me.
I suffered long, and I suffered sore:
  —What else can I think upon?
I fear no evil; but, oh!—the moon!
  She is seven days gone.'

'Peter!' she said, 'the night is long:
  The hours will not go by:
The moon is calm; but she meets her death
  Bitter as women die.
I think too much of the flowers. I dreamed
  I walked in a wedding gown,
Or was it a shroud? The moon! the moon!
  She is seven days down.'

'Woman!' he said, 'my ears could stand
  Much noise when I was young;
But year by year you have wearied me:
  Can you never stop your tongue?
Here am I, with my broken rest,
  To be up at the break of day:

—So much to do; and the sheep not shorn,
And the lambs not yet away.'

'Peter!' she said, 'your tongue is rude;
You have ever spoken so:
My aches and ills, they trouble you not
This many a year, I know:
You talk of your lambs and sheep and wool:
—'Tis all that you think upon:
I fear no evil; but, oh! the moon!
She is seven days gone.'

'Peter!' she said, 'the children went:
My children would not stay:
By the hard word and the hard work
You have driven them far away.
I suffered, back in the ten years
That I never saw a town:
—Oh! the moon is over her full glory!
She is seven days down!

'Woman!' he said, 'I want my rest.
'Tis the worst time of the year:
The weeds are thick in the top fallow,
And the hay will soon be here.
A man is a man, and a child a child:
From a daughter or a son
Or a man or woman I want no talk
For anything I have done.'

'Peter!' she said, ''twas told to me,
Long back, in a happy year,
That I should die in the turning time
When the wheat was in the ear;
That I should go in a plain coffin
And lie in a plain gown
When the moon had taken her full glory
And was seven days down.'

Peter, he rose and lit the lamp
    At the first touch of the day:
His mind was full of the top fallow,
    And the ripening of the hay.
He said, 'She sleeps,'—but the second look
    He knew how the dead can stare:
And there came a dance of last beauty
    That none of the living share.

How cool and straight and steady he was:
    He said, 'She seems so young!
Her face is fine—it was always fine—
    But, oh, by God! her tongue!
She always thought as the children thought:
    Her mind was made for a town.'
—And the moon was out in the pale sky:
    She was seven days down.

He sauntered out to the neighbour's place
    As the daylight came in clear:
'The wheat,' he said, 'it is filling well,'
    And he stopped at a heavy ear.
He said, 'A good strong plain coffin
    Is the one I am thinking on.'
—And the moon was over his shoulder:
    She was seven days gone.

THE POOR CAN FEED THE BIRDS

Ragged, unheeded, stooping, meanly shod,
The poor pass to the pond; not far away
The spires go up to God.

Shyly they come from the unpainted lane;
Coats have they made of old unhappiness
That keeps in every pain.

The rich have fear, perchance their God is dim;
'Tis with the hope of stored-up happiness
They build the spires to Him.

The rich go out in clattering pomp and dare
In the most holy places to insult
The deep Benevolence there.

But 'tis the poor who make the loving words.
Slowly they stoop; it is a sacrament:
The poor can feed the birds.

Old, it is old, this scattering of the bread,
Deep as forgiveness, or the tears that go
Out somewhere to the dead.

The feast of love, the love that is the cure
For all indignities—it reigns, it calls,
It chains us to the pure.

Seldom they speak of God, He is too dim;
So without thought of after happiness
They feed the birds for Him.

The rich men walk not here on the green sod,
But they have builded towers, the timorous
That still go up to God.

Still will the poor go out with loving words;
In the long need, the need for happiness
The poor can feed the birds.

THE SUNDOWNER

I know not when this tiresome man
With his shrewd, sable billy-can
And his unwashed Democracy
His boomed-up Pilgrimage began.

Sometimes he wandered far outback
On a precarious Tucker Track;
Sometimes he lacked Necessities
No gentleman would like to lack.

Tall was the grass, I understand,
When the old Squatter ruled the land.
Why were the Conquerors kind to him?
Ah, the Wax Matches in his hand!

Where bullockies with oaths intense
Made of the dragged-up trees a fence,
Gambling with scorpions he rolled
His Swag, conspicuous, immense.

In the full splendour of his power
Rarely he touched one mile an hour,
Dawdling at sunset, History says,
For the Pint Pannikin of flour.

Seldom he worked; he was, I fear,
Unreasonably slow and dear;
Little he earned, and that he spent
Deliberately drinking Beer.

Cheerful, sorefooted child of chance,
Swiftly we knew him at a glance;
Boastful and self-compassionate,
Australia's Interstate Romance.

Shall he not live in Robust Rhyme,
Soliloquies and Odes Sublime?
Strictly between ourselves, he was
A rare old Humbug all the time.

In many a Book of Bushland dim
Mopokes shall give him greeting grim;
The old swans pottering in the reeds
Shall pass the time of day to him.

On many a page our Friend shall take
Small sticks his evening fire to make;
Shedding his waistcoat, he shall mix
On its smooth back his Johnny-Cake.

'Mid the dry leaves and silvery bark
Often at nightfall will he park
Close to a homeless creek, and hear
The Bunyip paddling in the dark.

THE BARD AND THE LIZARD

The lizard leans in to October,
   He walks on the yellow and green,
The world is awake and unsober,
   It knows where the lovers have been:
The wind, like a violoncello,
   Comes up and commands him to sing:
He says to me, 'Courage, good fellow!
   We live by the folly of Spring!'

A fish that the sea cannot swallow,
   A bird that can never yet rise,
A dreamer no dreamer can follow,
   The snake is at home in his eyes.
He tells me the paramount treason,
   His words have the resolute ring:
'Away with the homage to Reason!
   We live by the folly of Spring!'

The leaves are about him; the berry
   Is close in the red and the green,
His eyes are too old to be merry,
   He knows where the lovers have been.
And yet he could never be bitter,
   He tells me no sorrowful thing:
'The Autumn is less than a twitter!
We live by the folly of Spring!'

As green as the light on a salad
He leans in the shade of a tree,
He has good breath of a ballad,
The strength that is down in the sea.
How silent he creeps in the yellow—
How silent! and yet can he sing:
He gives me, 'Good morning, good fellow!
We live by the folly of Spring!'

I scent the alarm of the faded
Who love not the light and the play,
I hear the assault of the jaded,
I hear the intolerant bray.
My friend has the face of a wizard,
He tells me no desolate thing:
I learn from the heart of the lizard,
We live by the folly of Spring!

LOVE'S COMING

Quietly as rosebuds
Talk to the thin air,
Love came so lightly
I knew not he was there.

Quietly as lovers
Creep at the middle moon,
Softly as players tremble
In the tears of a tune;

Quietly as lilies
Their faint vows declare
Came the shy pilgrim:
I knew not he was there;

Quietly as tears fall
On a wild sin,
Softly as griefs call
In a violin;

Without hail or tempest,
Blue sword or flame,
Love came so lightly
I knew not that he came.

SONG BE DELICATE

Let your song be delicate.
The skies declare
No war—the eyes of lovers
Wake everywhere.

Let your voice be delicate.
How faint a thing
Is Love, little Love crying
Under the Spring.

Let your song be delicate.
The flowers can hear:
Too well they know the tremble
Of the hollow year.

Let your voice be delicate.
The bees are home:
All their day's love is sunken
Safe in the comb.

Let your song be delicate.
Sing no loud hymn:
Death is abroad . . . Oh, the black season!
The deep—the dim!

THE SMOKER PARROT

He has the full moon on his breast,
The moonbeams are about his wing;
He has the colours of a king.
I see him floating unto rest
When all eyes wearily go west,
And the warm winds are quieting.
The moonbeams are about his wing:
He has the full moon on his breast.

ROBERT FROST
(1874–1963)

Born San Francisco, USA. Unnoticed in America, he moved to England where his poetry gained recognition. With his work then accepted in America, he returned there, spending most of the rest of his life in New England, where most of his poems are set.

MOWING

There was never a sound beside the wood but one,
And that was my long scythe whispering to the ground.
What was it it whispered? I knew not well myself;
Perhaps it was something about the heat of the sun,
Something, perhaps, about the lack of sound—
And that was why it whispered and did not speak.
It was no dream of the gift of idle hours,
fairy Or easy gold at the hand of fay▲ or elf:
Anything more than the truth would have seemed
    too weak
To the earnest love that laid the swale in rows,
Not without feeble-pointed spikes of flowers
(Pale orchises), and scared a bright green snake.
The fact is the sweetest dream that labor knows.
My long scythe whispered and left the hay to make.

10. swale: a moist or marshy depression in a tract of land, especially in the midst of rolling prairie.

MENDING WALL

Something there is that doesn't love a wall,
That sends the frozen-ground-swell under it
And spills the upper boulders in the sun,
And makes gaps even two can pass abreast.
The work of hunters is another thing:
I have come after them and made repair
Where they have left not one stone on a stone,
But they would have the rabbit out of hiding,
To please the yelping dogs. The gaps I mean,
No one has seen them made or heard them made,
But at spring mending-time we find them there.
I let my neighbour know beyond the hill;
And on a day we meet to walk the line
And set the wall between us once again.
We keep the wall between us as we go.
To each the boulders that have fallen to each.
And some are loaves and some so nearly balls
We have to use a spell to make them balance:
'Stay where you are until our backs are turned!'
We wear our fingers rough with handling them.
Oh, just another kind of out-door game,
One on a side. It comes to little more:
There where it is we do not need the wall:
He is all pine and I am apple orchard.
My apple trees will never get across
And eat the cones under his pines, I tell him.
He only says, 'Good fences make good neighbours.'
Spring is the mischief in me, and I wonder
If I could put a notion in his head:
'*Why* do they make good neighbours? Isn't it
Where there are cows? But here there are no cows.
Before I built a wall I'd ask to know
What I was walling in or walling out,
And to whom I was like to give offense.
Something there is that doesn't love a wall,
That wants it down.' I could say 'Elves' to him,
But it's not elves exactly, and I'd rather

He said it for himself. I see him there,
Bringing a stone grasped firmly by the top
In each hand, like an old-stone savage armed.
He moves in darkness as it seems to me,
Not of woods only and the shade of trees.
He will not go behind his father's saying,
And he likes having thought of it so well
He says again, 'Good fences make good neighbours.'

BIRCHES

When I see birches bend to left and right
Across the lines of straighter darker trees,
I like to think some boy's been swinging them.
But swinging doesn't bend them down to stay
As ice storms do. Often you must have seen them
Loaded with ice a sunny winter morning
After a rain. They click upon themselves
As the breeze rises, and turn many-colored
As the stir cracks and crazes their enamel.
Soon the sun's warmth makes them shed crystal shells
Shattering and avalanching on the snowcrust—
Such heaps of broken glass to sweep away
You'd think the inner dome of heaven had fallen.
They are dragged to the withered bracken by the load,
And they seem not to break, though once they are bowed
So low for long, they never right themselves:
You may see their trunks arching in the woods
Years afterwards, trailing their leaves on the ground
Like girls on hands and knees that throw their hair
Before them over their heads to dry in the sun.
But I was going to say when Truth broke in
With all her matter of fact about the ice storm,
I should prefer to have some boy bend them
As he went out and in to fetch the cows—
Some boy too far from town to learn baseball,

Whose only play was what he found himself,
Summer or winter, and could play alone.
One by one he subdued his father's trees
By riding them down over and over again
Until he took the stiffness out of them,
And not one but hung limp, not one was left
For him to conquer. He learned all there was
To learn about not launching out too soon
And so not carrying the tree away
Clear to the ground. He always kept his poise
To the top branches, climbing carefully
With the same pains you use to fill a cup
Up to the brim, and even above the brim.
Then he flung outward, feet first, with a swish,
Kicking his way down through the air to the ground.
So was I once myself a swinger of birches.
And so I dream of going back to be.
It's when I'm weary of considerations,
And life is too much like a pathless wood
Where your face burns and tickles with the cobwebs
Broken across it, and one eye is weeping
From a twig's having lashed across it open.
I'd like to get away from earth a while
And then come back to it and begin over.
May no fate willfully misunderstand me
And half grant what I wish and snatch me away
Not to return. Earth's the right place for love.
I don't know where it's likely to go better.
I'd like to go by climbing a birch tree,
And climb black branches up a snow-white trunk
Toward heaven, till the tree could bear no more,
But dipped its top and set me down again.
That would be good both going and coming back
One could do worse than be a swinger of birches.

'OUT, OUT—'

The buzz saw snarled and rattled in the yard
And made dust and dropped stove-length sticks of wood,
Sweet-scented stuff when the breeze drew across it.
And from there those that lifted eyes could count
Five mountain ranges one behind the other
Under the sunset far into Vermont.
And the saw snarled and rattled, snarled and rattled,
As it ran light, or had to bear a load.
And nothing happened: day was all but done.
Call it a day, I wish they might have said
To please the boy by giving him the half hour
That a boy counts so much when saved from work.
His sister stood beside them in her apron
To tell them 'Supper.' At the word, the saw,
As if to prove saws knew what supper meant,
Leaped out at the boy's hand, or seemed to leap—
He must have given the hand. However it was,
Neither refused the meeting. But the hand!
The boy's first outcry was a rueful laugh,
As he swung toward them holding up the hand
Half in appeal, but half as if to keep
The life from spilling. Then the boy saw all—
Since he was old enough to know, big boy
Doing a man's work, though a child at heart—
He saw all spoiled. 'Don't let him cut my hand off—
The doctor, when he comes. Don't let him, sister!'
So. But the hand was gone already.
The doctor put him in the dark of ether.
He lay and puffed his lips out with his breath.
And then—the watcher at his pulse took fright.
No one believed. They listened at his heart.
Little—less—nothing!—and that ended it.
No more to build on there. And they, since they
Were not the one dead, turned to their affairs.

STOPPING BY WOODS ON A SNOWY EVENING

Whose woods these are I think I know.
His house is in the village, though;
He will not see me stopping here
To watch his woods fill up with snow.

My little horse must think it queer
To stop without a farmhouse near
Between the woods and frozen lake
The darkest evening of the year.

He gives his harness bells a shake
To ask if there is some mistake.
The only other sound's the sweep
Of easy wind and downy flake.

The woods are lovely, dark, and deep,
But I have promises to keep,
And miles to go before I sleep,
And miles to go before I sleep.

DESIGN

I found a dimpled spider, fat and white,
On a white heal-all▲, holding up a moth
Like a white piece of rigid satin cloth—
Assorted characters of death and blight
Mixed ready to begin the morning right,
Like the ingredients of a witches' broth—
A snow-drop spider, a flower like froth,
And dead wings carried like a paper kite.
What had that flower to do with being white,
The wayside blue and innocent heal-all?
What brought the kindred spider to that height,
Then steered the white moth thither in the night?

plant used for many ailments

What but design of darkness to appall?—
If design govern in a thing so small.

THE MOST OF IT

He thought he kept the universe alone;
For all the voice in answer he could wake
Was but the mocking echo of his own
From some tree-hidden cliff across the lake.
Some morning from the boulder-broken beach
He would cry out on life, that what it wants
Is not its own love back in copy speech,
But counter-love, original response.
And nothing ever came of what he cried
Unless it was the embodiment that crashed
rubble at the base In the cliff's talus▲ on the other side,
And then in the far distant water splashed,
But after a time allowed for it to swim,
Instead of proving human when it neared
And someone else additional to him,
As a great buck it powerfully appeared,
Pushing the crumpled water up ahead,
And landed pouring like a waterfall,
And stumbled through the rocks with horny tread,
And forced the underbrush—and that was all.

PROVIDE, PROVIDE

The witch that came (the withered hag)
To wash the steps with pail and rag,
Was once the beauty Abishag,

The picture pride of Hollywood.
Too many fall from great and good
For you to doubt the likelihood.

Die early and avoid the fate.
Or if predestined to die late,
Make up your mind to die in state.

Make the whole stock exchange your own!
If need be occupy a throne,
Where nobody can call *you* crone.

Some have relied on what they knew;
Others on being simply true.
What worked for them might work for you.

No memory of having starred
Atones for later disregard,
Or keeps the end from being hard.

Better to go down dignified
With boughten friendship at your side
Than none at all. Provide, provide!

NEITHER OUT FAR NOR IN DEEP

The people along the sand
All turn and look one way.
They turn their back on the land.
They look at the sea all day.

As long as it takes to pass
A ship keeps raising its hull;
The wetter ground like glass
Reflects a standing gull.

The land may vary more;
But wherever the truth may be—
The water comes ashore,
And the people look at the sea.

They cannot look out far.
They cannot look in deep.
But when was that ever a bar
To any watch they keep?

THE ROAD NOT TAKEN

Two roads diverged in a yellow wood,
And sorry I could not travel both
And be one traveler, long I stood
And looked down one as far as I could
To where it bent in the undergrowth;

Then took the other, as just as fair,
And having perhaps the better claim,
Because it was grassy and wanted wear,
Though as for that the passing there
Had worn them really about the same,

And both that morning equally lay
In leaves no step had trodden black.
Oh, I kept the first for another day!
Yet knowing how way leads on to way,
I doubted if I should ever come back.

AFTER APPLE-PICKING

My long two-pointed ladder's sticking through a tree
Toward heaven still,
And there's a barrel that I didn't fill
Beside it, and there may be two or three
Apples I didn't pick upon some bough.
But I am done with apple-picking now.
Essence of winter sleep is on the night,
The scent of apples: I am drowsing off.

I cannot rub the strangeness from my sight
I got from looking through a pane of glass
I skimmed this morning from the drinking trough
And held against the world of hoary grass.
It melted, and I let it fall and break.
But I was well
Upon my way to sleep before it fell,
And I could tell
What form my dreaming was about to take.
Magnified apples appear and disappear,
Stem end and blossom end,
And every fleck of russet showing clear.
My instep arch not only keeps the ache,
It keeps the pressure of a ladder-round.
I feel the ladder sway as the boughs bend.
And I keep hearing from the cellar bin
The rumbling sound
Of load on load of apples coming in.
For I have had too much
Of apple-picking: I am overtired
Of the great harvest I myself desired.
There were ten thousand thousand fruit to touch,
Cherish in hand, lift down, and not let fall.
For all
That struck the earth,
No matter if not bruised or spiked with stubble,
Went surely to the cider-apple heap
As of no worth.
One can see what will trouble
This sleep of mine, whatever sleep it is.
Were he not gone,
The woodchuck could say whether it's like his
Long sleep, as I describe its coming on,
Or just some human sleep.

HOME BURIAL

He saw her from the bottom of the stairs
Before she saw him. She was starting down,
Looking back over her shoulder at some fear.
She took a doubtful step and then undid it
To raise herself and look again. He spoke
Advancing toward her: 'What is it you see
From up there always—for I want to know.'
She turned and sank upon her skirts at that,
And her face changed from terrified to dull.
He said to gain time: 'What is it you see,'
Mounting until she cowered under him.
'I will find out now—you must tell me, dear.'
She, in her place, refused him any help
With the least stiffening of her neck and silence.
She let him look, sure that he wouldn't see,
Blind creature; and awhile he didn't see.
But at last he murmured. 'Oh,' and again, 'Oh.'

'What is it—what?' she said.

'Just that I see.'

'You don't,' she challenged. 'Tell me what it is.'

'The wonder is I didn't see at once.
I never noticed it from here before.
I must be wonted to it—that's the reason.
The little graveyard where my people are!
So small the window frames the whole of it.
Not so much larger than a bedroom, is it?
There are three stones of slate and one of marble,
Broad-shouldered little slabs there in the sunlight
On the sidehill. We haven't to mind *those.*
But I understand: it is not the stones,
But the child's mound—'

'Don't, don't, don't, don't,' she cried.

She withdrew shrinking from beneath his arm
That rested on the bannister, and slid downstairs;
And turned on him with such a daunting look,
He said twice over before he knew himself:
'Can't a man speak of his own child he's lost?'

'Not you! Oh, where's my hat? Oh, I don't need it!
I must get out of here. I must get air.
I don't know rightly whether any man can.'

'Amy! Don't go to someone else this time.
Listen to me. I won't come down the stairs.'
He sat and fixed his chin between his fists.
'There's something I should like to ask you, dear.'

'You don't know how to ask it.'

'Help me, then.'

Her fingers moved the latch for all reply.

'My words are nearly always an offense.
I don't know how to speak of anything
So as to please you. But I might be taught
I should suppose. I can't say I see how.
A man must partly give up being a man
With women-folk. We could have some arrangement
By which I'd bind myself to keep hands off
Anything special you're a-mind to name.
Though I don't like such things 'twixt those that love.
Two that don't love can't live together without them.
But two that do can't live together with them.'
She moved the latch a little. 'Don't—don't go.
Don't carry it to someone else this time.
Tell me about it if it's something human.
Let me into your grief. I'm not so much
Unlike other folks as your standing there
Apart would make me out. Give me my chance.
I do think, though, you overdo it a little.

What was it brought you up to think it the thing
To take your mother-loss of a first child
So inconsolably—in the face of love.
You'd think his memory might be satisfied—'

'There you go sneering now!'

'I'm not, I'm not!
You make me angry. I'll come down to you.
God, what a woman! And it's come to this,
A man can't speak of his own child that's dead.'

'You can't because you don't know how to speak.
If you had any feelings, you that dug
With your own hand—how could you?—his little grave;
I saw you from that very window there,
Making the gravel leap and leap in air,
Leap up, like that, like that, and land so lightly
And roll back down the mound beside the hole.
I thought, Who is that man? I didn't know you.
And I crept down the stairs and up the stairs
To look again, and still your spade kept lifting.
Then you came in. I heard your rumbling voice
Out in the kitchen, and I don't know why,
But I went near to see with my own eyes.
You could sit there with the stains on your shoes
Of the fresh earth from your own baby's grave
And talk about your everyday concerns.
You had stood the spade up against the wall
Outside there in the entry, for I saw it.'

'I shall laugh the worst laugh I ever laughed.
I'm cursed. God, If I don't believe I'm cursed.'

'I can repeat the very words you were saying.
"Three foggy mornings and one rainy day
Will rot the best birch fence a man can build."
Think of it, talk like that at such a time!
What had how long it takes a birch to rot

To do with what was in the darkened parlor.
You *couldn't* care! The nearest friends can go
With anyone to death, comes so far short
They might as well not try to go at all.
No, from the time when one is sick to death,
One is alone, and he dies more alone.
Friends make pretense of following to the grave,
But before one is in it, their minds are turned
And making the best of their way back to life
And living people, and things they understand.
But the world's evil. I won't have grief so
If I can change it. Oh, I won't, I won't!'

'There, you have said it all and you feel better.
You won't go now. You're crying. Close the door.
The heart's gone out of it: why keep it up.
Amy! There's someone coming down the road!'

'*You*—oh, you think the talk is all. I must go—
Somewhere out of this house. How can I make you—'

'If—you—do!' She was opening the door wider.
'Where do you mean to go? First tell me that.
I'll follow and bring you back by force. I *will!*—'

WALLACE **S**TEVENS
(1879–1955)

Born Reading, Pennsylvania. The son of a lawyer, he himself graduated in law and became the vice-president of an insurance company. Stevens has influenced younger poets but his originality makes him very difficult to imitate.

DISILLUSIONMENT OF TEN O'CLOCK

The houses are haunted
By white night-gowns.
None are green,
Or purple with green rings,
Or green with yellow rings,
Or yellow with blue rings.
None of them are strange,
With socks of lace
girdles And beaded ceintures▲.
People are not going
To dream of baboons and periwinkles.
Only, here and there, an old sailor,
Drunk and asleep in his boots,
Catches tigers
In red weather.

ANECDOTE OF THE JAR

I placed a jar in Tennessee,
And round it was, upon a hill.
It made the slovenly wilderness
Surround that hill.

The wilderness rose up to it,
And sprawled around, no longer wild.
The jar was round upon the ground
And tall and of a port in air.

It took dominion everywhere.
The jar was gray and bare.
It did not give of bird or bush,
Like nothing else in Tennessee.

THE SNOW MAN

One must have a mind of winter
To regard the frost and the boughs
Of the pine-trees crusted with snow;

And have been cold a long time
To behold the junipers shagged with ice,
The spruces rough in the distant glitter

Of the January sun; and not to think
Of any misery in the sound of the wind,
In the sound of a few leaves,

Which is the sound of the land
Full of the same wind
That is blowing in the same bare place

For the listener, who listens in the snow,
And, nothing himself, beholds
Nothing that is not there and the nothing that is.

THE HOUSE WAS QUIET AND THE WORLD WAS CALM

The house was quiet and the world was calm.
The reader became the book; and summer night

Was like the conscious being of the book.
The house was quiet and the world was calm.

The words were spoken as if there was no book,
Except that the reader leaned above the page.

Wanted to lean, wanted much most to be
The scholar to whom his book is true, to whom

The summer night is like a perfection of thought.
The house was quiet because it had to be.

The quiet was part of the meaning, part of the mind:
The access of perfection to the page.

And the world was calm. The truth in a calm world,
In which there is no other meaning, itself

Is calm, itself is summer and night, itself
Is the reader leaning late and reading there.

SUNDAY MORNING

I

woman's dressing gown

Complacencies of the peignoir▲, and late
Coffee and oranges in a sunny chair,
And the green freedom of a cockatoo
Upon a rug mingle to dissipate
The holy hush of ancient sacrifice.
She dreams a little, and she feels the dark
Encroachment of that old catastrophe,

As a calm darkens among water-lights.
The pungent oranges and bright, green wings
Seem things in some procession of the dead,
Winding across wide water, without sound.
The day is like wide water, without sound,
Stilled for the passing of her dreaming feet
Over the seas, to silent Palestine,
Dominion of the blood and sepulchre.

II

Why should she give her bounty to the dead?
What is divinity if it can come
Only in silent shadows and in dreams?
Shall she not find in comforts of the sun,
In pungent fruit and bright, green wings, or else
In any balm or beauty of the earth,
Things to be cherished like the thought of heaven?
Divinity must live within herself:
Passions of rain, or moods in falling snow;
Grievings in loneliness, or unsubdued
Elations when the forest blooms; gusty
Emotions on wet roads on autumn nights;
All pleasures and all pains, remembering
The bough of summer and the winter branch.
These are the measures destined for her soul.

III

Jove in the clouds had his inhuman birth.
No mother suckled him, no sweet land gave
Large-mannered motions to his mythy mind.
He moved among us, as a muttering king,
Magnificent, would move among his hinds,
Until our blood, commingling, virginal,
With heaven, brought such requital to desire
The very hinds discerned it, in a star.
Shall our blood fail? Or shall it come to be
The blood of paradise? And shall the earth
Seem all of paradise that we shall know?
The sky will be much friendlier then than now,

A part of labour and a part of pain,
And next in glory to enduring love,
Not this dividing and indifferent blue.

IV

She says, 'I am content when wakened birds,
Before they fly, test the reality
Of misty fields, by their sweet questionings;
But when the birds are gone, and their warm fields
Return no more, where, then, is paradise?'
There is not any haunt of prophecy,
Nor any old chimera of the grave,
Neither the golden underground, nor isle
Melodious, where spirits gat them home,
Nor visionary south, nor cloudy palm
Remote on heaven's hill, that has endured
As April's green endures; or will endure
Like her remembrance of awakened birds,
Or her desire for June and evening, tipped
By the consummation of the swallow's wings

V

She says, 'But in contentment I still feel
The need of some imperishable bliss.'
Death is the mother of beauty; hence from her,
Alone, shall come fulfilment to our dreams
And our desires. Although she strews the leaves
Of sure obliteration on our paths,
The path sick sorrow took, the many paths
Where triumph rang its brassy phrase, or love
Whispered a little out of tenderness,
She makes the willow shiver in the sun
For maidens who were wont to sit and gaze
Upon the grass, relinquished to their feet.
She causes boys to pile new plums and pears
On disregarded plate. The maidens taste
And stray impassioned in the littering leaves.

VI

Is there no change of death in paradise?
Does ripe fruit never fall? Or do the boughs
Hang always heavy in that perfect sky,
Unchanging, yet so like our perishing earth,
With rivers like our own that seek for seas
They never find, the same receding shores
That never touch with inarticulate pang?
Why set the pear upon those river-banks
Or spice the shores with odours of the plum?
Alas, that they should wear our colours there,
The silken weavings of our afternoons,
And pick the strings of our insipid lutes!
Death is the mother of beauty, mystical,
Within whose burning bosom we devise
Our earthly mothers waiting, sleeplessly.

VII

Supple and turbulent, a ring of men
Shall chant in orgy on a summer morn
Their boisterous devotion to the sun,
Not as a god, but as a god might be,
Naked among them, like a savage source.
Their chant shall be a chant of paradise,
Out of their blood, returning to the sky;
And in their chant shall enter, voice by voice,
The windy lake wherein their lord delights,
angels The trees, like seraphim▲, and echoing hills,
That choir among themselves long afterward.
They shall know well the heavenly fellowship
Of men that perish and of summer morn.
And whence they came and whither they shall go
The dew upon their feet shall manifest.

VIII

She hears, upon that water without sound,
A voice that cries, 'The tomb in Palestine
Is not the porch of spirits lingering.
It is the grave of Jesus, where he lay.'

We live in an old chaos of the sun,
Or old dependency of day and night,
Or island solitude, unsponsored, free,
Of that wide water, inescapable.
Deer walk upon our mountains, and the quail
Whistle about us their spontaneous cries;
Sweet berries ripen in the wilderness;
And, in the isolation of the sky,
At evening, casual flocks of pigeons make
Ambiguous undulations as they sink,
Downward to darkness, on extended wings.

THE PLAIN SENSE OF THINGS

After the leaves have fallen, we return
To a plain sense of things. It is as if
We had come to an end of the imagination,
Inanimate in an inert savoir.

It is difficult even to choose the adjective
For this blank cold, this sadness without cause.
The great structure has become a minor house.
No turban walks across the lessened floors.

The greenhouse never so badly needed paint.
The chimney is fifty years old and slants to one side.
A fantastic effort has failed, a repetition
In a repetitiousness of men and flies.

Yet the absence of the imagination had
Itself to be imagined. The great pond,
The plain sense of it, without reflections, leaves,
Mud, water like dirty glass, expressing silence

Of a sort, silence of a rat come out to see,
The great pond and its waste of the liles, all this
Had to be imagined as an inevitable knowledge,
Required, as a necessity requires.

NO POSSUM, NO SOP, NO TATERS

He is not here, the old sun,
As absent as if we were asleep.

The field is frozen. The leaves are dry.
Bad is final in this light.

In this bleak air the broken stalks
Have arms without hands. They have trunks

Without legs or, for that, without heads.
They have heads in which a captive cry

Is merely the moving of a tongue.
Snow sparkles like eyesight falling to earth,

Like seeing fallen brightly away.
The leaves hop, scraping on the ground.

It is deep January. The sky is hard.
The stalks are firmly rooted in ice.

It is in this solitude, a syllable,
Out of these gawky flitterings,

Intones its single emptiness,
The savagest hollow of winter-sound.

It is here, in this bad, that we reach
The last purity of the knowledge of good.

The crow looks rusty as he rises up.
Bright is the malice in his eye . . .

One joins him there for company.
But at a distance, in another tree.

T.S. ELIOT
(1888–1965)

Born St Louis, USA, but moved to England in 1915 and became an English citizen in 1927. Eliot was influential as poet, critic, and publisher. In later years he also wrote plays, the best known being Murder in the Cathedral.

THE LOVE SONG OF J. ALFRED PRUFROCK

S'io credessi che mia risposta fosse
a persona che mai tornasse al mondo,
questa fiamma staria senza più scosse.
Ma per ciòche giammai di questo fondo
non tornò vivo alcun, s'i' odo il vero
senza tema d'infamia ti rispondo.

Let us go then, you and I,
When the evening is spread out against the sky
Like a patient etherised upon a table;
Let us go, through certain half-deserted streets,
The muttering retreats
Of restless nights in one-night cheap hotels
And sawdust restaurants with oyster-shells:
Streets that follow like a tedious argument

Epigraph: from Dante's *Inferno*. 'If I thought my reply were to someone who could ever return to the world, this flame would shake no longer. But since no-one ever returned alive from this pit, if what I hear is true, I answer thee without fear of infamy.'

Of insidious intent
To lead you to an overwhelming question...
Oh, do not ask, 'What is it?'
Let us go and make our visit.

In the room the women come and go
Talking of Michelangelo.

The yellow fog that rubs its back upon the
window-panes,
The yellow smoke that rubs its muzzle on the
window-panes,
Licked its tongue into the corners of the evening,
Lingered upon the pools that stand in drains,
Let fall upon its back the soot that falls from chimneys,
Slipped by the terrace, made a sudden leap,
And seeing that it was a soft October night,
Curled once about the house, and fell asleep.

And indeed there will be time
For the yellow smoke that slides along the street,
Rubbing its back upon the window-panes;
There will be time, there will be time
To prepare a face to meet the faces that you meet;
There will be time to murder and create,
And time for all the works and days of hands
That lift and drop a question on your plate;
Time for you and time for me,
And time yet for a hundred indecisions,
And for a hundred visions and revisions,
Before the taking of a toast and tea.

In the room the women come and go
Talking of Michelangelo.

And indeed, there will be time
To wonder, 'Do I dare?' and, 'Do I dare?'
Time to turn back and descend the stair,
With a bald spot in the middle of my hair—

(They will say: 'How his hair is growing thin!')
My morning coat, my collar mounting firmly to
the chin,
My necktie rich and modest, but asserted by a
simple pin—
(They will say: 'But how his arms and legs are thin!')
Do I dare
Disturb the universe?
In a minute there is time
For decisions and revisions which a minute will reverse.

For I have known them all already, known them all—
Have known the evenings, mornings, afternoons,
I have measured out my life with coffee spoons;
I know the voices dying with a dying fall
Beneath the music from a farther room.
So how should I presume?

And I have known the eyes already, known them all—
The eyes that fix you in a formulated phrase,
And when I am formulated, sprawling on a pin,
When I am pinned and wriggling on the wall,
Then how should I begin
To spit out all the butt-ends of my days and ways?
And how should I presume?

And I have known the arms already, known them all—
Arms that are braceleted and white and bare
(But in the lamplight, downed with light brown hair!)
Is it perfume from a dress
That makes me so digress?
Arms that lie along a table, or wrap about a shawl,
And should I then presume?
And how should I begin?

*

Shall I say, I have gone at dusk through narrow streets
And watched the smoke that rises from the pipes
Of lonely men in shirt-sleeves, leaning out of windows? . . .

I should have been a pair of ragged claws
Scuttling across the floors of silent seas.

*

And the afternoon, the evening, sleeps so peacefully!
Smoothed by long fingers,
Asleep... tired... or it malingers,
Stretched on the floor, here beside you and me.
Should I, after tea and cakes and ices,
Have the strength to force the moment to its crisis?
But though I have wept and fasted, wept and prayed,
Though I have seen my head (grown slightly bald)
brought in upon a platter,
I am no prophet—and here's no great matter;
I have seen the moment of my greatness flicker,
And I have seen the eternal Footman hold my coat,
and snicker,
And in short, I was afraid.

And would it have been worth it, after all,
After the cups, the marmalade, the tea,
Among the porcelain, among some talk of you and me,
Would it have been worth while,
To have bitten off the matter with a smile,
To have squeezed the universe into a ball
To roll it towards some overwhelming question,
To say: 'I am Lazarus, come from the dead,
Come back to tell you all, I shall tell you all'—
If one, settling a pillow by her head,
Should say: 'That is not what I meant at all.
That is not it, at all.'

And would it have been worth it, after all,
Would it have been worth while,
After the sunsets and the dooryards and the sprinkled
streets,

83. prophet: like John the Baptist whose head was presented on a platter to Salome. Matthew xiv, 1–12.

94. Lazarus, resurrected from the dead by Jesus. John xi.

After the novels, after the teacups, after the skirts that
  trail along the floor—
And this, and so much more?—
It is impossible to say just what I mean!
But as if a magic lantern threw the nerves in patterns
  on a screen:
Would it have been worth while
If one, settling a pillow or throwing off a shawl,
And turning toward the window, should say:
  'That is not it at all,
  That is not what I meant, at all.'

*

  No! I am not Prince Hamlet, nor was meant to be;
Am an attendant lord, one that will do
royal journey
To swell a progress▲, start a scene or two,
Advise the prince; no doubt, an easy tool,
Deferential, glad to be of use,
Politic, cautious, and meticulous;
Full of high sentence, but a bit obtuse;
At times, indeed, almost ridiculous—
Almost, at times, the Fool.

  I grow old... I grow old...
I shall wear the bottoms of my trousers rolled.

  Shall I part my hair behind? Do I dare to eat a peach?
I shall wear white flannel trousers, and walk upon
  the beach.
I have heard the mermaids singing, each to each.

I do not think that they will sing to me.

I have seen them riding seaward on the waves
Combing the white hair of the waves blown back
When the wind blows the water white and black.

We have lingered in the chambers of the sea
By sea-girls wreathed with seaweed red and brown
Till human voices wake us, and we drown.

PORTRAIT OF A LADY

Thou has committed—
Fornication: but that was in another country,
And besides, the wench is dead.
The Jew of Malta

I

Among the smoke and fog of a December afternoon
You have the scene arrange itself—as it will seem to do—
With 'I have saved this afternoon for you';
And four wax candles in the darkened room,
Four rings of light upon the ceiling overhead,
An atmosphere of Juliet's tomb
Prepared for all the things to be said, or left unsaid.
We have been, let us say, to hear the latest Pole
Transmit the Preludes, through his hair and finger-tips.
'So intimate, this Chopin, that I think his soul
Should be resurrected only among friends
Some two or three, who will not touch the bloom
That is rubbed and questioned in the concert room.'
—And so the conversation slips
Among velleities▲ and carefully caught regrets
Through attenuated tones of violins
Mingled with remote cornets
And begins.
'You do not know how much they mean to me,
    my friends,
And how, how rare and strange it is, to find
In a life composed so much, so much of odds and ends,
(For indeed I do not love it... you knew? you are
    not blind!
How keen you are!)
To find a friend who has these qualities,
Who has, and gives

inert aspirations

Epigraph: by Christopher Marlowe.

Those qualities upon which friendship lives.
How much it means that I say this to you—
nightmare Without these friendships—life, what *cauchemar*▲!'

Among the windings of the violins
little melodies And the ariettes▲
Of cracked cornets
Inside my brain a dull tom-tom begins
Absurdly hammering a prelude of its own,
Capricious monotone
That is at least one definite 'false note'.
—Let us take the air, in a tobacco trance,
Admire the monuments,
Discuss the late events,
Correct our watches by the public clocks.
a strong Bavarian beer Then sit for half an hour and drink our bocks▲.

II

Now that lilacs are in bloom
She has a bowl of lilacs in her room
And twists one in her fingers while she talks.
'Ah, my friend, you do not know, you do not know
What life is, you who hold it in your hands';
(Slowly twisting the lilac stalks)
'You let it flow from you, you let it flow,
And youth is cruel, and has no remorse
And smiles at situations which it cannot see.'
I smile, of course,
And go on drinking tea.

'Yet with these April sunsets, that somehow recall
My buried life, and Paris in the Spring,
I feel immeasurably at peace, and find the world
To be wonderful and youthful, after all.'

The voice returns like the insistent out-of-tune
Of a broken violin on an August afternoon:

'I am always sure that you understand
My feelings, always sure that you feel,
Sure that across the gulf you reach your hand.

You are invulnerable, you have no Achilles' heel.
You will go on, and when you have prevailed
You can say: at this point many a one has failed.
But what have I, but what have I, my friend,
To give you, what can you receive from me?
Only the friendship and the sympathy
Of one about to reach her journey's end.

I shall sit here, serving tea to friends...'

I take my hat: how can I make a cowardly amends
For what she has said to me?
You will see me any morning in the park
Reading the comics and the sporting page.
Particularly I remark
An English countess goes upon the stage.
A Greek was murdered at a Polish dance,
Another bank defaulter has confessed.
I keep my countenance,
I remain self-possessed
Except when a street-piano, mechanical and tired
Reiterates some worn-out common song
With the smell of hyacinths across the garden
Recalling things that other people have desired.
Are these ideas right or wrong?

III

The October night comes down; returning as before
Except for a slight sensation of being ill at ease
I mount the stairs and turn the handle of the door

61. Achilles' heel: Achilles' mother dipped him in a river which made him invulnerable except at the heel where she held him. He was killed by an arrow shot into the heel.

And feel as if I had mounted on my hands and knees.
'And so you are going abroad; and when do you return?
But that's a useless question.
You hardly know when you are coming back,
You will find so much to learn.'
My smile falls heavily among the bric-à-brac.

'Perhaps you can write to me.'
My self-possession flares up for a second;
This is as I had reckoned.
'I have been wondering frequently of late
(But our beginnings never know our ends!)
Why we have not developed into friends.'
I feel like one who smiles, and turning shall remark
Suddenly, his expression in a glass.
My self-possession gutters; we are really in the dark.

'For everybody said so, all our friends,
They all were sure our feelings would relate
So closely! I myself can hardly understand.
We must leave it now to fate.
You will write, at any rate.
Perhaps it is not too late.
I shall sit here, serving tea to friends.'

And I must borrow every changing shape
To find expression . . . dance, dance
Like a dancing bear,
Cry like a parrot, chatter like an ape.
Let us take the air, in a tobacco trance—

Well! and what if she should die some afternoon,
Afternoon grey and smoky, evening yellow and rose;
Should die and leave me sitting pen in hand
With the smoke coming down above the housetops;
Doubtful, for a while
Not knowing what to feel or if I understand
Or whether wise or foolish, tardy or too soon . . .
Would she not have the advantage, after all?

This music is successful with a 'dying fall'
Now that we talk of dying—
And should I have the right to smile?

PRELUDES

I

The winter evening settles down
With smell of steaks in passageways.
Six o'clock.
The burnt-out ends of smoky days.
And now a gusty shower wraps
The grimy scraps
Of withered leaves about your feet
And newspapers from vacant lots;
The showers beat
On broken blinds and chimney-pots,
At the corner of the street
A lonely cab-horse steams and stamps.

And then the lighting of the lamps.

II

The morning comes to consciousness
Of faint stale smells of beer
From the sawdust-trampled street
With all its muddy feet that press
To early coffee-stands.

With the other masquerades
That time resumes,
One thinks of all the hands
That are raising dingy shades
In a thousand furnished rooms.

III

You tossed a blanket from the bed,
You lay upon your back, and waited;
You dozed, and watched the night revealing
The thousand sordid images
Of which your soul was constituted;
They flickered against the ceiling.
And when all the world came back
And the light crept up between the shutters
And you heard the sparrows in the gutters,
You had such a vision of the street
As the street hardly understands;
Sitting along the bed's edge, where
You curled the papers from your hair,
Or clasped the yellow soles of feet
In the palms of both soiled hands.

IV

His soul stretched tight across the skies
That fade behind a city block,
Or trampled by insistent feet
At four and five and six o'clock;
And short square fingers stuffing pipes,
And evening newspapers, and eyes
Assured of certain certainties,
The conscience of a blackened street
Impatient to assume the world.

I am moved by fancies that are curled
Around these images, and cling:
The notion of some infinitely gentle
Infinitely suffering thing.

Wipe your hand across your mouth, and laugh;
The worlds revolve like ancient women
Gathering fuel in vacant lots.

JOURNEY OF THE MAGI

'A cold coming we had of it,
Just the worst time of the year
For a journey, and such a long journey:
The ways deep and the weather sharp,
The very dead of winter.'
And the camels galled, sore-footed, refractory,
Lying down in the melting snow.
There were times we regretted
The summer palaces on slopes, the terraces,
And the silken girls bringing sherbet.
Then the camel men cursing and grumbling
And running away, and wanting their liquor and women,
And the night-fires going out, and the lack of shelters,
And the cities hostile and the towns unfriendly
And the villages dirty and charging high prices:
A hard time we had of it.
At the end we preferred to travel all night,
Sleeping in snatches,
With the voices singing in our ears, saying
That this was all folly.

Then at dawn we came down to a temperate valley,
Wet, below the snow line, smelling of vegetation;
With a running stream and a water-mill beating
    the darkness,
And three trees on the low sky,
And an old white horse galloped away in the meadow.
Then we came to a tavern with vine-leaves over
    the lintel,
Six hands at an open door dicing for pieces of silver,
And feet kicking the empty wine-skins.
But there was no information, and so we continued
And arrived at evening, not a moment too soon
Finding the place; it was (you may say) satisfactory.

1–5: adapted from a sermon by Launcelot Andrewes, Christmas 1622.

All this was a long time ago, I remember,
And I would do it again, but set down
This set down
This: were we led all that way for
Birth or Death? There was a Birth, certainly,
We had evidence and no doubt. I had seen birth
and death,
But had thought they were different; this Birth was
Hard and bitter agony for us, like Death, our death.
We returned to our places, these Kingdoms,
But no longer at ease here, in the old dispensation,
With an alien people clutching their gods.
I should be glad of another death.

WILFRED OWEN
(1893—1918)

Born Shropshire, England. He enlisted in the British Army in 1915. He wrote poems while he was on leave, injured. He was killed in the final days of the War.

EXPOSURE

Our brains ache, in the merciless iced east winds that knive us...
Wearied we keep awake because the night is silent...
Low, drooping flares confuse our memory of the salient...
Worried by silence, sentries whisper, curious, nervous,
        But nothing happens.

Watching, we hear the mad gusts tugging on the wire,
Like twitching agonies of men among its brambles.
Northward, incessantly, the flickering gunnery rumbles,
Far off, like a dull rumour of some other war.
        What are we doing here?

The poignant misery of dawn begins to grow...
We only know war lasts, rain soaks, and clouds sag stormy.
Dawn massing in the east her melancholy army
Attacks once more in ranks on shivering ranks of gray,
        But nothing happens.

Sudden successive flights of bullets streak the silence.
Less deadly than the air that shudders black with snow,
With sidelong flowing flakes that flock, pause, and renew,

We watch them wandering up and down the wind's nonchalance,
        But nothing happens.

Pale flakes with fingering stealth come feeling for our faces—
We cringe in holes, back on forgotten dreams, and stare, snow-dazed,
Deep into grassier ditches. So we drowse, sun-dozed,
Littered with blossoms trickling where the blackbird fusses.
        Is it that we are dying?

Slowly our ghosts drag home: glimpsing the sunk fires, glozed
With crusted dark-red jewels; crickets jingle there;
For hours the innocent mice rejoice; the house is theirs;
Shutters and doors, all closed: on us the doors are closed,—
        We turn back to our dying.

Since we believe not otherwise can kind fires burn;
Nor ever suns smile true on child, or field, or fruit.
For God's invincible spring our love is made afraid;
Therefore, not loath, we lie out here; therefore were born,
        For love of God seems dying.

To-night, His frost will fasten on this mud and us,
Shrivelling many hands, puckering foreheads crisp.
The burying-party, picks and shovels in their shaking grasp,
Pause over half-known faces. All their eyes are ice,
        But nothing happens.

THE SEND-OFF

Down the close, darkening lanes they sang their way
To the siding-shed,
And lined the train with faces grimly gay.

Their breasts were stuck all white with wreath and spray
As men's are, dead.

Dull porters watched them, and a casual tramp
Stood staring hard,
Sorry to miss them from the upland camp.
Then, unmoved, signals nodded, and a lamp
Winked to the guard.

So secretly, like wrongs hushed-up, they went.
They were not ours:
We never heard to which front these were sent.

Nor there if they yet mock what women meant
Who gave them flowers.

Shall they return to beatings of great bells
In wild train-loads?
A few, a few, too few for drums and yells,
May creep back, silent, to village wells
Up half-known roads.

DULCE ET DECORUM EST

Bent double, like old beggars under sacks,
Knock-kneed, coughing like hags, we cursed through
  sludge,
Till on the haunting flares we turned our backs,
And towards our distant rest began to trudge.
Men marched asleep. Many had lost their boots,
But limped on, blood-shod. All went lame, all blind;
Drunk with fatigue; deaf even to the hoots
Of gas-shells dropping softly behind.

Gas! GAS! Quick, boys!—An ecstasy of fumbling,
Fitting the clumsy helmets just in time,
But someone still was yelling out and stumbling
And floundering like a man in fire or lime.—
Dim through the misty panes and thick green light,
As under a green sea, I saw him drowning.

In all my dreams before my helpless sight
He plunges at me, guttering, choking, drowning.

If in some smothering dreams, you too could pace
Behind the wagon that we flung him in,
And watch the white eyes writhing in his face,
His hanging face, like a devil's sick of sin;
If you could hear, at every jolt, the blood
Come gargling from the froth-corrupted lungs,
Bitter as the cud
Of vile, incurable sores on innocent tongues—
My friend, you would not tell with such high zest
To children ardent for some desperate glory,
The old Lie: Dulce et decorum est
Pro patria mori▲.

'It is sweet and fitting to die for one's native land'

FUTILITY

Move him into the sun—
Gently its touch awoke him once,
At home, whispering of fields unsown.
Always it woke him, even in France,
Until this morning and this snow.
If anything might rouse him now
The kind old sun will know.
Think how it wakes the seeds,—
Woke, once, the clays of a cold star.
Are limbs, so dear-achieved, are sides,
Full-nerved—still warm—too hard to stir?

Was it for this the clay grew tall?
—O what made fatuous sunbeams toil
To break earth's sleep at all?

ANTHEM FOR DOOMED YOUTH

What passing-bells for these who die as cattle?
Only the monstrous anger of the guns.
Only the stuttering rifles' rapid rattle
prayers Can patter out their hasty orisons▲.
No mockeries now for them; no prayers nor bells,
Nor any voice of mourning save the choirs,—
The shrill, demented choirs of wailing shells;
And bugles calling for them from sad shires.

What candles may be held to speed them all?
Not in the hands of boys, but in their eyes
Shall shine the holy glimmers of good-byes.
The pallor of girls' brows shall be their pall;
Their flowers the tenderness of patient minds,
And each slow dusk a drawing-down of blinds.

STRANGE MEETING

It seemed that out of battle I escaped
Down some profound dull tunnel, long since scooped
Through granites which titanic wars had groined.
Yet also there encumbered sleepers groaned,
Too fast in thought or death to be bestirred.
Then, as I probed them, one sprang up, and stared
With piteous recognition in fixed eyes,
Lifting distressful hands as if to bless.
And by his smile, I knew that sullen hall,

By his dead smile I knew we stood in Hell.
With a thousand pains that vision's face was grained;
Yet no blood reached there from the upper ground,
And no guns thumped, or down the flues made moan.
'Strange friend,' I said, 'here is no cause to mourn.'
'None,' said that other, 'save the undone years,
The hopelessness. Whatever hope is yours,
Was my life also; I went hunting wild
After the wildest beauty in the world,
Which lies not calm in eyes, or braided hair,
But mocks the steady running of the hour,
And if it grieves, grieves richlier than here.
For of my glee might many men have laughed,
And of my weeping something had been left,
Which must die now. I mean the truth untold,
The pity of war, the pity war distilled.
Now men will go content with what we spoiled,
Or, discontent, boil bloody, and be spilled.
They will be swift with swiftness of the tigress.
None will break ranks, though nations trek
  from progress.
Courage was mine, and I had mystery,
Wisdom was mine, and I had mastery:
To miss the march of this retreating world
Into vain citadels that are not walled.
Then, when much blood had clogged their
  chariot-wheels,
I would go up and wash them from sweet wells,
Even with truths that lie too deep for taint.
I would have poured my spirit without stint
But not through wounds; not on the cess of war.
Foreheads of men have bled where no wounds were.
I am the enemy you killed, my friend.
I knew you in this dark: for so you frowned
Yesterday through me as you jabbed and killed.
I parried; but my hands were loath and cold.
Let us sleep now...'

KENNETH SLESSOR
(1901–1971)

Born Sydney, Australia. He worked as a journalist and was an official war correspondent in the Second World War.

THE NIGHT-RIDE

Gas flaring on the yellow platform; voices running up
  and down;
Milk-tins in cold dented silver; half-awake I stare,
Pull up the blind, blink out—all sounds are drugged;
The slow blowing of passengers asleep;
Engines yawning; water in heavy drips;
Black, sinister travellers, lumbering up the station,
One moment in the window, hooked over bags;
Hurrying, unknown faces—boxes with strange labels—
All groping clumsily to mysterious ends,
Out of the gaslight, dragged by private Fates.
Their echoes die. The dark train shakes and plunges;
Bells cry out; the night-ride starts again.
Soon I shall look out into nothing but blackness,
Pale, windy fields. The old roar and knock of the rails
Melts in dull fury. Pull down the blind. Sleep. Sleep.
Nothing but grey, rushing rivers of bush outside.
Gaslight and milk-cans. Of Rapptown I recall
  nothing else.

SOUTH COUNTRY

After the whey-faced anonymity
Of river-gums and scribbly-gums and bush,
After the rubbing and the hit of brush,
You come to the South Country

As if the argument of trees were done,
The doubts and quarrelling, the plots and pains,
All ended by these clear and gliding planes
Like an abrupt solution.

And over the flat earth of empty farms
The monstrous continent of air floats back
Coloured with rotting sunlight and the black,
Bruised flesh of thunderstorms:

Air arched, enormous, pounding the bony ridge,
Ditches and hutches, with a drench of light,
So huge, from such infinities of height,
You walk on the sky's beach

While even the dwindled hills are small and bare,
As if, rebellious, buried, pitiful,
Something below pushed up a knob of skull,
Feeling its way to air.

FIVE BELLS

Time that is moved by little fidget wheels
Is not my Time, the flood that does not flow.
Between the double and the single bell
Of a ship's hour, between a round of bells
From the dark warship riding there below,
I have lived many lives, and this one Life
Of Joe, long dead, who lives between five bells.

Deep and dissolving verticals of light
Ferry the falls of moonshine down. Five bells
Coldly rung out in a machine's voice. Night and water
Pour to one rip of darkness, the Harbour floats
In air, the Cross hangs upside-down in water.

Why do I think of you, dead man, why thieve
These profitless lodgings from the flukes of thought
Anchored in Time? You have gone from earth,
Gone even from the meaning of a name;
Yet something's there, yet something forms its lips
And hits and cries against the ports of space,
Beating their sides to make its fury heard.

Are you shouting at me, dead man, squeezing your face
In agonies of speech on speechless panes?
Cry louder, beat the windows, bawl your name!

But I hear nothing, nothing... only bells,
Five bells, the bumpkin calculus of Time.
Your echoes die, your voice is dowsed by Life,
There's not a mouth can fly the pygmy strait—
Nothing except the memory of some bones
Long shoved away, and sucked away, in mud;
And unimportant things you might have done,
Or once I thought you did; but you forgot,
And all have now forgotten—looks and words
And slops of beer; your coat with buttons off,
Your gaunt chin and pricked eye, and raging tales
Of Irish kings and English perfidy,
And dirtier perfidy of publicans
Groaning to God from Darlinghurst.

Five bells.

Then I saw the road, I heard the thunder
Tumble, and felt the talons of the rain
The night we came to Moorebank in slab-dark,

14. flukes: broad triangular plates on the arms of anchors; lucky accidents.

So dark you bore no body, had no face,
But a sheer voice that rattled out of air
(As now you'd cry if I could break the glass),
A voice that spoke beside me in the bush,
Loud for a breath or bitten off by wind,
Of Milton, melons, and the Rights of Man,
And blowing flutes, and how Tahitian girls
Are brown and angry-tongued, and Sydney girls
Are white and angry-tongued, or so you'd found.
But all I heard was words that didn't join
So Milton became melons, melons girls,
And fifty mouths, it seemed, were out that night,
And in each tree an Ear was bending down,
Or something had just run, gone behind grass,
When, blank and bone-white, like a maniac's thought,
The naphtha-flash of lightning slit the sky,
Knifing the dark with deathly photographs.
There's not so many with so poor a purse
Or fierce a need, must fare by night like that,
Five miles in darkness on a country track,
But when you do, that's what you think.

Five bells.

In Melbourne, your appetite had gone,
Your angers too; they had been leeched▲ away
By the soft archery of summer rains
And the sponge-paws of wetness, the slow damp
That stuck the leaves of living, snailed the mind,
And showed your bones, that had been sharp with rage,
The sodden ecstasies of rectitude.
I thought of what you'd written in faint ink,
Your journal with the sawn-off lock, that stayed behind
With other things you left, all without use,
All without meaning now, except a sign
That someone had been living who now was dead:
'At Labassa. Room 6 x 8
On top of the tower; because of this, very dark
And cold in winter. Everything has been stowed
Into this room—500 books all shapes

dissolved and drained away

And colours, dealt across the floor
And over sills and on the laps of chairs;
Guns, photoes of many differant things
And differant curioes that I obtained...'

In Sydney, by the spent aquarium-flare
Of penny gaslight on pink wallpaper,
We argued about blowing up the world,
But you were living backward, so each night
You crept a moment closer to the breast,
And they were living, all of them, those frames
And shapes of flesh that had perplexed your youth,
And most your father, the old man gone blind,
With fingers always round a fiddle's neck,
That graveyard mason whose fair monuments
And tablets cut with dreams of piety
Rest on the bosoms of a thousand men
Staked bone by bone, in quiet astonishment
At cargoes they had never thought to bear,
These funeral-cakes of sweet and sculptured stone.

Where have you gone? The tide is over you,
The turn of midnight water's over you,
As Time is over you, and mystery,
And memory, the flood that does not flow.
You have no suburb, like those easier dead
In private berths of dissolution laid—
The tide goes over, the waves ride over you
And let their shadows down like shining hair,
But they are Water; and the sea-pinks bend
Like lilies in your teeth, but they are Weed;
And you are only part of an Idea.
I felt the wet push its black thumb-balls in,
The night you died, I felt your eardrums crack,
And the short agony, the longer dream,
The Nothing that was neither long nor short;
But I was bound, and could not go that way,
But I was blind, and could not feel your hand.
If I could find an answer, could only find

Your meaning, or could say why you were here
Who now are gone, what purpose gave you breath
Or seized it back, might I not hear your voice?
I looked out of my window in the dark
At waves with diamond quills and combs of light
That arched their mackerel-backs and smacked the sand
In the moon's drench, that straight enormous glaze,
And ships far off asleep, and Harbour-buoys
Tossing their fireballs wearily each to each,
And tried to hear your voice, but all I heard
Was a boat's whistle, and the scraping squeal
Of seabirds' voices far away, and bells,
Five bells. Five bells coldly ringing out.

Five bells.

BEACH BURIAL

Softly and humbly to the Gulf of Arabs
The convoys of dead sailors come;
At night they sway and wander in the waters far under,
But morning rolls them in the foam.

Between the sob and clubbing of the gunfire
Someone, it seems, has time for this,
To pluck them from the shallows and bury them
  in burrows
And tread the sand upon their nakedness;

And each cross, the driven stake of tidewood,
Bears the last signature of men,
Written with such perplexity, with such bewildered pity,
The words choke as they begin—

'*Unknown seaman*'—the ghostly pencil
Wavers and fades, the purple drips,
The breath of the wet season has washed their
  inscriptions
As blue as drowned men's lips,

Dead seamen, gone in search of the same landfall,
Whether as enemies they fought,
Or fought with us, or neither; the sand joins them
together,
Enlisted on the other front.

El Alamein.

El Alamein: In North Africa, site of one of the great battles of the Second World War.

STEVIE SMITH
(1902–1979)

Born Hull, England. She lived in London and worked as a secretary in a publishing firm. In later years, she was famous for public readings of her own verse.

THOUGHTS ABOUT THE CHRISTIAN DOCTRINE OF ETERNAL HELL

Is it not interesting to see
How the Christians continually
Try to separate themselves in vain
From the doctrine of eternal pain.

They cannot do it,
They are committed to it,
Their Lord said it,
They must believe it.

So, the vulnerable body is stretched without pity
On flames forever. Is this not pretty? 1

The religion of Christianity
Is mixed of sweetness and cruelty.
Reject this Sweetness, for she wears
A smoky dress out of hell fires.

Who makes a God? Who shows him thus?
Is it the Christian religion does,
Oh, oh, have none of it,
Blow it away, have done with it.

This God the Christians show
Out with him, out with him, let him go.

NOT WAVING BUT DROWNING

Nobody heard him, the dead man,
But still he lay moaning:
I was much further out than you thought
And not waving but drowning.

Poor chap, he always loved larking
And now he's dead
It must have been too cold for him his heart gave way,
They said.

Oh, no no no, it was too cold always
(Still the dead one lay moaning)
I was much too far out all my life
And not waving but drowning.

THE FACE

There is a face I know too well,
A face I dread to see,
So vain it is, so eloquent
Of all futility.

It is a human face that hides
A monkey soul within,
That bangs about, that beats a gong,
That makes a horrid din.

Sometimes the monkey soul will sprawl
Athwart the human eyes,
And peering forth, will flesh its pads,
And utter social lies.

So wretched is this face, so vain,
So empty and forlorn,
You well may say that better far
This face had not been born.

CHILDE ROLANDINE

Dark was the day for Childe Rolandine the artist
When she went to work as a secretary-typist
And as she worked she sang this song
Against oppression and the rule of wrong:

It is the privilege of the rich
To waste the time of the poor
To water with tears in secret
A tree that grows in secret
That bears fruit in secret
That ripened falls to the ground in secret
And manures the parent tree
Oh the wicked tree of hatred and the secret
The sap rising and the tears falling.

Likely also, sang the Childe, my soul will fry in hell
Because of this hatred, while in heaven my employer does
well
And why should he not, exacerbating though he be but
generous
Is it his fault I must work at a work that is tedious?
Oh heaven sweet heaven keep my thoughts in their night
den
Do not let them by day be spoken.

But then she sang, Ah why not? tell all, speak, speak,
Silence is vanity, speak for the whole truth's sake.

And rising she took the bugle and put it to her lips,
crying:
There is a Spirit feeds on our tears, I give him mine,
Mighty human feelings are his food
Passion and grief and joy his flesh and blood
That he may live and grow fat we daily die
This cropping One is our immortality.

Childe Rolandine bowed her head and in the evening
Drew the picture of the spirit from heaven.

THE LADS OF THE VILLAGE

The lads of the village, we read in the lay,
By medalled commanders are muddled away,
And the picture that the poet makes is not very gay.

Poet, let the red blood flow, it makes the pattern better,
And let the tears flow, too, and grief stand that is their
begetter,
And let man have his self-forged chain and hug every fetter.

For without the juxtaposition of muddles, medals and clay,
Would the picture be so very much more gay,
Would it not be a frivolous dance upon a summer's day?

Oh sing no more: Away with the folly of commanders.
This will not make a better song upon the field of
Flanders,
Or upon any field of experience where pain makes
patterns the poet slanders.

MOTHER, AMONG THE DUSTBINS

Mother, among the dustbins and the manure
I feel the measure of my humanity, an allure
As of the presence of God. I am sure

In the dustbins, in the manure, in the cat at play,
Is the presence of God, in a sure way
He moves there. Mother, what do you say?

I too have felt the presence of God in the broom
I hold, in the cobwebs in the room,
But most of all in the silence of the tomb.

Ah! but that thought that informs the hope of our kind
Is but an empty thing, what lies behind?—
Naught but the vanity of a protesting mind

That would not die. This is the thought that bounces
Within a conceited head and trounces
Inquiry. Man is most frivolous when he pronounces.

Well Mother, I shall continue to feel as I do,
And I think you would be wise to do so too,
Can you question the folly of man in the creation of God?
    Who are you?

VOICES AGAINST ENGLAND IN THE NIGHT

'England, you had better go,
There is nothing else that you ought to do,
You lump of survival value, you are too slow.

England, you have been here too long,
And the songs you sing are the songs you sung
On a braver day. Now they are wrong.

And as you sing the sliver slips from your lips,
And the governing garment sits ridiculously on your hips.
It is a pity that you are still too cunning to make slips.'

Nazi propaganda minister

Dr Goebbels▲, that is the point,
You are a few years too soon with your jaunt,
Time and the moment is not yet England's daunt.

Yes, dreaming Germany with your Urge and Night,
You must go down before English and American might.
It is well, it is well, cries the peace kite.

Perhaps England our darling will recover her lost thought
We must think sensibly about our victory and not be
distraught,
Perhaps America will have an idea, and perhaps not.

But they cried: Could not England, once the world's best,
Put off her governing garment and be better dressed
In a shroud, a shroud? O history turn thy pages fast!

LOT'S WIFE

'In that rich, oil-bearing region, it is probable that Lot's wife was turned into a pillar of asphalt—not salt.'

Sir William Whitebait, Member of the Institute of Mining Engineers

I long for the desolate valleys,
Where the rivers of asphalt flow,
For here in the streets of the living,
Where my footsteps run to and fro,
Though my smile be never so friendly,
I offend wherever I go.

TITLE: LOT'S WIFE: Genesis 19, 26.

Yes, here in the land of the living,
Though a marriage be fairly sprung,
And the heart be loving and giving,
In the end it is sure to go wrong.

Then take me to the valley of asphalt,
And turn me to a river of stone,
That no tree may shift to my sighing,
Or breezes convey my moan.

PAD, PAD

I always remember your beautiful flowers
And the beautiful kimono you wore
When you sat on the couch
With that tigerish crouch
And told me you loved me more.

What I cannot remember is how I felt when you were
  unkind
All I know is, if you were unkind now I should not mind.
Ah me, the power to feel exaggerated, angry and sad
The years have taken from me. Softly I go now, pad pad.

THE RIVER GOD

I may be smelly and I may be old,
Rough in my pebbles, reedy in my pools,
But where my fish float by I bless their swimming
And I like the people to bathe in me, especially women.
But I can drown the fools
Who bathe too close to the weir, contrary to rules.
And they take a long time drowning

As I throw them up now and then in a spirit of clowning.
Hy yih, yippity-yap, merrily I flow,
Oh I may be an old foul river but I have plenty of go.
Once there was a lady who was too bold
She bathed in me by the tall black cliff where the water
runs cold,
So I brought her down here
To be my beautiful dear.
Oh will she stay with me will she stay
This beautiful lady, or will she go away?
She lies in my beautiful deep river bed with many a weed
To hold her, and many a waving reed.
Oh who would guess what a beautiful white face lies there
Waiting for me to smooth and wash away the fear
She looks at me with. Hi yih, do not let her
Go. There is no one on earth who does not forget her
Now. They say I am a foolish old smelly river
But they do not know of my wide original bed
Where the lady waits, with her golden sleepy head.
If she wishes to go I will not forgive her.

W.H. AUDEN
(1907–1973)

Born York, England. He moved to America in 1939 and lived in New York. He was a Marxist in the thirties, but later became an Anglo-Catholic and conservative politically.

ONE EVENING

As I walked out one evening,
  Walking down Bristol Street,
The crowds upon the pavement
  Were fields of harvest wheat.

And down by the brimming river
  I heard a lover sing
Under an arch of the railway:
  'Love has no ending.

I'll love you, dear, I'll love you
  Till China and Africa meet,
And the river jumps over the mountain
  And the salmon sing in the street.

I'll love you till the ocean
  Is folded and hung up to dry,
And the seven stars go squawking
  Like geese about the sky.

The years shall run like rabbits,
  For in my arms I hold
The Flower of the Ages,
  And the first love of the world.'

But all the clocks in the city
    Began to whirr and chime:
'O let not Time deceive you,
    You cannot conquer Time.

'In the burrows of the Nightmare
    Where Justice naked is,
Time watches from the shadow
    And coughs when you would kiss.

'In headaches and in worry
    Vaguely life leaks away,
And Time will have his fancy
    To-morrow or to-day.

'Into many a green valley
    Drifts the appalling snow;
Time breaks the threaded dances
    And the diver's brilliant bow.

'O plunge your hands in water,
    Plunge them in up to the wrist;
Stare, stare in the basin
    And wonder what you've missed.

'The glacier knocks in the cupboard,
    The desert sighs in the bed,
And the crack in the tea-cup opens
    A lane to the land of the dead.

'Where the beggars raffle the banknotes
    And the Giant is enchanting to Jack,
And the Lily-white Boy is a Roarer,
    And Jill goes down on her back.

'O look, look in the mirror,
    O look in your distress;
Life remains a blessing
    Although you cannot bless.

'O stand, stand at the window
    As the tears scald and start;
You shall love your crooked neighbour
    With your crooked heart.'

It was late, late in the evening
    The lovers they were gone;
The clocks had ceased their chiming,
    And the deep river ran on.

GARE DU MIDI

A nondescript express in from the South,
Crowds round the ticket barrier, a face
To welcome which the mayor has not contrived
Bugles or braid: something about the mouth
Distracts the stray look with alarm and pity.
Snow is falling. Clutching a little case,
He walks out briskly to infect a city
Whose terrible future may have just arrived.

O WHAT IS THAT SOUND

O what is that sound which so thrills the ear
    Down in the valley drumming, drumming?
Only the scarlet soldiers, dear,
    The soldiers coming.

O what is that light I see flashing so clear
    Over the distance brightly, brightly?
Only the sun on their weapons, dear,
    As they step lightly.

O what are they doing with all that gear,
    What are they doing this morning, this morning?
Only their manoeuvres, dear,
    Or perhaps a warning.

O why have they left the road down there,
Why are they suddenly wheeling, wheeling?
Perhaps a change in their orders, dear.
Why are you kneeling?

O haven't they stopped for the doctor's care,
Haven't they reined their horses, their horses?
Why, they are none of them wounded, dear,
None of these forces.

O is it the parson they want, with white hair,
Is it the parson, is it, is it?
No, they are passing his gateway, dear,
Without a visit.

O it must be the farmer who lives so near.
It must be the farmer so cunning, so cunning?
They have passed the farmyard already, dear,
And now they are running.

O where are you going? Stay with me here!
Were the vows you swore deceiving, deceiving?
No, I promised to love you, dear,
But I must be leaving.

O it's broken the lock and splintered the door,
O it's the gate where they're turning, turning;
Their boots are heavy on the floor
And their eyes are burning.

MUSÉE DES BEAUX ARTS

About suffering they were never wrong,
The Old Masters: how well they understood
Its human position; how it takes place

TITLE: MUSÉE DES BEAUX ARTS The Museum of Fine Arts, Brussels.
16. Icarus: Icarus' father made him wings of feathers and wax. Icarus flew too close to the sun, the wax melted, and he fell into the sea.

While someone else is eating or opening a window or
just walking dully along;
How, when the aged are reverently, passionately waiting
For the miraculous birth, there always must be
Children who did not specially want it to happen, skating
On a pond at the edge of the wood:
They never forgot
That even the dreadful martyrdom must run its course
Anyhow in a corner, some untidy spot
Where the dogs go on with their doggy life and the
torturer's horse
Scratches its innocent behind on a tree.

In Brueghel's *Icarus*, for instance: how everything turns away
Quite leisurely from the disaster; the ploughman may
Have heard the splash, the forsaken cry,
But for him it was not an important failure; the sun shone
As it had to on the white legs disappearing into the green
Water; and the expensive delicate ship that must
have seen
Something amazing, a boy falling out of the sky,
Had somewhere to get to and sailed calmly on.

SEPTEMBER 1ST 1939

I sit in one of the dives
On Fifty-second Street
Uncertain and afraid
As the clever hopes expire
Of a low dishonest decade:
Waves of anger and fear
Circulate over the bright
and darkened lands of the earth,
Obsessing our private lives;
The unmentionable odour of death
Offends the September night.

TITLE: 1ST SEPTEMBER 1939 the beginning of the Second World War, the day Germany marched into Poland.

Accurate scholarship can
Unearth the whole offence
From Luther until now
That has driven a culture mad,
Find what occurred at Linz,
What huge imago made
A psychopathic god:
I and the public know
What all schoolchildren learn,
Those to whom evil is done
Do evil in return.

Exiled Thucydides knew
All that a speech can say
About Democracy.
And what dictators do.
The elderly rubbish they talk
To an apathetic grave:
Analysed all in his book.
The enlightenment driven away.
The habit-forming pain.
Mismanagement and grief:
We must suffer them all again.

Into this neutral air
Where blind skyscrapers use
Their full height to proclaim
The strength of Collective Man,
Each language pours its vain
Competitive excuse:
But who can live for long
In an euphoric dream;
Out of the mirror they stare,
Imperialism's face
And the international wrong.

Faces along the bar
Cling to their average day:

The lights must never go out,
The music must always play,
All the conventions conspire
To make this fort assume
The furniture of home;
Lest we should see where we are,
Lost in a haunted wood,
Children afraid of the night
Who have never been happy or good.

The windiest militant trash
Important Persons shout
Is not so crude as our wish:
What mad Nijinsky wrote
About Diaghilev
Is true of the normal heart;
For the error bred in the bone
Of each woman and each man
Craves what it cannot have,
Not universal love
But to be loved alone.

From the conservative dark
Into the ethical life
The dense commuters come,
Repeating their morning vow;
'I *will* be true to the wife,
I'll concentrate more on my work,'
And helpless governors wake
To resume their compulsory game:
Who can release them now,
Who can reach the deaf,
Who can speak for the dumb?

Defenceless under the night
Our world in stupor lies;
Yet, dotted everywhere,
Ironic points of light

Flash out wherever the Just
Exchange their messages:
May I, composed like them
Or Eros and of dust,
Beleaguered by the same
Negation and despair,
Show an affirming flame.

IN MEMORY OF W.B. YEATS

d. Jan. 1939

I

He disappeared in the dead of winter:
The brooks were frozen, the airports almost deserted,
And snow disfigured the public statues;
The mercury sank in the mouth of the dying day.
What instruments we have agree
The day of his death was a dark cold day.

Far from his illness
The wolves ran on through the evergreen forests,
The peasant river was untempted by the fashionable quays;
By mourning tongues
The death of the poet was kept from his poems.

But for him it was his last afternoon as himself,
An afternoon of nurses and rumours;
The provinces of his body revolted,
The squares of his mind were empty,
Silence invaded the suburbs,
The current of his feeling failed; he became his admirers.

Now he is scattered among a hundred cities
And wholly given over to unfamiliar affections;
To find his happiness in another kind of wood
And be punished under a foreign code of conscience.

The words of a dead man
Are modified in the guts of the living.

But in the importance and noise of to-morrow
When the brokers are roaring like beasts on the floor of the Bourse▲,
stock exchange
And the poor have the sufferings to which they are fairly accustomed,
And each in the cell of himself is almost convinced of his freedom,
A few thousand will think of this day
As one thinks of a day when one did something slightly unusual.
What instruments we have agree
The day of his death was a dark cold day.

II

You were silly like us; your gift survived it all;
The parish of rich women, physical decay,
Yourself: mad Ireland hurt you into poetry.
Now Ireland has her madness and her weather still,
For poetry makes nothing happen: it survives
In the valley of its saying where executives
Would never want to tamper; it flows south
From ranches of isolation and the busy griefs,
Raw towns that we believe and die in; it survives,
A way of happening, a mouth.

III

Earth, receive an honoured guest:
William Yeats is laid to rest.
Let the Irish vessel lie
Emptied of its poetry.
In the nightmare of the dark
All the dogs of Europe bark,
And the living nations wait,

Each sequestered in its hate;
Intellectual disgrace
Stares from every human face,
And the seas of pity lie
Locked and frozen in each eye.
Follow, poet, follow right
To the bottom of the night,
With your unconstraining voice
Still persuade us to rejoice;
With the farming of a verse
Make a vineyard of the curse,
Sing of human unsuccess
In a rapture of distress;
In the deserts of the heart
Let the healing fountain start,
In the prison of his days
Teach the free man how to praise.

IN PRAISE OF LIMESTONE

If it form the one landscape that we the inconstant ones
    Are consistently home sick for, this is chiefly
Because it dissolves in water. Mark these rounded slopes
    With their surface fragrance of thyme and beneath
A secret system of caves and conduits; hear these springs
    That spurt out everywhere with a chuckle
Each filling a private pool for its fish and carving
    Its own little ravine whose cliffs entertain
The butterfly and the lizard; examine this region
    Of short distances and definite places:
What could be more like Mother or a fitter background
    For her son, the flirtatious male who lounges
Against a rock in the sunlight, never doubting
    That for all his faults he is loved; whose works are but
Extensions of his power to charm? From weathered outcrop
    To hill-top temple, from appearing waters to
Conspicuous fountains, from a wild to a formal vineyard,

Are ingenious but short steps that a child's wish
To receive more attention than his brothers, whether
By pleasing or teasing, can easily take.
Watch then, the band of rivals as they climb up and down
Their steep stone gennels in twos and threes, sometimes
Arm in arm, but never, thank God, in step; or engaged
On the shady side of a square at midday in
Voluble discourse, knowing each other too well to think
There are any important secrets, unable
To conceive a god whose temper-tantrums are moral
And not to be pacified by a clever line
Or a good lay: for, accustomed to a stone that responds,
They have never had to veil their faces in awe
Of a crater whose blazing fury could not be fixed;
Adjusted to the local needs of valleys
Where everything can be touched or reached by walking,
Their eyes have never looked into infinite space
Through the lattice-work of a nomad's comb; born lucky,
Their legs have never encountered the fungi
And insects of the jungle, the monstrous forms and lives
With which we have nothing, we like to hope, in common.
So, when one of them goes to the bad, the way his mind works
Remains comprehensible: to become a pimp
Or deal in fake jewellery or ruin a fine tenor voice
For effects that bring down the house could happen to all
But the best and the worst of us...
That is why, I suppose,
The best and worst never stayed here long but sought
Immoderate soils where the beauty was not so external,
The light less public and the meaning of life
Something more than a mad camp. 'Come!' cried the granite wastes,
'How evasive is your humour, how accidental
Your kindest kiss, how permanent is death.' (Saints-to-be
Slipped away sighing.) 'Come!' purred the clays and gravels.
'On our plains there is room for armies to drill; rivers
Wait to be tamed and slaves to construct you a tomb
In the grand manner: soft as the earth is mankind and both
Need to be altered.' (Intendent Caesars rose and
Left, slamming the door.) But the really reckless were fetched

By an older colder voice, the oceanic whisper:
'I am the solitude that asks and promises nothing;
That is how I shall set you free. There is no love;
There are only the various envies, all of them sad.'

They were right my dear, all those voices were right
And still are; this land is not the sweet home that it looks,
Nor its peace the historical calm of a site
Where something was settled once and for all: A backward
And delapidated province, connected
To the big busy world by a tunnel, with a certain
Seedy appeal, is that all it is now? Not quite:
It has a wordly duty which in spite of itself
It does not neglect, but call into question
All the Great Powers assume; it disturbs our rights. The poet,
Admired for his earnest habit of calling
The sun the sun, his mind Puzzle, is made uneasy
By these solid statues which so obviously doubt
His antimythological myth; and these gamins,
Pursuing the scientist down the tiled colonnade
With such lively offers, rebuke his concern for Nature's
Remotest aspects: I, too, am reproached, for what
And how much you know. Not to lose time, not to get caught,
Not to be left behind, not, please! to resemble
The beasts who repeat themselves, or a thing like water
Or stone whose conduct can be predicted, these
Are our Common Prayer, whose greatest comfort is music
Which can be made anywhere, is invisible,
And does not smell. In so far as we have to look forward
To death as a fact, no doubt we are right: but if
Sins can be forgiven, if bodies rise from the dead,
These modifications of matter into
Innocent athletes and gesticulating fountains,
Made solely for pleasure, make a further point:
The blessed will not care what angle they are regarded from,
Having nothing to hide. Dear, I know nothing of
Either, but when I try to imagine a faultless love
Or the life to come, what I hear is the murmur
Of underground streams, what I see is a limestone landscape.

A.D. HOPE
(b. 1907)

Born in Cooma, NSW. He was Professor of English at the Australian National University, Canberra. He is a noted critic as well as a poet.

AUSTRALIA

A Nation of trees, drab green and desolate grey
In the field uniform of modern wars,
Darkens her hills, those endless, outstretched paws
Of Sphinx demolished or stone lion worn away.

They call her a young country, but they lie.
She is the last of lands, the emptiest.
A woman beyond her change of life, a breast
Still tender but within the womb is dry.

Without songs, architecture, history:
The emotions and superstitions of younger lands,
Her rivers of water drown among inland sands,
The river of her immense stupidity

Floods her monotonous tribes from Cairns to Perth.
In them at last the ultimate men arrive
Whose boast is not: 'We live' but 'we survive',
A type who will inhabit the dying earth.

And her five cities, like five teeming sores,
Each drains her: a vast parasite robber-state
Where second-hand Europeans pullulate▲
Timidly on the edge of alien shores.

pullulate: *teem, multiply*

Yet there are some like me turn gladly home
From the lush jungle of modern thought, to find
The Arabian desert of the human mind,
Hoping, if still from the deserts the prophets come,

Such savage and scarlet as no green hills dare
Springs in that waste, some spirit which escapes
The learned doubt, the chatter of cultured apes
Which is called civilization over there.

JUDITH WRIGHT
(b. 1915)

Born near Armidale, NSW, of a pioneer pastoral family. She is a conservationist and involved in the Aboriginal land rights movement. She has written a family history, Generations of Men, *stories and criticism.*

BROTHER AND SISTERS

The road turned out to be a cul-de-sac;
stopped like a lost intention at the gate
and never crossed the mountains to the coast.
But they stayed on. Years grew like grass and leaves
across the half-erased and dubious track
until one day they knew the plans were lost,
the blue-print for the bridge was out of date,
and now their orchards never would be planted.
The saplings sprouted slyly; day by day
the bush moved one step nearer, wondering when.
The polished parlour grew distrait and haunted
where Millie, Lucy, John each night at ten
wound the gilt clock that leaked the year away.

The pianola—oh, listen to the mocking-bird—
wavers on Sundays and has lost a note.
The wrinkled ewes snatch pansies through the fence
and stare with shallow eyes into the garden
where Lucy shrivels waiting for a word,
and Millie's cameos loosen round her throat.
The bush comes near, the ranges grow immense.

Feeding the lambs deserted in early spring
Lucy looked up and saw the stockman's eye
telling her she was cracked and old.
                                                  The wall
groans in the night and settles more awry.
O how they lie awake. Their thoughts go fluttering
from room to room like moths: 'Millie, are you awake?'
'Oh John, I have been dreaming.' 'Lucy, do you cry?'
—meet tentative as moths. Antennae stroke a wing.
'There is nothing to be afraid of. Nothing at all.'

SOUTH OF MY DAYS

South of my days' circle, part of my blood's country,
rises that tableland, high delicate outline
of bony slopes wincing under the winter,
low trees blue-leaved and olive, outcropping granite—
clean, lean, hungry country. The creek's leaf-silenced,
willow-choked, the slope a tangle of medlar and crabapple
branching over and under, blotched with a green lichen;
and the old cottage lurches in for shelter.

O cold the black-frost night. The walls draw in to the
    warmth
and the old roof cracks its joints; the slung kettle
hisses a leak on the fire. Hardly to be believed that summer
will turn up again some day in a wave of rambler roses,
thrust its hot face in here to tell another yarn—
a story old Dan can spin into a blanket against the winter.
Seventy years of stories he clutches round his bones.
Seventy summers are hived in him like old honey.

Droving that year, Charleville to the Hunter,
nineteen-one it was, and the drought beginning;
sixty head left at the McIntyre, the mud round them
hardened like iron; and the yellow boy died
in the sulky ahead with the gear, but the horse went on,

stopped at the Sandy Camp and waited in the evening.
It was the flies we seen first, swarming like bees.
Came to the Hunter, three hundred head of a thousand—
cruel to keep them alive—and the river was dust.

Or mustering up in the Bogongs in the autumn
when the blizzards came early. Brought them down;
 we brought them
down, what aren't there yet. Or driving for Cobb's
 on the run
up from Tamworth—Thunderbolt at the top of Hungry
 Hill,
and I give him a wink. I wouldn't wait long, Fred,
not if I was you; the troopers are just behind,
coming for that job at the Hillgrove. He went like a luny,
him on his big black horse.

Oh, they slide and they vanish
as he shuffles the years like a pack of conjuror's cards.
True or not, it's all the same; and the frost on the roof
cracks like a whip, and the back-log breaks into ash.
Wake, old man. This is winter, and the yarns are over.
No one is listening.
South of my days' circle
I know it dark against the stars, the high lean country
full of old stories that still go walking in my sleep.

WOMAN TO MAN

The eyeless labourer in the night,
the selfless, shapeless seed I hold,
builds for its resurrection day
silent and swift and deep from sight
foresees the unimagined light.

This is no child with a child's face:
this has no name to name it by:
yet you and I have known it well.
This is our hunter and our chase,
the third who lay in our embrace.

This is the strength that your arm knows,
The arc of flesh that is my breast,
the precise crystals of our eyes.
This is the blood's wild tree that grows
the intricate and folded rose.

This is the maker and the made:
this is the question and reply:
the blind head butting at the dark,
the blaze of light along the blade.
O hold me, for I am afraid.

THE BULL

In the olive darkness of the sally-trees
silently moved the air from night to day.
The summer-grass was thick with honey daisies
where he, a curled god, a red Jupiter*, *chief of the gods*
heavy with power among his women lay.

But summer's bubble-sound of sweet creek-water
dwindles and is silent, the seeding grasses
grow harsh, and wind and frost in the black sallies
roughen the sleek-haired slopes. Seek him out, then,
the angry god betrayed, whose godhead passes,

and down the hillsides drive him from his mob.
What enemy steals his strength—what rival steals
his mastered cows? His thunders powerless,
the red storm of his body shrunk with fear,
runs the great bull, the dogs upon his heels.

AT COOLOOLA

The blue crane fishing in Cooloola's twilight
has fished there longer than our centuries.
He is the certain heir of lake and evening,
and he will wear their colour till he dies,

but I'm a stranger, come of a conquering people.
I cannot share his calm, who watch his lake,
being unloved by all my eyes delight in,
and made uneasy, for an old murder's sake.

Those dark-skinned people who once named Cooloola
knew that no land is lost or won by wars,
for earth is spirit: the invader's feet will tangle
in nets there and his blood be thinned by fears.

Riding at noon and ninety years ago,
my grandfather was beckoned by a ghost—
a black accoutred warrior armed for fighting,
who sank into bare plain, as now into time past.

White shores of sand, plumed reed and paperbark,
clear heavenly levels frequented by crane and swan—
I know that we are justified only by love,
but oppressed by arrogant guilt, have room for none.

And walking on clean sand among the prints
of bird and animal, I am challenged by a driftwood spear
thrust from the water; and, like my grandfather,
must quiet a heart accused by its own fear.

EGRETS

Once I travelled through a quiet evening,
I saw a pool, jet-black and mirror-still.
Beyond, the slender paperbarks stood crowding;

each on its own white image looked its fill,
and nothing moved but thirty egrets wading—
thirty egrets in a quiet evening.

Once in a lifetime, lovely past believing,
your lucky eyes may light on such a pool.
As though for many years I had been waiting,
I watched in silence, till my heart was full
of clear dark water, and white trees unmoving,
and, whiter yet, those thirty egrets wading.

AUSTRALIA 1970

Die, wild country, like the eaglehawk,
dangerous till the last breath's gone,
clawing and striking. Die
cursing your captor through a raging eye.

Die like the tigersnake
that hisses such pure hatred from its pain
as fills the killer's dreams
with fear like suicide's invading stain.

Suffer, wild country, like the ironwood
that gaps the dozer-blade.
I see your living soil ebb with the tree
to naked poverty.

Die like the soldier-ant
mindless and faithful to your million years.
Though we corrupt you with our torturing mind,
stay obstinate; stay blind.

For we are conquerors and self-poisoners
more than scorpion or snake
and dying of the venoms that we make
even while you die of us.

I praise the scoring drought, the flying dust,
the drying creek, the furious animal,
that they oppose us still;
that we are ruined by the thing we kill.

EVE TO HER DAUGHTERS

It was not I who began it.
Turned out into draughty caves,
hungry so often, having to work for our bread,
hearing the children whining,
I was nevertheless not unhappy.
Where Adam went I was fairly contented to go.
I adapted myself to the punishment: it was my life.

But Adam, you know. . . !
He kept on brooding over the insult,
over the trick They had played on us, over the scolding.
He had discovered a flaw in himself
and he had to make up for it.

Outside Eden the earth was imperfect,
the seasons changed, the game was fleet-footed,
he had to work for our living, and he didn't like it.
He even complained of my cooking
(it was hard to compete with Heaven).

So he set to work.
The earth must be made a new Eden
with central heating, domesticated animals,
mechanical harvesters, combustion engines,
escalators, refrigerators,
and modern means of communication
and multiplied opportunities for safe investment
and higher education for Abel and Cain
and the rest of the family.
You can see how his pride had been hurt.

In the process he had to unravel everything,
because he believed that mechanism
was the whole secret—he was always mechanical-
  minded.
He got to the very inside of the whole machine
exclaiming as he went, So this is how it works!

And now that I know how it works, why, I must have
  invented it.
As for God and the Other, they cannot be demonstrated,
and what cannot be demonstrated
doesn't exist.
You see, he had always been jealous.

Yes, he got to the centre
where nothing at all can be demonstrated.
And clearly he doesn't exist; but he refuses
to accept the conclusion.
You see, he was always an egotist.

It was warmer than this in the cave;
there was none of this fall-out.
I would suggest, for the sake of the children,
that it's time you took over.

But you are my daughters, you inherit my own faults
  of character;
you are submissive, following Adam
even beyond existence.
Faults of character have their own logic
and it always works out.
I observed this with Abel and Cain.

Perhaps the whole elaborate fable
right from the beginning
is meant to demonstrate this; perhaps it's the whole secret.
Perhaps nothing exists but our faults?
At least they can be demonstrated.

But it's useless to make
such a suggestion to Adam.
He has turned himself into God,
who is faultless, and doesn't exist.

TABLEAU

Bent over, staggering in panic or despair
from post to parking-meter in the hurried street,
he seemed to gesture at me,
as though we had met again; had met somewhere
forgotten, and now for the last time had to meet.

And I debated with myself; ought I to go
over the road—since no one stopped to ask
or even stand and look—
abandon my own life awhile and show
I was too proud to shirk that ant-like task?

And finally went. His almost vanished voice
accepted me; he gave himself to my hold,
(*pain, cancer—keep me still*).
We leaned on a drinking-fountain, fused in the vice
of a double pain; his sweat dropped on me cold.

Holding him up as he asked till the ambulance came,
among the sudden curious crowd, I knew
his plunging animal heart,
against my flesh the shapes of his too-young bone,
the heaving pattern of ribs. As still I do.

Warding the questioners, bearing his rack of weight,
I drank our strange ten minutes of embrace,
and watched him whiten there,
the drenched poverty of his slender face.
We could have been desperate lovers met too late.

ROBERT LOWELL

(1917–1977)

Born Boston, USA, of a distinguished Massachusetts family. He was jailed for draft resistance in the Second World War, and was associated in the sixties and seventies with the civil rights and peace movements.

WAKING IN THE BLUE

Boston University

The night attendant, a B.U.▲ sophomore,
rouses from the mare's-nest of his drowsy head
propped on *The Meaning of Meaning*.
He catwalks down our corridor.
Azure day
makes my agonized blue window bleaker.
Crows maunder on the petrified fairway.
Absence! My heart grows tense
as though a harpoon were sparring for the kill.
(This is the house for the 'mentally ill'.)

What use is my sense of humour?
I grin at 'Stanley', now sunk in his sixties,
once a Harvard all-American fullback,
(if such were possible!)
still hoarding the build of a boy in his twenties,
as he soaks, a ramrod
with the muscle of a seal
in his long tub,
vaguely urinous from the Victorian plumbing.
A kingly granite profile in a crimson golf-cap,
worn all day, all night,
he thinks only of his figure,

of slimming on sherbet and ginger ale—
more cut off from words than a seal.

This is the way day breaks in Bowditch Hall at McLean's;
the hooded night lights bring out 'Bobbie',
an exclusive club at Harvard Porcellian '29▲,
a replica of Louis XVI
without the wig—
fragrant redolent▲ and roly-poly as a sperm whale,
as he swashbuckles about in his birthday suit
and horses at chairs.

These victorious figures of bravado ossified young.

In between the limits of day,
hours and hours go by under the crew haircuts
and slightly too little nonsensical bachelor twinkle
of the Roman Catholic attendants.
(There are no Mayflower
screwballs in the Catholic Church.)

After a hearty New England breakfast,
I weigh two hundred pounds
this morning. Cock of the walk,
I strut in my turtle-necked French sailor's jersey
before the metal shaving mirrors,
and see the shaky future grow familiar
in the pinched, indigenous faces
of these thoroughbred mental cases,
twice my age and half my weight.
We are all-old timers,
each of us holds a locked razor.

25. Bowditch Hall at McLean's: a fashionable sanatorium outside Boston.

MEMORIES OF WEST STREET AND LEPKE

Only teaching on Tuesdays, book-worming
in pajamas fresh from the washer each morning,
I hog a whole house on Boston's
'hardly passionate Marlborough Street'
where even the man
scavenging filth in the back alley trash cans,
has two children, a beach wagon, a helpmate,
and is a 'young Republican'.
I have a nine months' daughter,
young enough to be my granddaughter.
Like the sun she rises in her flame-flamingo infants' wear.

These are the tranquillized *Fifties*,
and I am forty. Ought I to regret my seedtime?
I was a fire-breathing Catholic C.O.▲,
and made my manic statement,
telling off the state and president, and then
sat waiting sentence in the bull pen
beside a Negro boy with curlicues
of marijuana in his hair.

conscientious objector to military service

Given a year,
I walked on the roof of the West Street Jail, a short
enclosure like my school soccer court,
and saw the Hudson River once a day
through sooty clothesline entanglements
and bleaching khaki tenements.

Strolling, I yammered metaphysics with Abramowitz,
a jaundice-yellow ('it's really tan')
and fly-weight pacifist,
so vegetarian,
he wore rope shoes and preferred fallen fruit.

TITLE: 'Czar Lepke' was a notorious gangland murderer.

He tried to convert Bioff and Brown,
the Hollywood pimps, to his diet.
Hairy, muscular, suburban,
wearing chocolate double-breasted suits,
they blew their tops and beat him black and blue.

I was so out of things, I'd never heard
of the Jehovah's Witnesses.
'Are you a C.O.?' I asked a jailbird.
'No,' he answered, 'I'm a J.W.'
He taught me the 'hospital tuck,'
and pointed out the T-shirted back
of *Murder Incorporated*'s Czar Lepke,
there piling towels on a rack,
or dawdling off to his little segregated cell full
of things forbidden the common man:
a portable radio, a dresser, two toy American
flags tied together with a ribbon of Easter palm.
Flabby, bald, lobotomized▲ *pacified by brain operation*
he drifted in a sheepish calm,
where no agonizing reappraisal
jarred his concentration on the electric chair—
hanging like an oasis in his air
of lost connections . . .

SKUNK HOUR

FOR ELIZABETH BISHOP

Nautilus Island's hermit
heiress still lives through winter in her Spartan cottage;
her sheep still graze above the sea.
Her son's a bishop. Her farmer
is first selectman in our village,
she's in her dotage.

TITLE: this poem is set in Castine, Maine, where Lowell had a summer house.
5. selectman: an elected member of the administrative body of a New England town.

Thirsting for
the hierarchic privacy
of Queen Victoria's century,
she buys up all
the eyesores facing her shore,
and lets them fall.

The season's ill—
we've lost our summer millionaire,
a mail order firm
who seemed to leap from an L. L. Bean▲
catalogue. His nine-knot yawl
was auctioned off to lobstermen.
A red fox stain covers Blue Hill.

And now our fairy
decorator brightens his shop for fall,
his fishnet's filled with orange cork,
orange, his cobbler's bench and awl,
there is no money in his work,
he'd rather marry.

One dark night,
my Tudor Ford climbed the hill's skull,
I watched for love-cars. Lights turned down,
they lay together, hull to hull,
where the graveyard shelves on the town...
My mind's not right.

A car radio bleats,
'Love, O careless Love...' I hear
my ill-spirit sob in each blood cell,
as if my hand were at its throat...
I myself am hell,
nobody's here—

only skunks, that search
in the moonlight for a bite to eat,
They march on their soles up Main Street:
white stripes, moonstruck eyes' red fire

under the chalk-dry and spar spire
of the Trinitarian Church.

I stand on top
of our back steps and breathe the rich air—
a mother skunk with her column of kittens swills the
    garbage pail.
She jabs her wedge-head in a cup
of sour cream, drops her ostrich tail,
and will not scare.

JAMES McAULEY
(1917–1976)

Born Sydney, Australia. He was founding editor of Quadrant, *and Professor of English at the University of Tasmania.*

ENVOI

There the blue-green gums are a fringe of remote disorder
And the brown sheep poke at my dreams along the hillsides;
And there in the soil, in the season, in the shifting airs,
Comes the faint sterility that disheartens and derides.

Where once was a sea is now a salty sunken desert,
A futile heart within a fair periphery;
The people are hard-eyed, kindly, with nothing inside them,
The men are independent but you could not call them free.

And I am fitted to that land as the soul is to the body,
I know its contractions, waste, and sprawling indolence;
They are in me and its triumphs are my own,
Hard-won in the thin and bitter years without pretence.

Beauty is order and good chance in the artesian heart
And does not wholly fail, though we impede;
Though the reluctant and uneasy land resent
The gush of waters, the lean plough, the fretful seed.

'ERN MALLEY'
'(1918–1943)'

'Ern Malley' was invented by James McAuley and Harold Stewart. They presented his 'posthumous' poems to Max Harris, editor of the magazine, Angry Penguins, *who published them in 1943. Intended to discredit modernists by showing that they could not distinguish sense from nonsense, the Ern Malley affair is Australia's most celebrated literary hoax.*

NIGHT PIECE

The swung torch scatters seeds
In the umbelliferous dark
And a frog makes guttural comment
On the naked and trespassing
Nymph of the lake.

The symbols were evident,
Though on park-gates
The iron birds looked disapproval
With rusty invidious beaks.

Among the water-lilies
A splash—white foam in the dark!
And you lay sobbing then
Upon my trembling intuitive arm.

ROSEMARY DOBSON
(b. 1920)

Born in Sydney, where she worked as a book editor, she moved to London, and now lives in Canberra. Many of her poems are influenced by her training and abiding interest in painting.

THE BYSTANDER

I am the one who looks the other way,
In any painting you may see me stand
Rapt at the sky, a bird, an angel's wing,
While others kneel, present the myrrh, receive
The benediction from the radiant hand.

I hold the horses while the knights dismount
And draw their swords to fight the battle out;
Or else in dim perspective you may see
My distant figure on the mountain road
When in the plains the hosts are put to rout.

I am the silly soul who looks too late,
The dullard dreaming, second from the right.
I hang upon the crowd, but do not mark
(Cap over eyes) the slaughtered Innocents,
Or Icarus, his downward-plunging flight.

Once in a Garden—back view only there—
How well the painter placed me, stroke on stroke,
Yet scarcely seen among the flowers and grass—
I heard a voice say, "Eat," and would have turned—
I often wonder who it was that spoke.

15. Icarus: cf Auden—Musée des Beaux Arts.

THE MARTYRDOM OF SAINT SEBASTIAN

My scarlet coat lies on the ground,
You note the texture of the fur,
What miracles of art, you say,
Those Flemish painters could command,
Each brush-stroke like a single hair.

How the eye focuses upon
The archer stiffly draped in black
Cutting the foreground to the right—
Masterly, that foreshortened arm,
Skilful, the modelling of the neck.

How colour, line, and form combine
To give the painting depth and space!
Beyond the stream, beyond the hill,
The village—each receding plane
Leads to the sky the travelling glance.

And in the sky the angels throng
Like glittering birds upon a tree—
Marvellous, you say, the mind that takes
A fantasy upon the wing
And out of prose makes poetry.

I am Sebastian. While you praise
I suffer and my lips are dumb,
The arrows pierce me through and through,
Yet you admire with abstract phrase
The torment of my martyrdom.

CHILD WITH A COCKATOO

Portrait of Anne, daughter of the Earl of Bedford, by S. Verelst

"Paid by my lord, one portrait, Lady Anne,
Full length with bird and landscape, twenty pounds
And framed withal. I say received. Verelst."

So signed the painter, bowed, and took his leave.
My Lady Anne smiled in the gallery
A small, grave child, dark-eyed, half turned to show
Her five bare toes beneath the garment's hem,
In stormy landscape with a swirl of drapes.
And, who knows why, perhaps my lady wept
To stand so long and watch the painter's brush
Flicker between the palette and the cloth
While from the sun-drenched orchard all the day
She heard her sisters calling each to each.
And someone gave, to drive the tears away,
That sulphur-crested bird with great white wings,
The wise, harsh bird—as old and wise as Time
Whose well-dark eyes the wonder kept and closed.
So many years to come and still he knew,
Brooded that great, dark island continent
Terra Australis.
                                    To those fabled shores
Not William Dampier, pirating for gold,
Nor Captain Cook his westward course had set
Jumped from the longboat, waded through the surf,
And clapt his flag ashore at Botany Bay.
Terra Australis, unimagined land—
Only that sulphur-crested bird could tell
Of dark men moving silently through trees,
Of stones and silent dawns, of blackened earth
And the long golden blaze of afternoon.
That vagrant which an ear-ringed sailor caught
(Dropped from the sky, near dead, far out to sea)
And caged and kept, till, landing at the docks,
Walked whistling up the Strand and sold it then,
The curious bird, its cynic eyes half closed,

To the Duke's steward, drunken at an inn.
And he lived on, the old adventurer,
And kept his counsel, was a sign unread,
A disregarded prologue to an age.
So one might find a meteor from the sun
Or sound one trumpet ere the play's begun.

THE ECOLOGY OF FISHES

Coming late to a study of ecology
I have learnt about the corrugated skin of sea-horses
Who abrade themselves constantly on the harsh branches of sea-shrubs, appearing
Very like branches themselves.
And certain fish disguise themselves as shadows over sand, passing without comment
Over the striped sea-floor. Others
Glide with a variable, sinuous movement, resembling
The faint demarcation of ripple and current,
Lacking the rigidity of pattern, as the lines of a poem may waver and tremble
Endeavouring the fluidity of fish.
Fish, it is said,
Cannot survive unless they adapt themselves to their environments,
And certain environments will not survive unless they are inhabited
By ecologically
Knowledgeable
Fish.
Am I not subject for a similar ecological case-history?
Striped like my kitchen floor with sunlight and shadow,
I stand by the sink and my fingers shoot forth teaspoons
As the light rays out from the silver sides of canisters.
I am admirably adapted to the shape required for comforting children,

I am perfectly evolved in length, breadth, and coloration to
  suit my environment.
Can it be true then—is it ecologically logical—
That my environment would not survive without me?

GHOST TOWN: NEW ENGLAND

The grass is bleached by summer sun
The dry pods rustle underfoot,
On quartz-bright rocks the lichens creep
Like frail anemones betrayed
Still trembling towards an unknown sea.
Up the steep shoulder of the hill
The wind goes scattering seeds of light.

Here at the edge the mind goes on,
The eyes go on, though steps must stop
At plunging scarps where dizzily
The plumes of haze shroud and unshroud
Knife-edge and scree; and down and down
Still sight must drop, be cut and grazed,
To find at last the dry creek-bed.

This is no landscape for the eye
Cupped by a hand to shield the mind
From earth's most naked cruelty.
Who looks the longest must take on
The fierceness of the eagle-hawk,
His hungry thought, his still intent,
His burnished, undeflected eye.

How fared they then who built and lived
Beneath the shoulder of the hill,
Who planted with their hopeful hands
The oak, the fruit, the sheltering hedge,
The store, the church, the bakery

Where still the letters are discerned
That here for man is meal, his bread.

The houses lean against the wind,
Their eyes are scarfed with sheets of tin,
I heard in all that stillness once
The cracked complaining of the bell.
A door that shut on nothing scraped,
And with a turning, sick unease
I saw a child's discarded shoe.

Was it on such a summer's day
They gathered from the bakery,
The store, the church, and, beckoned on
By the compulsion of the fall,
Plunged to those knife-edged silences?
His mind, as mine, will veer away
Who lacks the hawks' unwavering eye.

AUTOBIOGRAPHY

Time holds the glass the wrong way round:
I see a matchstick child, thin,
Dwindling through far-off summer days
Exhausted in a cotton dress,
Sustained by longing, burning still
With passion underneath the skin
For love, for words, for excellence.

She crouches over poetry,
Starts like a bird and trembling waits
The lightning-flash of love, exchange
Of name for name and known for known.
She learns that word and love are one
Though each assume a different form,
And she the seeker and the sought.

The good, indifferent and bad
She takes with equal joy, content
That all are shaped like poetry
And all can teach her excellence.
Now, chin on hand, I watch her make
Her wilful way to where I am.
How thin she is! How thin and grave!

NEW YORK SPRING

I was alert for crime
The quick knifing, death
The body spreadeagled, the turning
Away of the watchers
Wry avoidance of pity,
The dark stain spreading
As the dark stain spread
In a thousand old films.

Well, we took the subway
Battered by graffiti
And rose like muddy minnows
To the blue of the city
And lunchtime loiterers
In the first sun of springtime.

I saw a girl on roller-
Skates. She wore a button
Saying Save the Whales,
She wore a pair of headphones
Wired to a Walkman
In her top pocket
And a whole symphony orchestra
Played for her alone.

This was in New York
Along the Avenue
In the spring of April
Nineteen eighty-two.

CLERGYMAN

He took a tray and queued. She found a table,
Quiet, beside a window, and sat down
Watching his courtesy, his helpful hands
Thought of the place beyond Brewarrina
His earliest parish, and the three of them,
Herself, her parents, in that poky house.
And then the western suburbs: troubled years
His duties always coming first; his dogged,
Simple unquestioning beliefs. Her mother's death.

Grief, grief. How could he stand it? How would she?
Now, resident parson in a nursing-home
He eased the deaths and met the relatives,
And at each graveside bore it for them all.
"His coat's still good," she thought. "He stands so well."
He brought the laden tray, put down the plates,
A glass of wine for each—father and child,
Widow and widower, loving and loved.
She smiled. He nodded. Bowed his head. Said grace.

GWEN HARWOOD
(1920–1995)

Born Brisbane, Australia. As well as being a poet, she taught music, was a church organist, and wrote a libretto for an opera. She lived in Hobart.

THE OLD WIFE'S TALE

Summer, transpose your haunting themes
into a key that all can sing.
How soon will winter's gadfly air
dart through the empty streets to sting
those dancers from the crowded square,
to spear their hopes and spike their dreams.

When I was young I danced so long
the fireworks stars wheeled round and burst
and showered their fierce chromatic rain
about my feet so long rehearsed
in dancing that I felt no pain
but far outdanced the dancing throng

until, beside a glass, I turned
to fix my hair and smooth my lace.
Then terror had me by the throat—
a vacant, crazed old woman's face
stared from my own. One vibrant note
cracked folly's bowl. The music burned

one moment, then its prism tones
fused into silence. Dazed and halt
I called on Christ, kind nurse, to wean
my foolish lips from sweet to salt,
erase in mercy what had been,
and melt with ease my tortured bones.

Silence for answer. So I caught
a young man's hand. He smiled and said,
"God's old and foolish, we can steal
more than our share of heavenly bread.
Rest in my arms, and I'll reveal
in darkness the true mode of thought."

I bit the core of pain, to find
this world's true sweetness on my lips,
the virtuoso senses priced
at nothing, in one vast eclipse.
A moving fingertip sufficed
to draw love's orbit through the mind.

Better than love, what name for this:
our vanished childhood sealed in flesh,
the restless energy of joy
whipping a world still morning-fresh
to hum new notes, a spinning toy.
All sorrow mended in a kiss.

My children grew. Like wine I poured
knowledge and skill, fought love's long war
with trivial cares. My spirit gave
a cry of hunger: "Grant me more
than this bare sustenance, I crave
some combat worthy of my sword."

Powerless to temper or withhold
time's raining blows, I watched him break
my cherished moulds and shape his own,
give strangers back for children, take

my husband, and I stood alone,
a shepherd with an empty fold.

Now with divining age I seek
the hidden seminal springs of peace,
hold mercy's spiral to my ear,
or stand in silence and release
the falcon mind to hunt down fear.
I stare at clouds until they break

in paradigms of truth, and spell
decree my sentence at the sun's assize▲.
My bone-bare, stark endurance frames
terror for fools, but to the wise
my winter-landscape face proclaims
life's last, and death's first parable.

IN THE PARK

She sits in the park. Her clothes are out of date.
Two children whine and bicker, tug her skirt.
A third draws aimless patterns in the dirt.
Someone she loved once passes by—too late

to feign indifference to that casual nod.
"How nice," et cetera. "Time holds great surprises."
From his neat head unquestionably rises
a small balloon . . . "but for the grace of God . . ."

They stand a while in flickering light, rehearsing
the children's names and birthdays. "It's so sweet
to hear their chatter, watch them grow and thrive,"
she says to his departing smile. Then, nursing
the youngest child, sits staring at her feet.
To the wind she says, "They have eaten me alive."

SUBURBAN SONNET

She practises a fugue, though it can matter
to no one now if she plays well or not.
Beside her on the floor two children chatter,
then scream and fight. She hushes them. A pot
boils over. As she rushes to the stove
too late, a wave of nausea overpowers
subject and counter-subject. Zest and love
drain out with soapy water as she scours
the crusted milk. Her veins ache. Once she played
for Rubinstein, who yawned. The children caper
round a sprung mousetrap where a mouse lies dead.
When the soft corpse won't move they seem afraid.
She comforts them; and wraps it in a paper
featuring: *Tasty dishes from stale bread*.

FATHER AND CHILD

I BARN OWL

Daybreak: the household slept.
I rose, blessed by the sun.
A horny fiend, I crept
out with my father's gun.
Let him dream of a child
obedient, angel-mild—

old No-Sayer, robbed of power
by sleep. I knew my prize
who swooped home at this hour
with daylight-riddled eyes
to his place on a high beam
in our old stables, to dream

light's useless time away.
I stood, holding my breath,
in urine-scented hay,
master of life and death,
a wisp-haired judge whose law
would punish beak and claw.

My first shot struck. He swayed,
ruined, beating his only
wing, as I watched, afraid
by the fallen gun, a lonely
child who believed death clean
and final, not this obscene

bundle of stuff that dropped,
and dribbled through loose straw
tangling in bowels, and hopped
blindly closer. I saw
those eyes that did not see
mirror my cruelty

while the wrecked thing that could
not bear the light nor hide
hobbled in its own blood.
My father reached my side,
gave me the fallen gun.
"End what you have begun."

I fired. The blank eyes shone
once into mine, and slept.
I leaned my head upon
my father's arm, and wept,
owl-blind in early sun
for what I had begun.

II NIGHTFALL

Forty years, lived or dreamed:
what memories pack them home.
Now the season that seemed
incredible is come.
Father and child, we stand
in time's long-promised land.

Since there's no more to taste
ripeness is plainly all.
Father, we pick our last
fruits of the temporal.
Eighty years old, you take
this late walk for my sake.

Who can be what you were?
Link your dry hand in mine,
my stick-thin comforter.
Far distant suburbs shine
with great simplicities.
Birds crowd in flowering trees,

sunset exalts its known
symbols of transience.
Your passionate face is grown
to ancient innocence.
Let us walk for this hour
as if death had no power

or were no more than sleep.
Things truly named can never
vanish from earth. You keep
a child's delight for ever
in birds, flowers, shivery-grass—
I name them as we pass.

"*Be your tears wet?*" You speak
as if air touched a string

near breaking-point. Your cheek
brushes on mine. Old king,
your marvellous journey's done.
Your night and day are one

as you find with your white stick
the path on which you turn
home with the child once quick
to mischief, grown to learn
what sorrows, in the end,
no words, no tears can mend.

MOTHER WHO GAVE ME LIFE

Mother who gave me life
I think of women bearing
women. Forgive me the wisdom
I would not learn from you.

It is not for my children I walk
on earth in the light of the living.
It is for you, for the wild
daughters becoming women,

anguish of seasons burning
backward in time to those other
bodies, your mother, and hers
and beyond, speech growing stranger

on thresholds of ice, rock, fire,
bones changing, heads inclining
to monkey bosom, lemur breast,
guileless milk of the word.

I prayed you would live to see
Halley's Comet a second time.
The Sister said, When she died
she was folding a little towel.

You left the world so, having lived
nearly thirty thousand days:
a fabric of marvels folded
down to a little space.

At our last meeting I closed
the ward door of heavy glass
between us, and saw your face
crumple, fine threadbare linen

worn, still good to the last,
then, somehow, smooth to a smile
so I should not see your tears.
Anguish: remembered hours:

a lamp on embroidered linen,
my supper set out, your voice
calling me in as darkness
falls on my father's house.

THE SEA ANEMONES

Grey mountains, sea and sky. Even the misty
seawind is grey. I walk on lichened rock
in a kind of late assessment, call it peace.
Then the anemones, scarlet, gouts of blood.
There is a word I need, and earth was speaking.
I cannot hear. These seaflowers are too bright.
Kneeling on rock, I touch them through cold water.
My fingers meet some hungering gentleness.
A newborn child's lips moved so at my breast.

18. MOTHER WHO GAVE ME LIFE Halley's Comet is seen every 75 years.

I woke, once, with my palm across your mouth.
  The word is: *ever*. Why add salt to salt?
  Blood drop by drop among the rocks they shine.
  Anemos, wind. The spirit, where it will.
Not flowers, no, animals that must eat or die.

CLASS OF 1927

SLATE

Quite often in some trendy quarter
the passion to redecorate
those areas concerned with water
results in an expanse of slate.
Cork tiling's warmer, vinyl's neater.
Slate's forty dollars a square metre.
In kitchen, laundry, loo, I see
the stuff the State School gave us free,
and very soon my morbid, chronic
nostalgia swells to recreate
slate-pencil's piercing squeal on slate,
beloved of all those bored demonic
infants whose purpose was to make
mischief purely for mischief's sake.

We sat, ranked by examination,
those with the best marks at the back.
In undisguised discrimination
at the front sat the dim, the slack,
where they could not converse or fiddle;
and in the undistinguished middle
the hard triers, the fairly bright
laboured to get their set work right
not out of any love of study
but simply to escape the cane.
Somehow the teacher knew whose brain
was cleared by stirring, whose was muddy.

One vacant lad, condemned to go
from year to year in the front row,

was said to have three skulls, poor creature.
Everyone liked to feel his head
and demonstrate its curious feature:
ridge after ridge of bone instead
of brain. Bonehead was oddly charming.

His eagerness was so disarming
the whole class used him as a pet
though he was likely to forget
between instruction and retrieval
the object he was sent to find.
No angst stirred his unleavened mind.
He beamed, and hummed, and knew no evil.
The doctor's son, a clever skite,
found inexpressible delight

in cruelty. This boy collected,
or stole, unpleasant instruments;
with these, at playtime, he dissected
lizards and frogs, or spiked their vents
to see how long they took in dying.
One day the class, kept in for sighing
when Sir set homework, heard a squeak.
Being on our honour not to speak
while Sir was briefly absent (bearing
his cane as always) we turned round
and witnessed, as the source of sound,
a captive mouse, its torturer swearing
because the victim tried to bite.
The back row, silent out of fright,

did nothing, and the middle section
saw, but pretended not to look.
Bonehead, after a brief inspection,
stopped smiling; turned again and took
his slate out of its slot; descended

in fury, and with one blow ended
the wanton vivisector's sport.
Then revolution of a sort
broke out. The stricken head was gory.
We stamped and cheered our hero on.
The unhappy mouse was too far gone
to benefit from Bonehead's glory,
or squeak for victory, or curse
the arrangement of this universe.

When Sir returned the class was sitting
so quietly he racked his wits
and stroked his cane and walked round hitting
his leg, but didn't find the bits
of slate we hid in hasty cleaning.
Nor did he grasp the hidden meaning
of some congealing drops of red.

"Where did you get that bloody head?"
"Knocked it." "Go home. That cut needs dressing."
Our golden silence filled the room.
We sat preparing to resume
our work as if it were a blessing
to write on slate, for Sir to see,
the conjugation of *to be*.

THE SPELLING PRIZE

Every Child's Book of Animal Stories.
To compete, we stood on the wooden forms
that seated four in discomfort.
When you missed your word, you sat down
and wrote it out twenty times.
At last only two were left:
Ella and I, who had sailed
past *ghost, nymph, scheme, flight, nephew*,
the shoals of o - u - g - h

and i before e, stood waiting
for the final word, Whoever
put her hand up first when Sir
announced it, could try to spell it.
A pause, while Sir went outside.
Some of the girls started hissing,
"Give Ella a chance. Let her win."

Through the window I saw the playground
bare as a fowlyard, the ditch
in a paddock beyond where frogs
lived out whatever their life was
before the big boys impaled them
on wooden skewers, a glint
from a roof in the middle distance
that was Ella's home. I had been there

the week before, when my grandmother went
to take their baby, the ninth,
my brother's old shawl. Ella coaxed me
to a ramshackle tinroofed shed
where her father was killing a bull calf.
A velvety fan of blood
opened out on the concrete floor
as one of her brothers pumped the forelegs:
"You do this to empty the heart."

The father severed the head, and set it
aside on a bench where the eyes, still trusting,
looked back at what had become
of the world. It was not the sight
of the entrails, the deepening crimson
of blood that sent me crying
across the yard, but the calf's eyes watching
knife, whetstone, carcase, the hand that fed.

Ella followed. "I'll show you my toys."
In that house where nobody owned
a corner, a space they might call their own,

she kept two old dolls in a shoebox.
Below me the whispers continued:
"Let Ella win the prize."
Why, now, does memory brood
on Sir's return, and the moment

when he put down his cane and smoothed
his hair grease-tight on his skull
and snapped out the last word: MYSTIC,
a word never found in our Readers.
My innocent hand flew up.
Sheer reflex, but still, I knew it,
and knew I could slip in a k
or an i for a y and lose,

but did not, and sixty years
can't change it; I stand in the playground
and the pale dust stirs as my friends
of the hour before yell "Skite!"
and "Showoff!" and "Think you're clever!"
They gather round Ella, who turns
one hurt look from her red-rimmed eyes
at my coveted, worthless prize.

RELIGIOUS INSTRUCTION

The clergy came in once a week for Religious Instruction.
Divided by faith, not age, we were bidden to be,
(except for the Micks and a Jew) by some curious
    deduction,
Presbyterian, Methodist, Baptist or C of E.

The Micks were allowed to be useful, to tidy the
    playground.
But Micah, invited to join them, told Sir "They'd only
give me a hiding", and stayed inside; moved round
as he chose with his book of Hebrew letters, a lonely

example, among the tender lambs of Jesus,
of good behaviour. Handsome as a dark angel
he studied while the big boys laboured to tease us
with hair-tweak, nib-prick, Chinese burns, as the well

of boredom overflowed in games of noughts
and crosses, spitballs, and drawings so obscene
if Sir had found them they'd have earned us six cuts.
"You give me real insight into original sin,"

said one minister in despair, intercepting some verses
describing him as Old Swivelneck. Beaked like a
 sparrowhawk
he clawed at his collar and singled me out from his class.
I feared his anger rightly, feared he would talk

to our headmaster, or Sir. I stood in disgrace.
Then a quiet voice from the back interrupted his wrath:
"*I am ready to forgive.*" "Who said that? Stand up in your
 place!"
Micah stood. "It was said by the Lord God of Sabaoth."

Then we heard the monitor's footsteps. Saved by the bell!
In a tumult of voices we spilled into sunlight to play,
a host of rejoicing sinners, too young to feel
original darkness under that burning day.

THE TWINS

Three years old when their mother died
in what my grandmother called
accouchement, my father labour,
they heard the neighbours intone
"A mercy the-child went with her."

Their father raised them somehow.
No one could tell them apart.
At seven they sat in school

in their rightful place, at the top
of the class, the first to respond
with raised arm and finger-flick.

When one gave the answer, her sister
repeated it under her breath.
An inspector accused them of cheating,
but later, in front of the class,
declared himself sorry, and taught us
a marvellous word: *telepathic*.

On Fridays, the story went,
they slept in the shed, barred in
from their father's rage as he drank
his dead wife back to his house.
For the rest of the week he was sober
and proud. My grandmother gave them
a basket of fruit. He returned it.
"We manage. We don't need help."

They could wash their own hair, skin rabbits,
milk the cow, make porridge, clean boots.

Unlike most of the class I had shoes,
clean handkerchiefs, ribbons, a toothbrush.
We all shared the schoolsores and nits
and the language I learned to forget
at the gate of my welcoming home.

One day as I sat on the fence
fluted, crimped my pinafore goffered▲, my hair
still crisp from the curlers, the twins
came by. I scuttled away
so I should not have to share
my Saturday sweets. My mother
saw me, and slapped me, and offered
the bag to the twins, who replied
softly one aloud and one sotto voce▲,
"No thank you. We don't like lollies."

They lied in their greenish teeth
as they knew, and we knew.
Good angel
give me that morning again
and let me share, and spare me
the shame of my parents' rebuke.
If there are multiple worlds
then let there be one with an ending
quite other than theirs: leaving school
too early and coming to grief.

Or if this is our one life sentence,
hold them in innocence, writing
Our Father which art in Heaven
in copperplate, or drawing
(their work being done) the same picture
on the backs of their slates: a foursquare
house where a smiling woman
winged like an angel welcomes
two children home from school.

THE SECRET LIFE OF FROGS

Mr Gabriel Fur, my Siamese,
brings to the hearth a Common Toadlet,
Crinia tasmaniensis.
Mice are permitted, frogs forbidden.
It will live. I carry it outside.
Its heartbeat troubles my warm hand
and as I set it down I see
two small girls in a warmer land.

My friend Alice and I would sit
cradling our frogs behind the tankstand.
Other fathers would talk about
the Great War. Mine would only say,

"I used to be a stretcher-bearer."
Not seen, not heard, in childhood's earshot
of the women on the back veranda,
we knew about atrocities.
Some syllables we used as charms:
Passchendaele Mons Gallipoli.
We knew about Poor George, who cried
if any woman touched her hair.
He'd been inside a brothel when
the Jerries came and started shooting.
(We thought a brothel was a French
hotel that served hot broth to diggers.)
The girl that he'd been with was scalped.
Every Frog in the house was killed.

Well, that was life for frogs. At school
the big boys blew them up and spiked them.
One bully had the very knife
with which his father killed ten Germans—
twenty—a hundred—numbers blossomed.
Dad the Impaler! making work
for the more humble stretcher-bearers.

In safety by the dripping tankstand
our frogs with matchstick hands as pale
as the violet stems they lived among
cuddled their vulnerable bellies
in hands that would not do them wrong.

THE LION'S BRIDE

I loved her softness, her warm human smell,
her dark mane flowing loose. Sometimes stirred by
rank longing laid my muzzle on her thigh.
Her father, faithful keeper, fed me well,
but she came daily with our special bowl

barefoot into my cage, and set it down:
our love feast. We became the talk of town,
brute king and tender woman, soul to soul.

Until today: an icy spectre sheathed
in silk minced to my side on pointed feet.
I ripped the scented veil from its unreal
head and engorged the painted lips that breathed
our secret names. A ghost has bones, and meat!
Come soon my love, my bride, and share this meal.

OODGEROO NOONUCCAL (KATH WALKER)

(1920–1993)

She was raised on Stradbroke Island, Moreton Bay, Queensland. Her first book of poems, We Are Going, *made her the first Aboriginal poet to have a book published. In 1988 she rejected the European name by which her work had been known.*

WE ARE GOING

(FOR GRANNIE COOLWELL)

They came in to the little town
A semi-naked band subdued and silent,
All that remained of their tribe.
They came here to the place of their old bora▲ ground
Where now the many white men hurry about like ants.
Notice of estate agent reads: 'Rubbish May Be Tipped Here'.
Now it half covers the traces of the old bora ring.
They sit and are confused, they cannot say their thoughts:
'We are as strangers here now, but the white tribe are the strangers.
We belong here, we are of the old ways.
We are the corroboree and the bora ground,
We are the old sacred ceremonies, the laws of the elders.
We are the wonder tales of Dream Time, the tribal legends told.

sacred ground for initiation rites

We are the past, the hunts and the laughing games, the wandering camp fires.
We are the lightning-bolt over Gaphembah Hill
Quick and terrible,
And the Thunder after him, that loud fellow.

We are the quiet daybreak paling the dark lagoon.
We are the shadow-ghosts creeping back as the camp fires burn low.
We are nature and the past, all the old ways
Gone now and scattered.
The scrubs are gone, the hunting and the laughter.
The eagle is gone, the emu and the kangaroo are gone from this place.
The bora ring is gone.
The corroboree is gone.
And we are going.

COLOUR BAR

When vile men jeer because my skin is brown,
This I live down.

But when a taunted child comes home in tears,
Fierce anger sears.

The colour bar! It shows the meaner mind
Of moron kind.

Men are but medieval yet, as long
As lives this wrong.

Could he but see, the colour-baiting clod
Is blaming God

'Who made us all, and all His children He
Loves equally.

As long as brothers banned from brotherhood
You still exclude,

The Christianity you hold so high
Is but a lie.

Justice a cant of hypocrites, content
With precedent.

MUNICIPAL GUM

Gumtree in the city street,
Hard bitumen around your feet,
Rather you should be
In the cool world of leafy forest halls
And wild bird calls.
Here you seem to me
Like that poor cart-horse
Castrated, broken, a thing wronged,
Strapped and buckled, its hell prolonged,
Whose hung head and listless mien express
Its hopelessness.
Municipal gum, it is dolorous
To see you thus
Set in your black grass of bitumen—
O fellow citizen,
What have they done to us?

DAWN WAIL FOR THE DEAD

Dim light of daybreak now
Faintly over the sleeping camp.
Old lubra first to wake remembers:
First thing every dawn
Remember the dead, cry for them.
Softly at first her wail begins,
One by one as they wake and hear
Join in the cry, and the whole camp
Wails for the dead, the poor dead
Gone from here to the Dark Place:
They are remembered.
Then it is over, life now,
Fires lit, laughter now,
And a new day calling.

DIMITRIS TSALOUMAS
(b. 1921)

Born on the Greek island of Leros, brought up under Italian occupation, he worked for the underground during the Second World War. He has lived in Australia since 1952, but makes frequent trips to Greece. His earlier poems were first written in Greek.

A PROGRESSIVE MAN'S INDIGNATION

Why the hell do you grumble and blame tourism
for everything? What's wrong with it in any case?
Would you prefer hovels still and market-gardens
so you can ride between them on donkey-back and scratch
your knees on the withies? Or to creep around
hugging the wall of old Kalafatas's property, jumping
like a hare lest the wave should catch you and
you squelch to work as though you'd pissed yourself?
For sure, you folk would rather have the people
slaving for a crust of bread, so you could hear
the gentle evening clack of wheel-wells, tinkling bells
at dawn, and have the beach all to yourselves at noon.
If I had a property in the spot that yours is in,
I'd raise a fifty-room hotel, I'd...
That's how my fellow-countrymen go on, and truly
they've never yet had whiter bread to eat,
nor portlier corporations,
nor a glossier sheen on their bald heads.

FALCON DRINKING

Awakened to this other bleakness
I sit to read my daily portion

of the wall. Sometimes it's voices:
women disputing a place at the head

of public fountains in years of drought,
Orpheus pleading in the basement,

the anguished bidding at the 'Change.
Sometimes it's touch:

shuddering flesh and silken skin,
the clammy passage of darkness

in the night corridors, forgotten scars
and varnishes on old violins.

Today is seeing time. Knife-sharp,
a cruel blade of light cuts through

the brain's greyness, sweeps over mists
and hints at ridges, distantly.

Close in, at the stone-trough
hard by the spring of language where

the cypress stands, a falcon drinks.
The cypress ripples in shattered water

nights of many moons and nightingales.
The bird stoops shivering to sip

then tilts its head back skywards,
stammers its beak and trills

the narrow tongue. Spilt drops
hang bright in midair, hard as tears.

NOCTURNE

In the anteroom of sleep swing tails of rats
festoons and frills of mandrake
bitter is the cup and welcome the lullaby
of the bat my love, I told you
there is no bitterness like the music of verse
a nightingale sings in the cypress
starry coracles on the floods of night
waiting women shyly bearing myrrh
with sprigs of moon-drenched mint with
generals, politicians, spies—
don't let me fall asleep my love
first come and warm my spine
they'll come, they'll take deep breaths, I know,
they'll swallow all the air.

PRODIGAL

Fanatical mosquitoes and persistent fetid stench
hold absolute dominion
over the twilight bogs. Evening comes early
full of mutterings. Our days
were never rich—but now!
The ox is skin and bone and the goat
barely yields enough for the baby. Therefore
make no rash decision.
The other day Eros was seen in the market-place
unrecognised in cast-off clothes,
grown old. Come of course since you insist, but
whatever you remember, now forget.

NOCTURNE, PRODIGAL, THE RETURN, are all translated from Greek by Philip Grundy.

THE RETURN

The war's been over now for forty years
and you've still to take the enemy off the wire.
Who opened up his back so that his lungs hung out
from behind? Haven't you tired of his shallow moans
in a whole lifetime? I sent you word to empty out
the bucket with the arm and other bits,
to stop up all the cracks. The house
stinks like a shambles. You haven't even sealed
the holes in the cellar and who knows what
might suddenly creep out on us? I don't like
this weather at all. Already my sleep is taking
water, and there are tentacles stretching out,
feeling in the dark. I'm sorry to tell you,
brother, but I'm not spending summer here.
At our age some caution is called for.

THE DEBATE

The crisis rippled through the placid land
and the people's Deputies sat in debate

far into night. In the wintry yards
the Three Horsemen paced impatiently.

Rates had shot up beyond the need of banks,
inflation past the prick. The City Raiders,

the Services, were starved of funds:
dogs barked all night behind the city gates.

Some blamed the lack of action, others
wrong action, some said I told you so.

Buoyed up by TV-snack and beer, the Citizen,
his ears afloat upon the murky waters

looked on, agog for his own man to rise
and say again that he had all the brawn,

that for His vote he'd roll his trousers
and pull Him out and dry Him on the lawn.

from RHAPSODIC MEDITATION ON THE MELBOURNE SUBURB OF ST KILDA

1 THE PLACE

Summers out of alien tracts
in the chronicle of my days
rising now as though they'd never
been dead, to settle among
the proper seasons. Between
the seed and dubious harvest,
this calendar makes a desert rich.

There should be another meaning
for these words, but secret wear
has stripped them to a nakedness
that's of the beggared self.
As I reckon time discarded
in disbelief, stark to this door,
like fragments from some text
demanding restoration,
come vagrant faces, scraps
out of sleep; and from landscapes
obscured in darker folds
of the recording mind,
crowded places push to the front
to challenge the winter tedium
of a night.
Thus old St Kilda
comes back. Sea-skirted,

reeking at low tide
with rotten mussels, sand-stung
and thirsting in the bronze days
of cloud and north winds;
city of droning hotels, of gloomy
wine saloons and men of character,
alive with ambulant
cop-fearing tarts, discreet
with privet havens
in its beach parks after dark.

A brass band cheered the crowds
on Sundays while at the beach
a thousand burnished girls
shuddered and reared like mares
at the water's touch. At night
men from impossible countries
saw scarlet bolts crack their sleep,
and there was a smell of roses
upon their pillows, a bitterness
of sage in their mouths.

2 THE HOUSE

It's after six. Back from the pub
the landlord, tall and gruff
and medal-proud on Anzac Days,
sits in the porch drunk royally.
He nods with sentiment to all
his boarding Dagos as they come in
from work. The times were hard,
the house, decaying in stucco,
was where that tower stands.

They sat in coffee shops, talking
till words grew darker with night.
Many saw women or buildings rising
from their steaming cups. Sometimes

it was the turning belly of a girl,
and they'd steady the wobbly table
and clear the top. Many witnessed
such miracles. On summer nights
they'd sleep-walk, and from the pier
gaze long at the far-lighted ships.

4 REFFO

Stiff with age and recent memories
from the death camps, she'd come
down the stairs, teapot in hand,
and cross the kitchen gloom
with a smile so imponderable
we thought it meant for others,
despite the cupboard-hung walls.
She was fond of black bread
and pickled herring, and talked
of recipes too difficult to test
in the pot. Often the night
was alerted to the sounds
of preparation. She shuffled about
in her balcony room and noises
of opening and shutting, of things
dragged on the floor, would slip
the guard of her discretion. Also,
the rustle of paper and hushed,
torn words. She'd found the sun
too strong in this country,
the family bonds too loose.
I was refused time off to attend
the funeral. She was neither relative
nor friend but she didn't go
beyond the vague periphery
of my living, where shadows lurk
and break through secret gaps
to body forth their bitter meaning.

WAITING FOR WAR

I pull the blinds down and sit in the gloom
to think. Time frowns on my hands:

there'll be war. The desert's ploughed deep
with mighty chains yet my garden sheds leaves

in the height of summer, many small birds
drop to the bitumen, dead. Rat poison,

they say, the pink grain of death. I know
its other colours but this is not a time

for memory. I must shut my ears to weakness.
Out in the melting heat all voices

protesting innocence are flawed. Therefore
hard men sit by the shimmer of pools

reviewing the situation, and in my head
the whole day long three ravens fat as swans

cross back and forth a wilderness,
and others rise like flies from its ravines.

I must reach the shadier places, its verdant
tracts. The world is running out of patience.

ADRIENNE RICH
(b. 1929)

Born in Baltimore, she has travelled extensively. She is well known for her feminist writing as well as for her poetry, which combines personal experience and social issues.

AUNT JENNIFER'S TIGERS

Aunt Jennifer's tigers prance across a screen,
Bright topaz denizens of a world of green.
They do not fear the men beneath the tree;
They pace in sleek chivalric certainty.

Aunt Jennifer's fingers fluttering through her wool
Find even the ivory needle hard to pull.
The massive weight of Uncle's wedding band
Sits heavily upon Aunt Jennifer's hand.

When Aunt is dead, her terrified hands will lie
Still ringed with ordeals she was mastered by.
The tigers in the panel that she made
Will go on prancing, proud and unafraid.

AFTER TWENTY YEARS

FOR A.P.C.

Two women sit at a table by a window. Light breaks
unevenly on both of them.
Their talk is a striking of sparks
which passers-by in the street observe

as a glitter in the glass of that window.
Two women in the prime of life.
Their babies are old enough to have babies.
Loneliness has been part of their story for twenty years,
the dark edge of the clever tongue,
the obscure underside of the imagination.
It is snow and thunder in the street.
While they speak the lightning flashes purple.
It is strange to be so many women,
eating and drinking at the same table,
those who bathed their children in the same basin
who kept their secrets from each other
walked the floors of their lives in separate rooms
and flow into history now as the women of their time
living in the prime of life
as in a city where nothing is forbidden
and nothing permanent.

MOTHER-RIGHT

FOR M.H.

Woman and child   running
in a field   A man planted
on the horizon

Two hands   one long, slim   one
small, starlike   clasped
in the razor wind

Her hair cut short for faster travel
the child's curls grazing his shoulders
the hawk-winged cloud   over their heads

The man is walking boundaries
measuring   He believes in what is his
the grass   the waters underneath   the air

the air   through which child and mother
are running   the boy singing

the woman   eyes sharpened in the light
heart stumbling   making for the open

DIVING INTO THE WRECK

First having read the book of myths,
and loaded the camera,
and checked the edge of the knife-blade,
I put on
the body-armor of black rubber
the absurd flippers
the grave and awkward mask.
I am having to do this
not like Cousteau with his
assiduous team
aboard the sun-flooded schooner
but here alone.

There is a ladder.
The ladder is always there
hanging innocently
close to the side of the schooner.
We know what it is for,
we who have used it.
Otherwise
it's a piece of maritime floss
some sundry equipment.

I go down.
Rung after rung and still
the oxygen immerses me
the blue light
the clear atoms
of our human air.
I go down.
My flippers cripple me,
I crawl like an insect down the ladder
and there is no one

to tell me when the ocean
will begin.

First the air is blue and then
it is bluer and then green and then
black I am blacking out and yet
my mask is powerful
it pumps my blood with power
the sea is another story
the sea is not a question of power
I have to learn alone
to turn my body without force
in the deep element.

And now: it is easy to forget
what I came for
among so many who have always
lived here
swaying their crenellated fans
between the reefs
and besides
you breathe differently down here.

I came to explore the wreck.
The words are purposes.
The words are maps.
I came to see the damage that was done
and the treasures that prevail.
I stroke the beam of my lamp
slowly along the flank
of something more permanent
than fish or weed

the thing I came for:
the wreck and not the story of the wreck
the thing itself and not the myth
the drowned face always staring
toward the sun
the evidence of damage
worn by salt and sway into this threadbare beauty

the ribs of the disaster
curving their assertion
among the tentative haunters.

This is the place.
And I am here, the mermaid whose dark hair
streams black, the merman in his armored body
We circle silently
about the wreck
we dive into the hold.
I am she: I am he

whose drowned face sleeps with open eyes
whose breasts still bear the stress
whose silver, copper, vermeil cargo lies
obscurely inside barrels
half-wedged and left to rot
we are the half-destroyed instruments
that once held to a course
the water-eaten log
the fouled compass

We are, I am, you are
by cowardice or courage
the one who find our way
back to this scene
carrying a knife, a camera
a book of myths
in which
our names do not appear.

PHANTASIA FOR ELVIRA SHATAYEV

Leader of a women's climbing team, all of whom died in a storm on Lenin Peak, August 1974. Later, Shatayev's husband found and buried the bodies.

The cold felt cold until our blood
grew colder   then the wind
died down and we slept

If in this sleep I speak
it's with a voice no longer personal
(I want to say *with voices*)
When the wind tore our breath from us at last
we had no need of words
For months for years each one of us
had felt her own *yes* growing in her
slowly forming as she stood at windows waited
for trains mended her rucksack combed her hair
What we were to learn was simply what we had
up here as out of all words that *yes* gathered
its forces fused itself and only just in time
to meet a *No* of no degrees
the black hole sucking the world in

I feel you climbing toward me
your cleated bootsoles leaving their geometric bite
colossally embossed on microscopic crystals
as when I trailed you in the Caucasus
Now I am further
ahead than either of us dreamed anyone would be
I have become
the white snow packed like asphalt by the wind
the women I love lightly flung against the mountain
that blue sky
our frozen eyes unribboned through the storm
we could have stitched that blueness together like a quilt

You come (I know this) with your love your loss
strapped to your body with your tape-recorder camera
ice-pick against advisement
to give us burial in the snow and in your mind
While my body lies out here
flashing like a prism into your eyes
how could you sleep You climbed here for yourself
we climbed for ourselves

When you have buried us told your story
ours does not end we stream
into the unfinished the unbegun

the possible
Every cell's core of heat   pulsed out of us
into the thin air   of the universe
the armature of rock beneath these snows
this mountain   which has taken   the imprint of our minds
through changes elemental and minute
as those we underwent
to bring each other here
choosing ourselves   each other   and this life
whose every breath   and grasp   and further foothold
is somewhere   still enacted   and continuing

In the diary I wrote: *Now we are ready*
and each of us knows it   I have never loved
like this   I have never seen
my own forces so taken up and shared
and given back
After the long training   the early sieges
we are moving almost effortlessly in our love

In the diary as the wind   began to tear
at the tents over us   I wrote:
We know now we have always been in danger
down in our separateness
and now up here together   but till now
we had not touched our strength

In the diary torn from my fingers I had written:
What does love mean
what does it mean   "to survive"
A cable of blue fire ropes our bodies
burning together in the snow   We will not live
to settle for less   We have dreamed of this
all of our lives

ORIGINS AND HISTORY OF CONSCIOUNESS

I

Night-life. Letters, journals, bourbon
sloshed in the glass. Poems crucified on the wall,
dissected, their bird-wings severed
like trophies. No one lives in this room
without living through some kind of crisis.

No one lives in this room
without confronting the whiteness of the wall
behind the poems, planks of books,
photographs of dead heroines.
Without contemplating last and late
the true nature of poetry. The drive
to connect. The dream of a common language.

Thinking of lovers, their blind faith, their
experienced crucifixions,
my envy is not simple. I have dreamed of going to bed
as walking into clear water ringed by a snowy wood
white as cold sheets, thinking, *I'll freeze in there*.
My bare feet are numbed already by the snow
but the water
is mild, I sink and float
like a warm amphibious animal
that has broken the net, has run
through fields of snow leaving no print;
this water washes off the scent—
You are clear now
of the hunter, the trapper
the wardens of the mind—

yet the warm animal dreams on
of another animal
swimming under the snow-flecked surface of the pool,
and wakes, and sleeps again.

No one sleeps in this room without
the dream of a common language.

II

It was simple to meet you, simple to take your eyes
into mine, saying: these are eyes I have known
from the first . . . It was simple to touch you
against the hacked background, the grain of what we
had been, the choices, years . . . It was even simple
to take each other's lives in our hands, as bodies.

What is not simple: to wake from drowning
from where the ocean beat inside us like an afterbirth
into this common, acute particularity
these two selves who walked half a lifetime untouching—
to wake to something deceptively simple: a glass
sweated with dew, a ring of the telephone, a scream
of someone beaten up far down in the street
causing each of us to listen to her own inward scream

knowing the mind of the mugger and the mugged
as any woman must who stands to survive this city,
this century, this life . . .
each of us having loved the flesh in its clenched or
  loosened beauty
better than trees or music (yet loving those too
as if they were flesh—and they are—but the flesh
of beings unfathomed as yet in our roughly literal life).

III

It's simple to wake from sleep with a stranger,
dress, go out, drink coffee,
enter a life again. It isn't simple
to wake from sleep into the neighborhood
of one neither strange nor familiar
whom we have chosen to trust. Trusting, untrusting,
we lowered ourselves into this, let ourselves
downward hand over hand as on a rope that quivered
over the unsearched . . . We did this. Conceived
of each other, conceived each other in a darkness
which I remember as drenched in light.
                                        I want to call this, life.

But I can't call it life until we start to move
beyond this secret circle of fire
where our bodies are giant shadows flung on a wall
where the night becomes our inner darkness, and sleeps
like a dumb beast, head on her paws, in the corner.

HUNGER

FOR AUDRE LORDE

1.

A fogged hill-scene on an enormous continent,
intimacy rigged with terrors,
a sequence of blurs the Chinese painter's ink-stick planned,
a scene of desolation comforted
by two human figures recklessly exposed,
leaning together in a sticklike boat
in the foreground. Maybe we look like this,
I don't know. I'm wondering
whether we even have what we think we have—
lighted windows signifying shelter,
a film of domesticity
over fragile roofs. I know I'm partly somewhere else—
huts strung across a drought-stretched land
not mine, dried breasts, mine and not mine, a mother
watching my children shrink with hunger.
I live in my Western skin,
my Western vision, torn
and flung to what I can't control or even fathom.
Quantify suffering, you could rule the world.

2.

They cán rule the world while they can persuade us
our pain belongs in some order.
Is death by famine worse than death by suicide,

than a life of famine and suicide, if a black lesbian dies,
if a white prostitute dies, if a woman genius
starves herself to feed others,
self-hatred battening on her body?
Something that kills us or leaves us half-alive
is raging under the name of an 'act of god'
in Chad, in Niger, in the Upper Volta—
yes, that male god that acts on us and on our children,
that male State that acts on us and on our children
till our brains are blunted by malnutrition,
yet sharpened by the passion for survival,
our powers expended daily on the struggle
to hand a kind of life on to our children,
to change reality for our lovers
even in a single trembling drop of water.

3.

We can look at each other through both our lifetimes
like those two figures in the sticklike boat
flung together in the Chinese ink-scene;
even our intimacies are rigged with terror.
Quantify suffering? My guilt at least is open,
I stand convicted by all my convictions—
you, too. We shrink from touching
our power, we shrink away, we starve ourselves
and each other, we're scared shitless
of what it could be to take and use our love,
hose it on a city, on a world,
to wield and guide its spray, destroying
poisons, parasites, rats, viruses—
like the terrible mothers we long and dread to be.

4.

The decision to feed the world
is the real decision. No revolution

has chosen it. For that choice requires
that women shall be free.
I choke on the taste of bread in North America
but the taste of hunger in North America
is poisoning me. Yes, I'm alive to write these words,
to leaf through Kollwitz's women
huddling the stricken children into their stricken arms
the 'mothers' drained of milk, the 'survivors' driven
to self-abortion, self-starvation, to a vision
bitter, concrete, and wordless.
I'm alive to want more than life,
want it for others starving and unborn,
to name the deprivations boring
into my will, my affections, into the brains
of daughters, sisters, lovers caught in the crossfire
of terrorists of the mind.
In the black mirror of the subway window
hangs my own face, hollow with anger and desire.
Swathed in exhaustion, on the trampled newsprint,
a woman shields a dead child from the camera.
The passion to be inscribes her body.
Until we find each other, we are alone.

from TWENTY-ONE LOVE POEMS

1.

Wherever in this city, screens flicker
with pornography, with science-fiction vampires,
victimized hirelings bending to the lash,
we also have to walk . . . if simply as we walk
through the rainsoaked garbage, the tabloid cruelties
of our own neighborhoods.
We need to grasp our lives inseparable
from those rancid dreams, that blurt of metal, those
disgraces,
and the red begonia perilously flashing
from a tenement sill six stories high,

or the long-legged young girls playing ball
in the junior highschool playground.
No one has imagined us. We want to live like trees,
sycamores blazing through the sulfuric air,
dappled with scars, still exuberantly budding,
our animal passion rooted in the city.

5.

This apartment full of books could crack open
to the thick jaws, the bulging eyes
of monsters, easily: Once open the books, you have to face
the underside of everything you've loved—
the rack and pincers held in readiness, the gag
even the best voices have had to mumble through,
the silence burying unwanted children—
women, deviants, witnesses—in desert sand.
Kenneth tells me he's been arranging his books
so he can look at Blake and Kafka while he types;
yes; and we still have to reckon with Swift
loathing the woman's flesh while praising her mind,
Goethe's dread of the Mothers, Claudel vilifying Gide,
and the ghosts—their hands clasped for centuries—
of artists dying in childbirth, wise-women charred at the
stake,
centuries of books unwritten piled behind these shelves;
and we still have to stare into the absence
of men who would not, women who could not, speak
to our life—this still unexcavated hole
called civilization, this act of translation, this half-world.

TOWARD THE SOLSTICE

The thirtieth of November.
Snow is starting to fall.
A peculiar silence is spreading
over the fields, the maple grove.

It is the thirtieth of May,
rain pours on ancient bushes, runs
down the youngest blade of grass.
I am trying to hold in one steady glance
all the parts of my life.
A spring torrent races
on this old slanting roof,
the slanted field below
thickens with winter's first whiteness.
Thistles dried to sticks in last year's wind
stand nakedly in the green,
stand sullenly in the slowly whitening,
field.

My brain glows
more violently, more avidly
the quieter, the thicker
the quilt of crystals settles,
the louder, more relentlessly
the torrent beats itself out
on the old boards and shingles.
It is the thirtieth of May,
the thirtieth of November,
a beginning or an end,
we are moving into the solstice
and there is so much here
I still do not understand.

If I could make sense of how
my life is still tangled
with dead weeds, thistles,
enormous burdocks, burdens
slowly shifting under
this first fall of snow,
beaten by this early, racking rain
calling all new life to declare itself strong
or die,
if I could know
in what language to address
the spirits that claim a place

beneath these low and simple ceilings,
tenants that neither speak nor stir
yet dwell in mute insistence
till I can feel utterly ghosted in this house.

If history is a spider-thread
spun over and over though brushed away
it seems I might some twilight
or dawn in the hushed country light
discern its greyness stretching
from molding or doorframe, out
into the empty dooryard
and following it climb
the path into the pinewoods,
tracing from tree to tree
in the failing light, in the slowly
lucidifying day
its constant, purposive trail,
till I reach whatever cellar hole
filling with snowflakes or lichen,
whatever fallen shack
or unremembered clearing
I am meant to have found
and there, under the first or last
star, trusting to instinct
the words would come to mind
I have failed or forgotten to say
year after year, winter
after summer, the right rune
to ease the hold of the past
upon the rest of my life
and ease my hold on the past.

If some rite of separation
is still unaccomplished
between myself and the long-gone
tenants of this house,
between myself and my childhood,
and the childhood of my children,

it is I who have neglected
to perform the needed acts,
set water in corners, light and eucalyptus
in front of mirrors,
or merely pause and listen
to my own pulse vibrating
lightly as falling snow,
relentlessly as the rainstorm,
and hear what it has been saying.
It seems I am still waiting
for them to make some clear demand
some articulate sound or gesture,
for release to come from anywhere
but from inside myself.

A decade of cutting away
dead flesh, cauterizing
old scars ripped open over and over
and still it is not enough.
A decade of performing
the loving humdrum acts
of attention to this house
transplanting lilac suckers,
washing panes, scrubbing
wood-smoke from splitting paint,
sweeping stairs, brushing the thread
of the spider aside,
and so much yet undone,
a woman's work, the solstice nearing,
and my hand still suspended
as if above a letter
I long and dread to close.

TRANSCENDENTAL ETUDE

(FOR MICHELLE CLIFF)

This August evening I've been driving
over backroads fringed with queen anne's lace
my car startling young deer in meadows—one
gave a hoarse intake of her breath and all
four fawns sprang after her
into the dark maples.
Three months from today they'll be fair game
for the hit-and-run hunters, glorying
in a weekend's destructive power,
triggers fingered by drunken gunmen, sometimes
so inept as to leave the shattered animal
stunned in her blood. But this evening deep in summer
the deer are still alive and free,
nibbling apples from early-laden boughs
so weighted, so englobed
with already yellowing fruit
they seem eternal, Hesperidean
in the clear-tuned, cricket-throbbing air.

Later I stood in the dooryard,
my nerves singing the immense
fragility of all this sweetness,
this green world already sentimentalized, photographed,
advertised to death. Yet, it persists
stubbornly beyond the fake Vermont
of antique barnboards glazed into discothèques,
artificial snow, the sick Vermont of children
conceived in apathy, grown to winters
of rotgut violence,
poverty gnashing its teeth like a blind cat at their lives.
Still, it persists. Turning off onto a dirt road
from the raw cuts bulldozed through a quiet village
for the tourist run to Canada,
I've sat on a stone fence above a great, soft, sloping field
of musing heifers, a farmstead
slanting its planes calmly in the calm light,
a dead elm raising bleached arms

above a green so dense with life,
minute, momentary life—slugs, moles, pheasants, gnats,
spiders, moths, hummingbirds, groundhogs, butterflies—
a lifetime is too narrow
to understand it all, beginning with the huge
rockshelves that underlie all that life.

No one ever told us we had to study our lives,
make of our lives a study, as if learning natural history
or music, that we should begin
with the simple exercises first
and slowly go on trying
the hard ones, practicing till strength
and accuracy became one with the daring
to leap into transcendence, take the chance
of breaking down in the wild arpeggio
or faulting the full sentence of the fugue.
—And in fact we can't live like that: we take on
everything at once before we've even begun
to read or mark time, we're forced to begin
in the midst of the hardest movement,
the one already sounding as we are born.
At most we're allowed a few months
of simply listening to the simple line
of a woman's voice singing a child
against her heart. Everything else is too soon,
too sudden, the wrenching-apart, that woman's
heartbeat
heard ever after from a distance,
the loss of that ground-note echoing
whenever we are happy, or in despair.

Everything else seems beyond us,
we aren't ready for it, nothing that was said
is true for us, caught naked in the argument,
the counterpoint, trying to sightread
what our fingers can't keep up with, learn by heart
what we can't even read. And yet
it *is* this we were born to. We aren't virtuosi
or child prodigies, there are no prodigies

in this realm, only a half-blind, stubborn
cleaving to the timbre, the tones of what we are
—even when all the texts describe it differently.

And we're not performers, like Liszt, competing
against the world for speed and brilliance
(the 79-year-old pianist said, when I asked her
What makes a virtuoso?—Competitiveness.)
The longer I live the more I mistrust
theatricality, the false glamour cast
by performance, the more I know its poverty beside
the truths we are salvaging from
the splitting-open of our lives.
The woman who sits watching, listening,
eyes moving in the darkness
is rehearsing in her body, hearing-out in her blood
a score touched off in her perhaps
by some words, a few chords, from the stage:
a tale only she can tell.

But there come times—perhaps this is one of them—
when we have to take ourselves more seriously or die;
when we have to pull back from the incantations,
rhythms we've moved to thoughtlessly,
and disenthrall ourselves, bestow
ourselves to silence, or a severer listening, cleansed
of oratory, formulas, choruses, laments, static
crowding the wires. We cut the wires,
find ourselves in free-fall, as if
our true home were the undimensional
solitudes, the rift
in the Great Nebula.
No one who survives to speak
new language, has avoided this:
the cutting-away of an old force that held her
rooted to an old ground
the pitch of utter loneliness
where she herself and all creation
seem equally dispersed, weightless, her being a cry
to which no echo comes or can ever come.

But in fact we were always like this,
rootless, dismembered: knowing it makes the difference.
Birth stripped our birthright from us,
tore us from a woman, from women, from ourselves
so early on
and the whole chorus throbbing at our ears
like midges, told us nothing, nothing
of origins, nothing we needed
to know, nothing that could re-member us.

Only: that it is unnatural,
the homesickness for a woman, for ourselves,
for that acute joy at the shadow her head and arms
cast on a wall, her heavy or slender
thighs on which we lay, flesh against flesh,
eyes steady on the face of love; smell of her milk, her sweat,
terror of her disappearance, all fused in this hunger
for the element they have called most dangerous, to be
lifted breathtaken on her breast, to rock within her
—even if beaten back, stranded again, to apprehend
in a sudden brine-clear thought
trembling like the tiny, orbed, endangered
egg-sac of a new world:
This is what she was to me, and this
is how I can love myself—
as only a woman can love me.

Homesick for myself, for her—as, after the heatwave
breaks, the clear tones of the world
manifest: cloud, bough, wall, insect, the very soul of light:
homesick as the fluted vault of desire
articulates itself: *I am the lover and the loved,*
home and wanderer, she who splits
firewood and she who knocks, a stranger
in the storm, two women, eye to eye
measuring each other's spirit, each other's
limitless desire,
a whole new poetry beginning here.

Vision begins to happen in such a life
as if a woman quietly walked away
from the argument and jargon in a room
and sitting down in the kitchen, began turning in her lap
bits of yarn, calico and velvet scraps,
laying them out absently on the scrubbed boards
in the lamplight, with small rainbow-colored shells
sent in cotton-wool from somewhere far away,
and skeins of milkweed from the nearest meadow—
original domestic silk, the finest findings—
and the darkblue petal of the petunia,
and the dry darkbrown lace of seaweed;
not forgotten either, the shed silver
whisker of the cat,
the spiral of paper-wasp-nest curling
beside the finch's yellow feather.
Such a composition has nothing to do with eternity,
the striving for greatness, brilliance—
only with the musing of a mind
one with her body, experienced fingers quietly pushing
dark against bright, silk against roughness,
pulling the tenets of a life together
with no mere will to mastery,
only care for the many-lived, unending
forms in which she finds herself,
becoming now the sherd of broken glass
slicing light in a corner, dangerous
to flesh, now the plentiful, soft leaf
that wrapped round the throbbing finger, soothes the
  wound;
and now the stone foundation, rockshelf further
forming underneath everything that grows.

BRUCE DAWE
(b. 1930)

Born Geelong, Victoria. He attended Northcote High School until he was sixteen, and then worked at many jobs. He served in the RAAF for nine years, and then moved to teach English at Toowoomba.

THE FLASHING OF BADGES

The first thing the dead-beat does
Is flash his badge. . .
                                        If you're in uniform,
I'm an old digger myself, he says. If coming from Mass,
He's Catholic of course and loyal as hell,
While if you're wearing corduroys, carrying books,
He'll grimace towards learning's obscure god,
And—like a child opening its hand revealing
A pet frog for your wonderment—disclose
Literacy squatting somewhere in his family.

Which makes you wish to God he'd only stop
Long enough for you to acknowledge freely
(Via your pocket) the world's rank injustice.
Yet if by such magnanimous means you should
Cut him off halfway through some bleary anecdote,
You do him double harm, since what sustains him
In that Tierra del Fuego which distinguishes

17. Tierra del Fuego: 'Land of Fire', an island at the southern tip of South America, of volcanic origin, but now bleak, cold, windy.

Dignity's southern limits is the faith
That somewhere still, in a sheltered corner of the bleak
Island, in the lee of the storm, it's possible
For a frail personal herb of deception
To take root and survive where awareness shrieks
Nothing but wintry truths from year to year
And value, the essential topsoil, sluices
Seaward with every small indifferent stream.

THE NOT-SO-GOOD EARTH

For a while there we had 25-inch Chinese peasant families
famishing in comfort on the 25-inch screen
and even Uncle Billy whose eyesight's going fast
by hunching up real close to the convex glass
could just about make them out—the riot scene
in the capital city for example
he saw that better than anything, using the contrast knob
to bring them up dark—all those screaming faces
and bodies going under the horses' hooves—he did a terrific job
on that bit, not so successful though
on the quieter parts where they're just starving away
digging for roots in the not-so-good earth
cooking up a mess of old clay
and coming out with all those Confucian analects
to everybody's considerable satisfaction
(if I remember rightly Grandmother dies
with naturally a suspenseful break in the action
for a full symphony orchestra plug for Craven A
neat as a whistle probably damn glad
to be quit of the whole gang with their marvellous patience.)
We never did find out how it finished up... Dad

TITLE: *The Good Earth* by Pearl Buck is the novel upon which the film is based.

at this stage tripped over the main lead in the dark
hauling the whole set down smack on its inscrutable face,
wiping out in a blue flash and curlicue of smoke
600 million Chinese without a trace. . .

HOMECOMING

All day, day after day, they're bringing them home,
they're picking them up, those they can find, and bringing them home,
they're bringing them in, piled on the hulls of Grants, in trucks, in convoys,
they're zipping them up in green plastic bags,
they're tagging them now in Saigon, in the mortuary coolness
they're giving them names, they're rolling them out of
the deep-freeze lockers—on the tarmac at Tan Son Nhut
the noble jets are whining like hounds,
they are bringing them home
—curly-heads, kinky-hairs, crew-cuts, balding non-coms
—they're high, now, high and higher, over the land, the steaming *chow mein*,
their shadows are tracing the blue curve of the Pacific
with sorrowful quick fingers, heading south, heading east,
home, home, home—and the coasts swing upward, the old ridiculous curvatures
of earth, the knuckled hills, the mangrove-swamps, the desert emptiness. . .
in their sterile housing they tilt towards these like skiers
—taxiing in, on the long runways, the howl of their homecoming rises
surrounding them like their last moments (the mash, the splendour)
then fading at length as they move
on to small towns where dogs in the frozen sunset
raise muzzles in mute salute,

and on to cities in whose wide web of suburbs
telegrams tremble like leaves from a wintering tree
and the spider grief swings in his bitter geometry
—they're bringing them home, now, too late, too early.

THE ROCK-THROWER

Out in the suburbs I hear
trains rocketing to impossible destinations
cry out against the intolerable waste,
at 3.40 in the morning hear the dog-frost
bark over the dark back-yards with their young trees
and tubular-steel swings where tomorrow's children
laughingly dangle their stockinged feet already
and the moon coats with white primer
the youthful lawns, the thirtyish expectations.

Midway between the hills and the sea
our house rocks quietly in the flow of time, each morning
we descend to sandy loam, the birds
pipe us ashore, on the rimed grass
someone has left four sets of footprints
as a sign to us that we are not alone
but likely to be visited
at some unearthly hour by a dear friend
who bears a love for us, wax-wrapped and sealed,
sliced, white, starch-reduced . . .

Sometimes I wake at night, thinking:
Even now he may be at work,
the rock-thrower in the neighbouring suburb, turning
the particular street of his choice
back to an earlier settlement—the men armed,
mounting guard, eyeing the mysterious skies,
tasting the salt of siege, the cleansing sacrament
of bombardment, talking in whispers, breaking humbly

the bread of their small fame,
as the planes going north and south
wink conspiratorially overhead
and the stones rain down. . .
And sometimes, too, dieselling homewards
when the bruised blue look of evening
prompts speculations upon the reasons for existence
and sets the apprehensive traveller to fingering thoughtfully
his weekly ticket, when the sun draws its bloody
knuckles back from the teeth of roof-tops
and the wounded commuter limps finally up the cement
path
—I think of the rock-thrower, the glazier's benefactor,
raining down meaning from beyond the subdivisions,
proclaiming the everlasting evangel of vulnerability
—and the suburbs of men shrink to one short street
where voices are calling now from point to point:
'Is that you, Frank?'
'Is that you, Les?'
'Is that you, Harry?'
'See anything?'
'Nup. . .'
'Nup. . .'
'Nup. . .'

DRIFTERS

One day soon he'll tell her it's time to start packing,
and the kids will yell 'Truly?' and get wildly excited for
no reason,
and the brown kelpie pup will start dashing about, tripping
everyone up,
and she'll go out to the vegetable-patch and pick all the
green tomatoes from the vines,
and notice how the oldest girl is close to tears because she
was happy here,
and how the youngest girl is beaming because she wasn't.

And the first thing she'll put on the trailer will be the
  bottling-set she never unpacked from Grovedale,
and when the loaded ute bumps down the drive past the
  blackberry-canes with their last shrivelled fruit,
she won't even ask why they're leaving this time, or where
  they're heading for
—she'll only remember how, when they came here,
she held out her hands bright with berries,
the first of the season, and said:
'Make a wish, Tom, make a wish.'

SUBURBAN LOVERS

Every morning they hold hands
on the fleet diesel that interprets them
like music on a roller-piano as they move
over the rhythmic rails. Her thoughts lie
kitten-curled in his while the slats of living
racket past them, back yards greying
with knowledge, embankments blazoned
with pig-face whose hardihood
be theirs, mantling with pugnacious flowers
stratas of clay, blank sandstone, sustaining them
against years' seepage, rain's intolerance.

Each evening they cross the line
while the boom-gate's slender arms constrain
the lines of waiting cars.
Stars now have flown up out of the east.
They halt at her gate. Next-door's children
scatter past, laughing. They smile. The moon,
calm as a seashore, raises its pale face.
Their hands dance in the breeze blowing
from a hundred perfumed gardens. On the cliff
  of kissing
they know this stillness come down upon them like a cone.
All day it has been suspended there, above their heads.

TED HUGHES
(b. 1930)

Born Yorkshire, England. With Philip Larkin, he is one of the two most prominent poets to emerge in Britain since the Second World War. He was married to Sylvia Plath until her death in 1963.

HAWK ROOSTING

I sit in the top of the wood, my eyes closed.
Inaction, no falsifying dream
Between my hooked head and hooked feet:
Or in sleep rehearse perfect kills and eat.

The convenience of the high trees!
The air's buoyancy and the sun's ray
Are of advantage to me;
And the earth's face upward for my inspection.

My feet are locked upon the rough bark.
It took the whole of Creation
To produce my foot, my each feather:
Now I hold Creation in my foot

Or fly up, and revolve it all slowly—
I kill where I please because it is all mine.
There is no sophistry in my body:
My manners are tearing off heads—

The allotment of death.
For the one path of my flight is direct
Through the bones of the living.
No arguments assert my right:

The sun is behind me.
Nothing has changed since I began.
My eye has permitted no change.
I am going to keep things like this.

THISTLES

Against the rubber tongues of cows and the hoeing hands of men
Thistles spike the summer air
Or crackle open under a blue-black pressure.

Every one a revengeful burst
Of resurrection, a grasped fistful
Of splintered weapons and Icelandic frost thrust up

From the underground stain of a decayed Viking.
They are like pale hair and the gutturals of dialects.
Every one manages a plume of blood.

Then they grow grey, like men.
Mown down, it is a feud. Their sons appear,
Stiff with weapons, fighting back over the same ground.

THRUSHES

Terrifying are the attent sleek thrushes on the lawn,
More coiled steel than living—a poised
Dark deadly eye, those delicate legs
Triggered to stirrings beyond sense—with a start, a bounce, a stab

Overtake the instant and drag out some writhing thing.
No indolent procrastinations and no yawning stares.
No sighs or head-scratchings. Nothing but bounce and stab
And a ravening second.

Is it their single-minded-sized skulls, or a trained
Body, or genius, or a nestful of brats
Gives their days this bullet and automatic
Purpose? Mozart's brain had it, and the shark's mouth
That hungers down the blood-smell even to a leak of its own
Side and devouring of itself: efficiency which
Strikes too streamlined for any doubt to pluck at it
Or obstruction deflect.

With a man it is otherwise. Heroisms on horseback,
Outstripping his desk-diary at a broad desk,
Carving at a tiny ivory ornament
For years: his act worships itself—while for him,
Though he bends to be blent in the prayer, how loud and above what
Furious spaces of fire do the distracting devils
Orgy and hosannah, under what wilderness
Of black silent waters weep.

THE THOUGHT-FOX

I imagine this midnight moment's forest:
Something else is alive
Beside the clock's loneliness
And this blank page where my fingers move.

Through the window I see no star:
Something more near
Though deeper within darkness
Is entering the loneliness:

Cold, delicately as the dark snow
A fox's nose touches twig, leaf;
Two eyes serve a movement, that now
And again now, and now, and now

Sets neat prints into the snow
Between trees, and warily a lame
Shadow lags by stump and in hollow
Of a body that is bold to come

Across clearings, an eye,
A widening deepening greenness,
Brilliantly, concentratedly,
Coming about its own business

Till, with a sudden sharp hot stink of fox
It enters the dark hole of the head.
The window is starless still; the clock ticks,
The page is printed.

WIND

This house has been far out at sea all night,
The woods crashing through darkness, the booming hills,
Winds stampeding the fields under the window
Floundering black astride and blinding wet

Till day rose; then under an orange sky
The hills had new places, and wind wielded
Blade-like, luminous black and emerald,
Flexing like the lens of a mad eye.

At noon I scaled along the house-side as far as
The coal-house door. I dared once to look up—
Through the brunt wind that dented the balls of my eyes
The tent of the hills drummed and strained its guyrope,

The fields quivering, the skyline a grimace,
At any second to bang and vanish with a flap:
The wind flung a magpie away and a black-
Back gull bent like an iron bar slowly. The house

Rang like some fine green goblet in the note
That any second would shatter it. Now deep
In chairs, in front of the great fire, we grip
Our hearts and cannot entertain book, thought,

Or each other. We watch the fire blazing,
And feel the roots of the house move, but sit on,
Seeing the window tremble to come in,
Hearing the stones cry out under the horizons.

SHEEP

I

The sheep has stopped crying,
All morning in her wire-mesh compound
On the lawn, she has been crying
For her vanished lamb. Yesterday they came.
Then her lamb could stand, in a fashion,
And make some tiptoe cringing steps.
Now he has disappeared.
He was only half the proper size.
And his cry was wrong. It was not
A dry little hard bleat, a baby-cry
Over a flat tongue, it was human,
It was a despairing human smooth Oh!
Like no lamb I ever heard. Its hindlegs
Cowered in under its lumped spine,
Its feeble hips leaned towards
Its shoulders for support. Its stubby
White wool pyramid head, on a tottery neck,
Had sad and defeated eyes, pinched, pathetic,

Too small, and it cried all the time
Oh! Oh! staggering towards
Its alert, baffled, stamping, storming mother
Who feared our intentions. He was too weak
To find her teats, or to nuzzle up in under,
He hadn't the gumption. He was fully
Occupied just standing, then shuffling
Towards where she'd removed to. She knew
He wasn't right, she couldn't
Make him out. Then his rough-curl legs,
So stoutly built, and hooved
With real quality tips,
Just got in the way, like a loose bundle
Of firewood he was cursed to manage,
Too heavy for him, lending sometimes
Some support, but no strength, no real help.
When we sat his mother on her tail, he mouthed her teat,
Slobbered a little, but after a minute
Lost aim and interest, his muzzle wandered,
He was managing a difficulty
Much more urgent and important. By evening
He could not stand. It was not
That he could not thrive, he was born
With everything but the will—
That can be deformed, just like a limb.
Death was more interesting to him.
Life could not get his attention.
So he died, with the yellow birth-mucus
Still in his cardigan.
He did not survive a warm summer night.
Now his mother has started crying again.
The wind is oceanic in the elms
And the blossom is all set.

SYLVIA **P**LATH
(1932–1963)

Born Boston, USA. In 1955 she went to Cambridge. She married Ted Hughes in 1956, and they had two children. Most of her best verse was written in a brief period of brilliant intensity. Her death was by suicide. Apart from verse, she also wrote stories and a novel.

MUSHROOMS

Overnight, very
Whitely, discreetly,
Very quietly

Our toes, our noses
Take hold on the loam,
Acquire the air.

Nobody sees us,
Stops us, betrays us;
The small grains make room.

Soft fists insist on
Heaving the needles,
The leafy bedding,

Even the paving.
Our hammers, our rams,
Earless and eyeless,

Perfectly voiceless,
Widen the crannies,
Shoulder through holes. We

Diet on water,
On crumbs of shadow,
Bland-mannered, asking

Little or nothing.
So many of us!
So many of us!

We are shelves, we are
Tables, we are meek,
We are edible,

Nudgers and shovers
In spite of ourselves.
Our kind multiplies:

We shall by morning
Inherit the earth.
Our foot's in the door.

MORNING SONG

Love set you going like a fat gold watch.
The midwife slapped your footsoles, and your bald cry
Took its place among the elements.

Our voices echo, magnifying your arrival. New statue.
In a drafty museum, your nakedness
Shadows our safety. We stand round blankly as walls.

I'm no more your mother
Than the cloud that distils a mirror to reflect its own slow
Effacement at the wind's hand.

All night your moth-breath
Flickers among the flat pink roses. I wake to listen:
A far sea moves in my ear.

One cry, and I stumble from bed, cow-heavy and floral
In my Victorian nightgown.
Your mouth opens clean as a cat's. The window square

Whitens and swallows its dull stars. And now you try
Your handful of notes;
The clear vowels rise like balloons.

THE APPLICANT

First, are you our sort of person?
Do you wear
A glass eye, false teeth or a crutch,
A brace or a hook,
Rubber breasts or a rubber crotch,

Stitches to show something's missing? No, no? Then
How can we give you a thing?
Stop crying.
Open your hand.
Empty? Empty. Here is a hand

To fill it and willing
To bring teacups and roll away headaches
And do whatever you tell it.
Will you marry it?
It is guaranteed

To thumb shut your eyes at the end
And dissolve of sorrow.
We make new stock from the salt.
I notice you are stark naked.
How about this suit—

Black and stiff, but not a bad fit.
Will you marry it?
It is waterproof, shatterproof, proof
Against fire and bombs through the roof.
Believe me, they'll bury you in it.

Now your head, excuse me, is empty.
I have the ticket for that.
Come here, sweetie, out of the closet.
Well, what do you think of *that?*
Naked as paper to start

But in twenty-five years she'll be silver,
In fifty, gold.
A living doll, everywhere you look.
It can sew, it can cook,
It can talk, talk, talk.

It works, there is nothing wrong with it.
You have a hole, it's a poultice.
You have an eye, it's an image.
My boy, it's your last resort.
Will you marry it, marry it, marry it.

THE ARRIVAL OF THE BEE BOX

I ordered this, this clean wood box
Square as a chair and almost too heavy to lift.
I would say it was the coffin of a midget
Or a square baby
Were there not such a din in it.

The box is locked, it is dangerous
I have to live with it overnight
And I can't keep away from it.
There are no windows, so I can't see what is in there.
There is only a little grid, no exit.

I put my eye to the grid.
It is dark, dark,
With the swarmy feeling of African hands
Minute and shrunk for export,
Black on black, angrily clambering.

How can I let them out?
It is the noise that appals me most of all,
The unintelligible syllables.
It is like a Roman mob,
Small, taken one by one, but my god, together!

I lay my ear to furious Latin.
I am not a Caesar.
I have simply ordered a box of maniacs.
They can be sent back.
They can die, I need feed them nothing, I am the owner.

I wonder how hungry they are.
I wonder if they would forget me
If I just undid the locks and stood back and turned
    into a tree.
There is the laburnum, its blond colonnades,
And the petticoats of the cherry.

They might ignore me immediately
In my moon suit and funeral veil.
I am no source of honey
So why should they turn on me?
Tomorrow I will be sweet God, I will set them free.

The box is only temporary.

TULIPS

The tulips are too excitable, it is winter here.
Look how white everything is, how quiet, how snowed-in.
I am learning peacefulness, lying by myself quietly
As the light lies on these white walls, this bed, these hands.
I am nobody; I have nothing to do with explosions.
I have given my name and my day-clothes up to the nurses
And my history to the anesthetist and my body to surgeons.

They have propped my head between the pillow and the sheet-cuff
Like an eye between two white lids that will not shut.
Stupid pupil, it has to take everything in.
The nurses pass and pass, they are no trouble,
They pass the way gulls pass inland in their white caps,
Doing things with their hands, one just the same as another,
So it is impossible to tell how many there are.

My body is a pebble to them, they tend it as water
Tends to the pebbles it must run over, smoothing them gently.
They bring me numbness in their bright needles, they bring me sleep.
Now I have lost myself I am sick of baggage—
My patent leather overnight case like a black pillbox,
My husband and child smiling out of the family photo;
Their smiles catch onto my skin, little smiling hooks.

I have let things slip, a thirty-year-old cargo boat
Stubbornly hanging on to my name and address.
They have swabbed me clear of my loving associations.
Scared and bare on the green plastic-pillowed trolley
I watched my teaset, my bureaus of linen, my books
Sink out of sight, and the water went over my head.
I am a nun now, I have never been so pure.

I didn't want any flowers, I only wanted
To lie with my hands turned up and be utterly empty.
How free it is, you have no idea how free—
The peacefulness is so big it dazes you,
And it asks nothing, a name tag, a few trinkets.

It is what the dead close on, finally; I imagine them
Shutting their mouths on it, like a Communion tablet.

The tulips are too red in the first place, they hurt me.
Even through the gift paper I could hear them breathe
Lightly, through their white swaddlings, like an awful baby.
Their redness talks to my wound, it corresponds.
They are subtle: they seem to float, though they weigh
    me down,
Upsetting me with their sudden tongues and their color,
A dozen red lead sinkers round my neck.

Nobody watched me before, now I am watched.
The tulips turn to me, and the window behind me
Where once a day the light slowly widens and slowly thins,
And I see myself, flat, ridiculous, a cut-paper shadow
Between the eye of the sun and the eyes of the tulips,
And I have no face, I have wanted to efface myself.
The vivid tulips eat my oxygen.

Before they came the air was calm enough,
Coming and going, breath by breath, without any fuss.
Then the tulips filled it up like a loud noise.
Now the air snags and eddies round them the way a river
Snags and eddies round a sunken rust-red engine.
They concentrate my attention, that was happy
Playing and resting without committing itself.

The walls, also, seem to be warming themselves.
The tulips should be behind bars like dangerous animals;
They are opening like the mouth of some great African cat,
And I am aware of my heart: it opens and closes
Its bowl of red blooms out of sheer love of me.
The water I taste is warm and salt, like the sea,
And comes from a country far away as health.

THE MUNICH MANNEQUINS

Perfection is terrible, it cannot have children.
Cold as snow breath, it tamps the womb

Where the yew trees blow like hydras,
The tree of life and the tree of life

Unloosing their moons, month after month,
  to no purpose.
The blood flood is the flood of love,

The absolute sacrifice.
It means: no more idols but me,

Me and you.
So, in their sulphur loveliness, in their smiles

These mannequins lean tonight
In Munich, morgue between Paris and Rome,

Naked and bald in their furs,
Orange lollies on silver sticks,

Intolerable, without mind.
The snow drops its pieces of darkness,

Nobody's about. In the hotels
Hands will be opening doors and setting

Down shoes for a polish of carbon
Into which broad toes will go tomorrow.

O the domesticity of these windows,
The baby lace, the green-leaved confectionery,

The thick Germans slumbering in their bottomless
  Stolz.
And the black phones on hooks

Glittering
Glittering and digesting

Voicelessness. The snow has no voice.

KINDNESS

Kindness glides about my house.
Dame Kindness, she is so nice!
The blue and red jewels of her rings smoke
In the windows, the mirrors
Are filling with smiles.

What is so real as the cry of a child?
A rabbit's cry may be wilder
But it has no soul.
Sugar can cure everything, so Kindness says.
Sugar is a necessary fluid,

Its crystals a little poultice.
O kindness, kindness
Sweetly picking up pieces!
My Japanese silks, desperate butterflies,
May be pinned any minute, anaesthetized.

And here you come, with a cup of tea
Wreathed in steam.
The blood jet is poetry,
There is no stopping it.
You hand me two children, two roses.

EDGE

The woman is perfected.
Her dead

Body wears the smile of accomplishment,
The illusion of a Greek necessity

Flows in the scrolls of her toga,
Her bare

Feet seem to be saying:
We have come so far, it is over.

Each dead child coiled, a white serpent,
One at each little

Pitcher of milk, now empty.
She has folded

Them back into her body as petals
Of a rose close when the garden

Stiffens and odours bleed
From the sweet, deep throats of the night flower.

The moon has nothing to be sad about,
Staring from her hood of bone.

She is used to this sort of thing.
Her blacks crackle and drag.

FAY ZWICKY
(b. 1933)

Born in Melbourne, she has been a concert pianist, then lectured in literature at the University of Western Australia. She is now a freelance writer.

TO A SEA-HORSE

The male has a pouch on the underside of the tail into which the female injects the eggs. When the eggs hatch it looks as if the male is giving birth to the young. Even after hatching, the young remain near the father, darting back into his pouch if danger threatens.

Wall-eyed snouter, sweet feeble translucent
Tiny eunuch teetering on your rocker,
Pouting, corseted in
Rings of bone, flesh flaps
Fanning the tides as you totter and roll
Forward, but never so forward as
She.
Flex your pipes for the winter.
Keep an upright house.
Pucker piped lips for her, flex,
Flex your rings, flash your fin
If you can, man. Watch it!
Your love's bearing down with
Transparent efficiency, that
Abrasive lady's been starching her
Dorsal for meeting, nudges
Neatly your ring-tailed poise;
Totter and flex, finny vibrato for
Sex (can't afford to go off your
Rocker at this stage),
FLEX!
Chess knights collide:
A shuddering pouchful of eggs.
Nuzzle your snouters, sweet
Sons and daughters, tip to

Your tiny transparencies,
Hatched in your warmth,
Flexed in your strength.
They'd be mad to trust women
After this.

LEAR, CLASS '71

Trendy misses
In your gypsy dresses
Combing down your
Images of death,
Today's theme is
Renunciation:
Violets dwindle
On your breath,
Sunlight lilts upon
Your hair. *Look, will*
You a moment at the
Sequence of suffering . . .
Have you, Miss Hardcastle,
Another word for it?
Avoid it, then, by
All means—the
Rest of you
Take
Note.
Miss Hardcastle's father,
Bauxite magnate, knows
Never to give away:
(a) lands
(b) knights
(c) retainers for:
To be powerless
Invites
Attack.
He countenanced violence
In the nursery; Miss
Hardcastle orders her fear
With a moral, and young

Mr Middleton there, wandering
In the meadows of her hair
Yields to
Formal justice.
As they (and you) grow older
Your teachers will become
Somewhat evasive
On the subject, resort to
Delicate stratagems
To give the iron ball a miss,
To skip the rack, to pare
The teeth of:
Serpent
Vulture
Tiger
Bear
Wolf
Kite and,
Need I remind you,
Dog, coiled
In the obedient mind,
Images merely.
"Microcosm of the Human Race"—
Regrettable overstatement but
One suggestive of profound
Truth to be:
Defined
Analysed
Expanded
Qualified
For next
Week.
To suffer ripeness,
If it come,
Extends at present
Beyond the bounds of
Your curriculum and
The Administration
Chooses to
Grant us
No Extension.

SUMMER POGROM

Spade-bearded Grandfather, squat Lenin
In the snows of Donna Buang.
Your bicycle a wiry crutch, nomadic homburg
Alien, black, correct. Beneath, the curt defiant
Filamented eye. Does it count the dead
Between the Cossack horses' legs in Kovno?

Those dead who sleep in me, me dry
In a garden veiled with myrtle and oleander,
Desert snows that powder memory's track
Scoured by burning winds from eastern rocks,
Flushing the lobes of mind,
Fat white dormant flowrets.

Aggressive under dappled shade, girl in a glove;
Collins street in autumn,
Mirage of clattering crowds: Why don't you speak English?
I don't understand, *I don't understand!*
Sei nicht so ein Dummerchen, nobody cares.
Not for you the upreared hooves of Nikolai,
Eat your icecream, Kleine, *may his soul rot*,
These are good days.

Flared candles; the gift of children; love,
Need fulfilled, a name it has to have—how else to feel?
A radiance in the garden, the Electrolux man chats,
Cosy spectre of the afternoon's decay.
My eye his eye, the snows of Kovno cover us.
Is that my son bloodied against Isaac the Baker's door?

The tepid river's edge, reeds creak, rats' nests fold and
quiver,
My feet sink in sand; the children splash and call, sleek
Little satyrs diamond-eyed reined to summer's roundabout,
Hiding from me. Must I excavate you,
Agents of my death? Hushed snows are deep, the
Dead lie deep in me.

JACK FROST

To sit upon her belly warm
Jack Frost has come.
His cold sweet weight
Does not alarm the night
Or shake belief.

Too cold to ache
She parts her leaves
And welcomes thrust of snow
And stretches fingers past all pain
To stroke the teasing foe.

The cold creeps on
The buds unfold and burn
Her into night. Traversed
She lies and powerless to
Thaw the subtle guest.

from ARK VOICES

1. MRS NOAH SPEAKS

Lord, the cleaning's nothing.
What's a pen or two?
Even if the tapir's urine
Takes the paint clean off
There's nothing easier.

But sir, the care!

I used to dream perpetually
About a boat I had to push
(yes, *push*) through a stony town
without water
There was no river and no sea and yet
I pushed a boat against a tide.
It wouldn't float although I pulled and
hauled, my flesh eddying,
drifting with the strain of it.
Is *this* a dream?
Fibre my blood, sir.

The speckled pigeon and the tawny owl
swoop by
They coax me to the edge.

To save to save merely—no matter
what or whom—to save.

Sweep and push of waves against the sides.
Our raft is delicate and our fire
turns wood to ashes.

He takes it well
and Shem and Ham do help—you can't expect
too much of anyone can you and
Japhet's still a kid. Their wives are
young and tremble in the rain
their wits astray.
As soon as we're born
we're all astray—at least
you seem to think it's so or else
why this?

I know you promised us a landing but
what a price!
We're dashed from side to side
we strike through spray
the foam blinds Noah till he
cannot steer.
Even the mightiest creature cowers in his
stall panting, snorting in the welter,
bursting prayers upon your path
of righteousness.

Comfort enough I'm not.
To feed and clothe, to bind a scratch I can.

We once moved quiet in our lives
Looked steadily ahead. When I was small
there were no roads across the mountains
no boats or bridges over water.
We farmed, live simple, circumscribed.

Our birds and beasts delivered their young
in peace. The trees grew tall and now and
then I pocketed a speckled egg, could climb
and peer into the nests of starlings.
Height and blossom.
Then we lived neighbourly with our birds.
Creation, your handiwork, was one.
No good and bad—just men and women.
But with your sages came the rub.
                                        We tripped
over our charity. Duty-fettered, love
tumbled like a lightning-stricken tower.

Noah is incorruptible and good, a large
sweet soul.
Sir, I have tried to be!
But does the frog whose home was in a well
assail an ocean?
How does the summer gnat approach the ice?
The flood in which you throne us is to the
universe a puddle in a marsh.
                                        Of all the myriad
creatures you have made, man is but one, the
merest tip of hair upon a stallion's rump.

Noah looks into space.
He sees the small as small
The great as great.
He sees, goes fearless at the sight.
I see the small as too little
the great as too much.
Does this diminish me?

He looks back to the past
grieves not over what is distant.
I mourn the wrack, the rock under the
blue sea, our old wound, the
dismantling storm and cannot
thank you.
                    Helpless with what I am
what can I do? This pitted flesh and

madness in my heart, rage at my fear
of you. Am I thus harmless?

Strangers in this ark, this one small 'Yes'
afloat on a vast "No", your watery negative.

Noah stares impassive through the foam.
I trust in him although our woe, the
trap of my young body, cracked his trust
in me.
            I bend but do not break under your
chilling stars.

Even the wolves, the tigers must be fed
in these deep-laden waters. Else we are
all drowned bones.
                    Intercede with him
for me, speechless and unspoken to, the
comic keeper of his house.
My sons are fraught with wives, have
waded into deep waters.
A full ship and homeward bound—Yes,
I'm just about to lance the horse's leg.
A large sweet soul and incorruptible
I said. Or have I seen the great as
too much yet again?
                    The speckled pigeon
and the tawny owl have drawn me to the edge.
The drowned folk call to me:
Deliver us from harm!

Deliver, sir, deliver them
and all of us...

TIANANMEN SQUARE JUNE 4, 1989

Karl Marx, take your time,
looming over Highgate on your plinth.
Snow's falling on your beard,

exiled, huge, hairy, genderless.
Terminally angry, piss-poor,
stuffed on utopias and cold,
cold as iron.

I'm thinking of your loving wife,
your desperate children and your grandchild
dead behind the barred enclosure of your brain.
Men's ideas the product, not the cause
of history, you said?

The snow has killed the lilacs.
Whose idea?
The air is frozen with theory.

What can the man be doing all day
in that cold place?
What can he be writing?
What can he be reading?
What big eyes you have, mama!
Next year, child, we will eat.

I'm thinking of my middle-class German grandmother
soft as a pigeon, who wept
when Chamberlain declared a war.
Why are you crying, grandma?
It's only the big bad wolf, my dear.
It's only a story.

There's no end to it.
The wolves have come again.
What shall I tell my grandchildren?

No end to the requiems, the burning trains,
the guns, the shouting in the streets,
the outraged stars, the anguished face
of terror under ragged headbands
soaked in death's calligraphy.

Don't turn your back, I'll say.
Look hard.

Move into that frozen swarming screen.
How far can you run with a bullet in your brain?

And forgive, if you can, the safety of a poem
sharpened on a grieving night.

A story has to start somewhere.

SOUP AND JELLY

"Feed Fred and sit with him
and mind he doesn't walk about.
He falls. Tell him his ute is safe
back home. Thinks someone's pinched it,
peers around the carpark all the time.
His family brought him in it and
he thinks it's gone.
He was a farmer once . . ."

I take the tray. The ice-cream's almost
melted round the crumbled orange jelly
and the soup's too hot. I know
I'll have to blow on it.

Hunched, trapped behind a tray,
he glances sideways, face as brown
and caverned as the land itself,
long thin lips droop ironic
at the corners, gaunt nose.
The blue and white pyjamas cage
the restless rangy legs.
In and out they go, the feet
in cotton socks feeling for the ground.

"Are you a foreigner?"
"Not exactly. Just a little sunburnt,"
and I put the jelly down. I mustn't feel
a thing: my smile has come unstuck.
I place a paper napkin on his lap. He winces.

"You're a foreigner all right," he says.
"OK," I say. What's one displacement more or less,
wishing I were a hearty flat-faced Fenian
with a perm and nothing doing in the belfry.
Someone like his mother. Or a wife who
spared him the sorrow of himself.
Now he grabs the spoon. "I'll do it."
"Right," I say, "You go ahead. Just ask me
if you want some help." The tone's not right.
I watch the trembling progress of the spoon
for what seems years, paralysed with pity
for his pride.

How does a dark-faced woman give a man called Fred
who cropped a farm and drove a battered ute
a meal of soup and jelly?

Outside the window, clouds are swelling
into growing darkness and there's a man
hard on his knees planting something in the rain.

LETTING GO

Tell the truth of experience
they say they also
say you must let
go learn to let go
let your children
go

and they go
and you stay
letting them go
because you are obedient and
respect everyone's freedom
to go and you stay

and you want to tell the truth
because you are yours truly

its obedient servant
but you can't because
you're feeling what you're not
supposed to feel you have
let them go and go and

you can't say what you feel
because they might read
this poem and feel guilty
and some post-modern hack
will back them up
and make you feel guilty
and stop feeling which is
post-modern and what
you're meant to feel

so you don't write a poem
you line up words in prose
inside a journal trapped
like a scorpion in a locked
drawer to be opened by
your children let go
after lived life and all the time
a great wave bursting
howls and rears and

you have to let go
or you're gone you're
gone gasping you
let go
till the next wave
towers crumbles
shreds you to lace—

When you wake
your spine is twisted
like a sea-bird
inspecting the sky,
stripped by lightning.

JUDITH RODRIGUEZ
(b. 1936)

Born in Perth, raised in Brisbane, she has taught literature in Jamaica, London, and Australia.

NU-PLASTIK FANFARE RED

I declare myself:
I am painting my room red.
Because they haven't any
flat red suitable for interiors,
because their acres of colour-card
are snowy with daylight only,
because it will look like Danger! Explosives,
or would you prefer a basement cabaret?
a decent home where Italians moved in,
Como perhaps (yes, I've gilded the mirror)
or simply infernal—

I rejoice to be doing it
with quick-drying plastic,
for small area decoration.
I tear at the wall, brush speeding:
let's expand this limited stuff!
It dries impetuously in patches,
I at edges too late scrub; this is a fight.
I sought the conditions,
and the unbroken wall is yet to come.
Clear stretches screech into clots,
streak into smokiness.

Botched job this, my instant
hell! and no re-sale value, Dad;
cliché too. Well, too bad.
It's satisfying to note
this mix is right for pottery.
Good glad shock of seeing
that red-figure vases *are*.
Not 4th-edition-earthy, but stab-colour,
new vine, red-Attis-flower, the full howl.
My inward amphora!

Even thus shyly to surface:
up we go red, flag-balloon,
broomstick-rocket!
Brandishing blood and fire, pumping
lungs external as leaves!
This is a red land, sour
with blood it has not shed,
money not lost, risks evaded,
blood it has forgotten, dried
in furnace airs that vainly
figure (since mines are doing well)
the fire. Torpor
of a disallowed abortion.

Why not a red room?

LES MURRAY
(b. 1938)

Born Bunya, NSW. For a time he worked as a translator at the Australian National University. He is now a full-time writer and lives in the country in NSW.

THE BALLAD OF JIMMY GOVERNOR

H.M. PRISON, DARLINGHURST, 18TH JANUARY 1901

You can send for my breakfast now, Governor.
The colt from Black Velvet's awake
and the ladies all down from the country
are gathered outside for my sake.

Soon be all finished, the running.
No tracks of mine lead out of here.
Today, I take that big step
on the bottom rung of the air
and be in Heaven for dinner.
Might be the first jimbera there.

The Old People don't go to Heaven,
good thing. My mother might meet
that stockman feller my father
and him cut her dead in the street.
Mother, today I'll be dancing
your way and his way on numb feet.

10. jimbera: half-caste Aboriginal.

But a man's not a rag to wipe snot on,
I got that much into their heads,
them hard white sunbonnet ladies
that turned up their short lips and said
my wife had a slut's eye for colour.
I got that into their head

and the cow-cockies' kids plant up chimneys
they got horse soldiers out with the Law
after Joe and lame Jack and tan Jimmy—
but who learnt us how to make war
on women, old men, babies?
It ain't all one way any more.

The papers, they call us bushrangers:
That would be our style, I daresay,
bushrangers on foot with our axes.
It sweetens the truth, anyway.
They don't like us killing their women.
Their women kill us every day.

And the squatters are peeing their moleskins,
that's more than a calf in the wheat,
it's Jimmy the fencer, running
along the top rail in the night,
it's the Breelong mob crossing the ranges
with rabbitskins soft on their feet.

*

But now Jack in his Empire brickyard
has already give back his shoes
and entered the cleanliness kingdom,
the Commonwealth drums through the walls
and I'm weary of news.

I'm sorry, old Jack, I discharged you,
you might have enjoyed running free
of plonk and wet cornbags and colour
with us pair of outlaws. But see,

you can't trust even half a whitefeller.
You died of White Lady through me.

They tried me once running, once standing:
one time ought to do for the drop.
It's more trial than you got, I hear, Joe,
your tommyhawk's chipped her last chop.
I hope you don't mind I got lazy
when the leaks in my back made me stop.

If any gin stands in my print
I'll give her womb sorrow and dread,
if a buck finds our shape in the tussocks
I'll whiten the hair in his head,
but a man's not a rag to wipe boots on
and I got that wrote up, bright red,

where even fine ladies can read it
who never look at the ground
for a man that ain't fit to breed from
may make a terrible bound
before the knacker's knife gets him.
Good night to you, father. Sleep sound.

Fetch in my breakfast, Governor,
I have my journey to make
and the ladies all down from the country
are howling outside for my sake.

AN ABSOLUTELY ORDINARY RAINBOW

The word goes round Repins, the murmur goes round
  Lorenzinis,
At Tattersalls, men look up from sheets of numbers,
The Stock Exchange scribblers forget the chalk in their hands

51. White Lady: methylated spitits and powdered milk.

And men with bread in their pockets leave thc Greek Club:
There's a fellow crying in Martin Place. They can't stop him.

The traffic in George Street is banked up for half a mile
And drained of motion. The crowds are edgy with talk
And more crowds come hurrying. Many run in the
back streets
Which minutes ago were busy main streets, pointing:
There's a fellow weeping down there. No one can
stop him.

The man we surround, the man no one approaches
Simply weeps, and does not cover it, weeps
Not like a child, not like the wind, like a man
And does not declaim it, nor beat his breast, nor even
Sob very loudly—yet dignity of his weeping

Holds us back from his space, the hollow he makes
about him
In the midday light, in his pentagram of sorrow,
And uniforms back in the crowd who tried to seize him
Stare out at him, and feel, with amazement, their minds
Longing for tears as children for a rainbow.

Some will say, in the years to come, a halo
Or force stood around him. There is no such thing.
Some will say they were shocked and would have
stopped him
But they will not have been there. The fiercest manhood,
The toughest reserve, the slickest wit amongst us

Trembles with silence, and burns with unexpected
Judgements of peace. Some in the concourse scream
Who thought themselves happy. Only the smallest children
And such as look out of Paradise come near him
And sit at his feet, with dogs and dusty pigeons.

Ridiculous, says a man near me, and stops
His mouth with his hands, as if it uttered vomit—

And I see a woman, shining, stretch her hand
And shake as she receives the gift of weeping;
As many as follow her also receive it

And many weep for sheer acceptance, and more
Refuse to weep for fear of all acceptance,
But the weeping man, like the earth, requires nothing,
The man who weeps ignores us, and cries out
Of his writhen face and ordinary body

Not words, but grief, not messages, but sorrow
Hard as the earth, sheer, present as the sea—
And when he stops, he simply walks between us
Mopping his face with the dignity of one
Man who has wept, and now has finished weeping.

Evading believers, he hurries off down Pitt Street.

THE CONQUEST

Phillip was a kindly, rational man:
Friendship and Trust will win the natives, Sir.
Such was the deck the Governor walked upon.

One deck below, lieutenants hawked and spat.
One level lower, and dank nightmares grew.
Small floating Englands where our world began.

⋆

And what was trust when the harsh dead swarmed ashore
and warriors, trembling, watched the utterly strange
hard clouds, dawn beings, down there where time began,

so alien the eye could barely fix
blue parrot-figures wrecking the light with change,
man-shapes digging where no yam roots were?

⋆

The Governor proffers cloth and English words,
the tribesmen defy him in good Dhuruwal.
Marines stand firm, known warriors bite their beards.

Glass beads are scattered in that gulf of style
but pickpockets squeal, clubbed in imagination
as naked Indians circle them like birds.

*

They won't Respond. They threaten us. Drive them off.
In genuine grief, the Governor turns away.
Blowflies form trinkets for a harsher grief.

As the sickness of the earth bites into flesh
trees moan like women, striplings collapse like trees—
fever of Portsmouth hulks, the Deptford cough.

*

It makes dogs furtive, what they find to eat
but the noonday forest will not feed white men.
Capture some Natives, quick. Much may be learned

indeed, on both Sides. Sir! And Phillip smiles.
Two live to tell the back lanes of his smile
and the food ships come, and the barracks rise as planned.

*

And once again the Governor goes around
with his Amity. The yeasts of reason work,
triangle screams confirm the widening ground.

No one records what month the first striped men
mounted a clawing child, then slit her throat
but the spear hits Phillip with a desperate sound.

*

The thoughtful savage with Athenian flanks
fades from the old books here. The sketchers draw
pipe-smoking cretins jigging on thin shanks

poor for the first time, learning the Crown Lands tune.
The age of unnoticed languages begins
and Phillip, recovering, gives a nodded thanks.

McEntire speared! My personal huntsman, Speared!
Ten Heads for this, and two alive to hang!
A brave lieutenant cools it, bid by bid,

to a decent six. The punitive squads march off
without result, but this quandong of wrath
ferments in slaughters for a hundred years.

*

They couldn't tell us how to farm their skin.
They camped with dogs in the rift glens of our mind
till their old men mumbled who the stars had been.

They had the noon trees' spiritual walk.
Pathetic with sores, they could be suddenly not,
the low horizon strangely concealing them.

*

A few still hunt way out beyond philosophy
where nothing is sacred till it is your flesh
and the leaves, the creeks shine through their poverty

or so we hope. We make our conquests, too.
The ruins at our feet are hard to see.
For all the generous Governor tried to do

the planet he had touched began to melt
though he used much Reason; and foreshadowed more
before he recoiled into his century.

THE DOORMAN

The man applying rules to keep me out
knows if I have to deal with him the rules
apply to me. I am to be kept out.
Naive to think that he respects the rules;
he knows their purpose. Complicity is out:
if I were his sort I would know the rules.

His genes have seeped down a hundred centuries;
in a slave-ship's hold they pooled to form his eyes,
on a Sunday school mop they collected to a face
and they formed a skin in the dry air of a palace.
In stripes, in armour, in pinstripes, he stays the same man
and I know his sister, that right-thinking woman.

He is a craftsman, and these are his tools:
unyielding correctness, thin mouth, a nose for clout,
modulations of boredom (let the blusterers threaten).
He guards the status quo as he guards mankind's salvations
and those he protects need never learn the rules:
his contempt is reserved for those who are In, and Out.

THE BROAD BEAN SERMON

Beanstalks, in any breeze, are a slack church parade
without belief, saying *trespass against us* in unison,
recruits in mint Air Force dacron, with unbuttoned leaves.

Upright with water like men, square in stem-section
they grow to great lengths, drink rain, keel over all ways,
kink down and grow up afresh, with proffered new greenstuff.

Above the cat-and-mouse floor of a thin bean forest
snails hang rapt in their food, ants hurry through several dimensions,
spiders tense and sag like little black flags in their cordage.

Going out to pick beans with the sun high as fence-tops, you find
plenty, and fetch them. An hour or a cloud later
you find shirtfulls more. At every hour of daylight

appear more that you missed: ripe, knobbly ones, fleshy-sided,
thin-straight, thin-crescent, frown-shaped, bird-shouldered,
  boat-keeled ones,
beans knuckled and single-bulged, minute green dolphins
  at suck,

beans upright like lecturing, outstretched like blessing fingers
in the incident light, and more still, oblique to your notice
that the noon glare or cloud-light or afternoon slants will
  uncover

till you ask yourself Could I have overlooked so many, or
do they form in an hour? unfolding into reality
like templates for subtly broad grins, like unique caught
  expressions,

like edible meanings, each sealed around with a string
and affixed to its moment, an unceasing colloquial assembly,
the portly, the stiff, and those lolling in pointed green
  slippers....

Wondering who'll take the spare bagfulls, you grin with
  happiness
—it is your health—you vow to pick them all
even the last few, weeks off yet, misshapen as toes.

SEAMUS HEANEY
(b. 1939)

Born in Northern Ireland. Raised on a farm in Londonderry, he attended university in Belfast, and became a teacher. A Catholic, he moved to live in Eire in 1972. He was awarded the Nobel Prize for Literature in 1995.

DIGGING

Between my finger and my thumb
The squat pen rests; snug as a gun.

Under my window, a clean rasping sound
When the spade sinks into gravelly ground;
My father, digging, I look down

Till his straining rump among the flowerbeds
Bends low, comes up twenty years away
Stooping in rhythm through potato drills
Where he was digging.

The coarse boot nestled on the lug, the shaft
Against the inside knee was levered firmly.
He rooted out tall tops, buried the bright edge deep
To scatter new potatoes that we picked
Loving their cool hardness in our hands.

By God, the old man could handle a spade.
Just like his old man.

My grandfather cut more turf in a day
Than any other man on Toner's bog.
Once I carried him milk in a bottle
Corked sloppily with paper. He straightened up
To drink, then fell to right away

Nicking and slicing neatly, heaving sods
Over his shoulder, going down and down
For the good turf. Digging.

The cold smell of potato mould, the squelch and slap
Of soggy peat, the curt cuts of an edge
Through living roots awaken in my head.
But I've no spade to follow men like them.

Between my finger and my thumb
The squat pen rests.
I'll dig with it.

BLACKBERRY PICKING

(FOR PHILIP HOBSBAUM)

Late August, given heavy rain and sun
For a full week, the blackberries would ripen.
At first, just one, a glossy purple clot
Among others, red, green, hard as a knot.
You ate that first one and its flesh was sweet
Like thickened wine: summer's blood was in it
Leaving stains upon the tongue and lust for
Picking. Then red ones inked up and that hunger
Sent us out with milk-cans, pea-tins, jam-pots
Where briars scratched and wet grass bleached
    our boots.
Round hayfields, cornfields and potato-drills

We trekked and picked until the cans were full,
Until the tinkling bottom had been covered
With green ones, and on top big dark blobs burned
Like a plate of eyes. Our hands were peppered
With thorn pricks, our palms sticky as Bluebeard's.
We hoarded the fresh berries in the byre.
But when the bath was filled we found a fur,
A rat-grey fungus, glutting on our cache.
The juice was stinking too. Once off the bush
The fruit fermented, the sweet flesh would turn sour.
I always felt like crying. It wasn't fair
That all the lovely canfuls smelt of rot.
Each year I hoped they'd keep, knew they would not.

UNDINE

He slashed the briars, shovelled up grey silt
To give me right of way in my own drains
And I ran quick for him, cleaned out my rust.

He halted, saw me finally disrobed,
Running clear, with apparent unconcern.
Then he walked by me. I rippled and I churned

Where ditches intersected near the river
Until he dug a spade deep in my flank
And took me to him. I swallowed his trench

Gratefully, dispersing myself for love
Down in his roots, climbing his brassy grain—
But once he knew my welcome, I alone

Could give him subtle increase and reflection.
He explored me so completely, each limb
Lost its cold freedom. Human, warmed to him.

TITLE: Female water sprite.

THE TOLLUND MAN

I

Some day I will go to Aarhus
To see his peat-brown head,
The mild pods of his eye-lids,
His pointed skin cap.

In the flat country nearby
Where they dug him out,
His last gruel of winter seeds
Caked in his stomach,

Naked except for
The cap, noose and girdle,
I will stand a long time.
Bridegroom to the goddess,

She tightened her torc on him
And opened her fen,
Those dark juices working
Him to a saint's kept body,

Trove of the turfcutter's
Honeycombed workings.
Now his stained face
Reposes at Aarhus.

II

I could risk blasphemy,
Consecrate the cauldron bog
Our holy ground and pray
Him to make germinate

TITLE: Discovered by peat diggers at Tollund in Jutland, part of Denmark, in 1950, his body had been preserved in the peat bog for about two thousand years. He was probably a sacrifice to the Earth Goddess at the conclusion of Spring Festival ceremonies.

The scattered, ambushed
Flesh of labourers,
Stockinged corpses
Laid out in the farmyards,

Tell-tale skin and teeth
Flecking the sleepers
Of four young brothers, trailed
For miles along the lines.

III

Something of his sad freedom
a cart As he rode the tumbril▲
Should come to me, driving,
Saying the names

Tollund, Grauballe, Nebelgard,
Watching the pointing hands
Of country people,
Not knowing their tongue.

Out there in Jutland
In the old man-killing parishes
I will feel lost,
Unhappy and at home.

THE GRAUBALLE MAN

As if he had been poured
in tar, he lies
on a pillow of turf
and seems to weep

37. Grauballe, Nebelgard: near Tollund and also sites of discoveries of long-preserved bodies of victims of ritual killings.

the black river of himself.
The grain of his wrists
is like bog oak,
the ball of his heel

like a basalt egg.
His instep has shrunk
cold as a swan's foot
or a wet swamp root.

His hips are the ridge
and purse of a mussel,
his spine an eel arrested
under a glisten of mud.

The head lifts,
the chin is a visor
raised above the vent
of his slashed throat

that has tanned and toughened.
The cured wound
opens inwards to a dark
elderberry place.

Who will say 'corpse'
to his vivid cast?
Who will say 'body'
to his opaque repose?

And his rusted hair,
a mat unlikely
as a foetus's.
I first saw his twisted face

in a photograph,
a head and shoulder
out of the peat,
bruised like a forceps baby,

but now he lies
perfected in my memory,
down to the red horn
of his nails,

hung in the scales
with beauty and atrocity:
with the Dying Gaul
too strictly compassed

on his shield,
with the actual weight
of each hooded victim,
slashed and dumped.

PUNISHMENT

I can feel the tug
of the halter at the nape
of her neck, the wind
on her naked front.

It blows her nipples
to amber beads,
it shakes the frail rigging
of her ribs.

I can see her drowned
body in the bog,
the weighing stone,
the floating rods and boughs.

Under which at first
she was a barked sapling
that is dug up
oak-bone, brain-firkin:

her shaved head
like a stubble of black corn,
her blindfold a soiled bandage,
her noose a ring

to store
the memories of love.
Little adulteress,
before they punished you

you were flaxen-haired,
undernourished, and your
tar-black face was beautiful.
My poor scapegoat,

I almost love you
but would have cast, I know,
the stones of silence.
I am the artful voyeur

of your brain's exposed
and darkened combs,
your muscles' webbing
and all your numbered bones:

I who have stood dumb
when your betraying sisters,
cauled in tar,
wept by the railings,

who would connive
in civilized outrage
yet understand the exact
and tribal, intimate revenge.

16. A firkin is a small container. Brain-firken i.e. skull.

THATCHER

Bespoke for weeks, he turned up some morning
Unexpectedly, his bicycle slung
With a light ladder and a bag of knives.
He eyed the old rigging, poked at the eaves,

Opened and handled sheaves of lashed wheat-straw.
Next, the bundled rods: hazel and willow
Were flicked for weight, twisted in case they'd snap.
It seemed he spent the morning warming up:

Then fixed the ladder, laid out well-honed blades
And snipped at straw and sharpened ends of rods
That, bent in two, made a white-pronged staple
For pinning down his world, handful by handful.

Couchant for days on sods above the rafters,
He shaved and flushed the butts, stitched all together
Into a sloped honeycomb, a stubble patch,
And left them gaping at his Midas touch.

THE BARN

Threshed corn lay piled like grit of ivory
Or solid as cement in two-lugged sacks.
The musty dark hoarded an armoury
Of farmyard implements, harness, plough-socks.

The floor was mouse-grey, smooth, chilly concrete.
There were no windows, just two narrow shafts
Of gilded motes, crossing, from air-holes slit
High in each gable. The one door meant no draughts

1. THATCHER Bespoke: reserved, booked for a particular day.

All summer when the zinc burned like an oven.
A scythe's edge, a clean spade, a pitch-fork's prongs:
Slowly bright objects formed when you went in.
Then you felt cobwebs clogging up your lungs

And scuttled fast into the sunlit yard.
And into nights when bats were on the wing
Over the rafters of sleep, where bright eyes stared
From piles of grain in corners, fierce, unblinking.

The dark gulfed like a roof-space. I was chaff
To be pecked up when birds shot through the air-slits.
I lay face-down to shun the fear above.
The two-lugged sacks moved in like great blind rats.

CASUALTY

I

He would drink by himself
And raise a weathered thumb
Towards the high shelf,
Calling another rum
And blackcurrant, without
Having to raise his voice,
Or order a quick stout
By a lifting of the eyes
And a discreet dumb-show
Of pulling off the top;
At closing time would go
In waders and peaked cap
Into the showery dark,
A dole-kept breadwinner
But a natural for work.
I loved his whole manner,
Sure-footed but too sly,
His deadpan sidling tact,
His fisherman's quick eye
And turned observant back.

Incomprehensible
To him, my other life.
Sometimes, on his high stool,
Too busy with his knife
At a tobacco plug
And not meeting my eye,
In the pause after a slug
He mentioned poetry.
We would be on our own
And, always politic
And shy of condescension,
I would manage by some trick
To switch the talk to eels
Or lore of the horse and cart
Or the Provisionals▲.

Provisional Irish Republican Army

But my tentative art
His turned back watches too:
He was blown to bits
Out drinking in a curfew
Others obeyed, three nights
After they shot dead
The thirteen men in Derry.
PARAS▲ THIRTEEN, the walls said,
BOGSIDE NIL. That Wednesday
Everybody held
His breath and trembled.

Paramilitary forces

II

It was a day of cold
Raw silence, wind-blown
Surplice and soutane:
Rained-on, flower-laden
Coffin after coffin
Seemed to float from the door
Of the packed cathedral

42. Derry: thus called by Irish nationalists; called Londonderry by those who support union with the United Kingdom.
44. Bogside: a part of Derry with republican allegiance.

Like blossoms on slow water.
The common funeral
Unrolled its swaddling band,
Lapping, tightening
Till we were braced and bound
Like brothers in a ring.

But he would not be held
At home by his own crowd
Whatever threats were phoned,
Whatever black flags waved.
I see him as he turned
In that bombed offending place,
Remorse fused with terror
In his still knowable face,
His cornered outfaced stare
Blinding in the flash.

He had gone miles away
For he drank like a fish
Nightly, naturally
Swimming towards the lure
Of warm lit-up places,
The blurred mesh and murmur

Drifting among glasses
In the gregarious smoke.
How culpable was he
That last night when he broke
Our tribe's complicity?
'Now you're supposed to be
An educated man,'
I hear him say. 'Puzzle me
The right answer to that one.'

III

I missed his funeral,
Those quiet walkers
And sideways talkers

Shoaling out of his lane
To the respectable
Purring of the hearse . . .
They move in equal pace
With the habitual
Slow consolation
Of a dawdling engine,
The line lifted, hand
Over fist, cold sunshine
On the water, the land
Banked under fog: that morning
I was taken in his boat,
The screw purling, turning
Indolent fathoms white,
I tasted freedom with him.
To get out early, haul
Steadily off the bottom,
Dispraise the catch, and smile
As you find a rhythm
Working you, slow mile by mile,
Into your proper haunt
Somewhere, well out, beyond . . .
Dawn-sniffing revenant▲,
Plodder through midnight rain,
Question me again.

one who returns especially from the dead

NORTH

I returned to a long strand,
the hammered curve of a bay,
and found only the secular
powers of the Atlantic thundering.

I faced the unmagical
invitations of Iceland,
the pathetic colonies
of Greenland, and suddenly

those fabulous raiders,
those lying in Orkney and Dublin
measured against
their long swords rusting,

those in the solid
belly of stone ships,
those hacked and glinting
in the gravel of thawed streams

were ocean-deafened voices
warning me, lifted again
revelation in violence and epiphany▲.
The longship's swimming tongue

was buoyant with hindsight—
god of thunder it said Thor's▲ hammer swung
to geography and trade,
thick-witted couplings and revenges,

the hatreds and behindbacks
general assembly of Iceland of the althing▲, lies and women,
exhaustions nominated peace,
memory incubating the spilled blood.

It said, 'Lie down
in the word-hoard, burrow
the coil and gleam
of your furrowed brain.

Compose in darkness.
Expect aurora borealis
in the long foray
but no cascade of light.

Keep your eye clear
bubble as the bleb▲ of the icicle,
trust the feel of what nubbed treasure
your hands have known.'

34. Play of light seen near north pole, electro-magnetic activity in the sky.

GLANMORE SONNETS

For Ann Saddlemyer
our heartiest welcomer

I

Vowels ploughed into other: opened ground.
The mildest February for twenty years
Is mist bands over furrows, a deep no sound
Vulnerable to distant gargling tractors.
Our road is steaming, the turned-up acres breathe.
Now the good life could be to cross a field
And art a paradigm of earth new from the lathe
Of ploughs. My lea is deeply tilled.
Old ploughsocks gorge the subsoil of each sense
And I am quickened with a redolence
Of farmland as a dark unblown rose.
Wait then . . . Breasting the mist, in sowers' aprons,
My ghosts come striding into their spring stations.
The dream grain whirls like freakish Easter snows.

II

Sensings, mountings from the hiding places,
Words entering almost the sense of touch,
Ferreting themselves out of their dark hutch—
'These things are not secrets but mysteries,'
Oisin Kelly told me years ago
In Belfast, hankering after stone
That connived with the chisel, as if the grain
Remembered what the mallet tapped to know.
Then I landed in the hedge-school of Glanmore
And from the backs of ditches hoped to raise
A voice caught back off slug-horn and slow chanter
That might continue, hold, dispel, appease:
Vowels ploughed into other, opened ground,
Each verse returning like the plough turned round.

from CLEARANCES

In memoriam M.K.H. 1911–1984

3

When all the others were away at Mass
I was all hers as we peeled potatoes.
They broke the silence, let fall one by one
Like solder weeping off the soldering iron:
Cold comforts set between us, things to share
Gleaming in a bucket of clean water.
And again let fall. Little pleasant splashes
From each other's work would bring us to our senses.

So while the parish priest at her bedside
Went hammer and tongs at the prayers for the dying
And some were responding and some crying
I remembered her head bent towards my head,
Her breath in mine, our fluent dipping knives—
Never closer the whole rest of our lives.

4

Fear of affectation made her affect
Inadequacy whenever it came to
Pronouncing words 'beyond her'. *Bertold Brek.*
She'd manage something hampered and askew
Every time, as if she might betray
The hampered and inadequate by too
Well-adjusted a vocabulary.
With more challenge than pride, she'd tell me, 'You
Know all them things.' So I governed my tongue
In front of her, a genuinely well-
adjusted adequate betrayal
Of what I knew better. I'd *naw* and *aye*
And decently relapse into the wrong
Grammar which kept us allied and at bay.

BOBBI SYKES
(b. 1945)

Born Townsville, Queensland. A Harvard graduate with a Doctorate of Education she is a long-time activist for land rights for Blacks and for human and women's rights.

MONOPOLY

The trip to England is a mighty success,
                    rah, rah, rah,
Militant Black Leader ARRIVES screams the Press;
Cold, wet, ugly, sprawling, grey
                    London,
Never mind the view—it's work you're here to do!

Railway stations, strange faces,
Performing black doll alights,
Here's the platform—
Talk, doll; rage, doll; rant, doll;
Horrors in Australia,
                    rah, rah, rah,
Tell it like it is, tell it like it is.

From home the news—
          'Police are out to get you'
          'Blacks are out to get you'
          'Whore, prostitute, deserter of children'
          'Wealthy, posing as poor'
          'Poor, posing as wealthy'
          'Left-wing communist extremist'
          'Counter-revolutionary, opportunist, elitist'.

The cry rings in my ears,
        Paul Coe, Denis Walker,
        Gary Williams, Norma Williams,
        Gary Foley, Billy Craigie,
        Lyn Thompson—
        collective voices:
            'We are discriminated against because we are black!'

Quietly now—
        Bobbi Sykes is not as black as us,
                    white as us,
                    poor as us,
        Let us discriminate because we think she is
            'not the right kind of Black'.

Back to the platform—
Talk, doll; dance, doll;
Tears on black doll's face,
            rah, rah rah,
Emote, doll, 'tis a sad tale of starvation and hunger that you tell
            and tell well.

Blacks in Australia need money to combat starvation,
  malnutrition,
            (Whore, prostitute,)
We have been beaten into the grass by the Government fascist
  pigs,
            (Deserter of children,)
We need help from abroad—
            (Wealthy, posing as poor,)
We appeal to people around the globe to rally to our aid.
            (Poor, posing as wealthy.)
Police victimization is acute,
            (Left wing extremist,)

Our country sisters are raped by white stockmen,
            (Counter-revolutionary,)
For political action on just claims we are flung into gaol,
            (Opportunist,)
The Government oppresses the people.
                (Elitist.)

Tears on black doll's face,
            rah, rah, rah,
Cry, sister, tell it like it is!
Is the sorrow for the head-lice on the babies heads
        And children in rubbish bins in Alice?
Or for the knife which protrudes from your back?

Blacks have no monopoly on pain,
For within a black group an un-black black doll
Writhes, hurts, screams, cries out—
In soundless agony,
A hand at the throat blocks off the sound,
A black hand,
            rah, rah, rah.

In slow motion in a troubled mind,
        Token nigger, spit on her,
        Uppity nigger, slap her down,
        Cheeky nigger, don't play with her,
        Faces of attackers—clear, then waning,
        Black and white faces, taut and straining.

White groups huddled over candles,
Playing games with life and riches,
Black doll knocking on the door,
'Let her in, she will amuse us',
Talk, doll; rave, doll; rant, doll;
            rah, rah, rah.

Black group huddled in the night,
Making decisions which must be right,
Black doll knocking on the door,
'Let me in, let me help',
Go away, un-black black,
Only black blacks can help

There is no monopoly on discrimination,
There is no monopoly on pain!
Play it one more time, black doll,

This time with tears,
rah, rah, rah.

AMBROSE

They say you took your life/
With your
Own hand:
But I been looking
At your life
These past
Four years
And I see other
Hands
In the taking
Of your life.

Your mother was
helping
You
To die
Since
Your first breath.

You showed me
Her picture
Once/
Taken with you

As a babe
You lay, pretty boy,
On a table
Behind you she stood
Your bottle in one hand/
Her bottle in the other/
Symbol of your childhood.

Your father helped
By the hole

He left in your life
When he split/
&
You
Only seven months in
Foetaldom.

Teachers had a hand:
Laying hands
Upon you
(not in love)
In punishment
For your dirty clothes
& later
For your lies
(your survival kit, haha—
you told me later.)

Incorrigible:
You lived more
A uniformed life
Contained
By uniformed men
Than in the free air
Of which you
Often spoke.

I don't like to talk
About

How the 'helpers'
Helped—
Moving you closer
& closer
To your inevitable fall
(or were you pushed?)

Helpers who
Let you know so soon
That your best

Wasn't good enough/
for them

The many hands
That reached out
To you
Reached out
To tear off
Strips.

You lost another piece
'cause you failed
to be a
'splendid example of your race'
In an education project
For
Already failed
Aboriginal Boys of Twelve Years.

Everybody helped you
Ambrose—
Helped you inch
Closer to your end.

'There is no place
For me here'
You told me/
already 17,
And floating now

In the only space
You could see open.

There were handmarks
& fingerprints
All over you/
When they found you;
But you died
By your own hand/
They said

KATE JENNINGS
(b. 1949)

Born, New South Wales. Edited 'Mother I'm Rooted', an anthology that greatly influenced Australian women poets. She lives and works as a writer in New York.

COUPLES

celebrating a wedding
this is a song an epithalamium▲ it is also
celebrating a death
a requiem▲ this is a poem about couples it
is called *racked and ranked*
the title comes from william faulkner
who said

'and thank God you can flee, can escape from that
massy five-foot-thick maggot-cheesy solidarity which
overlays the earths, in which men and women in couples
are racked and ranked like ninepins.'

this is a poem for couples from which i cannot escape
this is a poem for people who are not couples but who
want to be couples from which i cannot escape a poem
for all you out there people who are coupling up or
breaking up just to couple up again and giving me
second prize because

kate jennings, lose him, weep him, couldn't catch a man
much less keep him

couples create obstacle courses to prevent me from doing
all sorts of things easily

couples make sure i'm not comfortable with myself
because
i'm only half a potential couple
couples point accusing right index fingers at me
couples make me guilty of loneliness, insecurity, or
worse still, lack of ambition.

what do i do at the end of the day?
lose him, weep him, think of catching a man,
and eating him.

LIONEL FOGARTY
(b. 1958)

Born in Cherbourg Aboriginal Reserve, Queensland. A prominent advocate for his people, he is an editor, and has had several books of poetry published.

REMEMBER SOMETHING LIKE THIS

Long ago a brown alighted story was told
As a boy, looked up on the hall walls
water flowed to his eyes
for Starlight was carrying snake in his shirt
gut belly
and around the fires a tall man
frightened the mobs that black eyes promised
that night at giant tree, way up
bushes crept in the ant hill
was the wild blackfella
from up north, they said.
Soldier cained him down at the waterhole
but as they bent to dip, sip
behind their backs, old man Waterflow
flew clear, magic
undoing the shackles, without keys
or sounds of saw
saw . . . nah . . . you didn't saw him.
He's old Waterflow, even I'm too young
to remember everything.
Yet clever than pictures them show off
making fun of old Boonah
sitting outside waiting for dreaming
to come to reality.

After that somebody broke into the store.
Oh, the police were everywhere
at every door, roof, in laws
Where's this and that, you know.
So they find out where him came from
by looking at the tracks.
He's headed for the caves
just near milky way.
Happy in strength, we took off
but the hills hid this tribal
bull-roaring feather foot
underJimmys Scrub
place up deep
where you have to leave smoke
if you want to hunt there
If you don't, you'll get slewed . . .
On earth our people are happy
but we couldn't find that food.
Musta been up the Reservoir
or expecting a life to run over near Yellow Bar cave
again.
But we bin told, one man got baldy porcupine.
Bring him home and not supposed to.
So him get sick, all life time
like green hands touch murri legs
that's why you don't swim too late
at this creek created.
A spoiled boy one aftemoon, went repeating
the bell bird singing.
And he went and went
and sent to Green Swamp, back of the grid.
Then as eels were caught
Aunties sang out, this the biggest
I've ever seen.
Come boys get more wood, we'll stay
here all night.
So sat waiting, a bit dark, tired light
the lines pulling in slowly
for fish seem to be in message

but two-headed creature appeared
legs chucked back
fires went out
the fish swam back
we raced home.
All cold that night, back of the bend
and rocks.
Just near the bunya tree you can see
this middle age woman, long black hair
walk past our Nana Rosies place
up to the graveyards
but she flows
and many a moons came shone in our minds
watching Dimmydum and Kingy doing corroboree
on stage
in front of the children.
A light story past thru windows
on to you all
never forget
remember more . . .

PHILIP HODGINS
(1959–1995)

Born on a farm in Victoria, farm life, and his long battle with leukaemia, were central facts of his life and of his poetry.

MAKING HAY

In rectangular vertigo the balepress
gives prodigious birth.
From conception to delivery
takes less than a minute.
Humming down slow rows
of lucerne and paspalum it chews grass,
snakeskins, thistles, feathers, anything.
By midday it can do no more.
The paddock is a maze of compression
soon to be unravelled
by hay-carters starting at the edges.
Shirtless in cowskin chaps and gloves
they perform their complex dance
with eighty-pound bales
on an earthquaking load that shoves
a slackchained,
bouncing, banging, balesucking escalator
down bays of the marvellous smell
of cut grass.
When the dance is done,
easing to the monolith, they sit
with cigarettes on what they've made.
After the hay has been restacked
they take a big tyre tube
to the swimming hole and muddy the water

worse than cattle,
slushing after the slippery tube.
With one stye eye and sleek
black skin it is the nearest thing
to a leviathan in this billabong.

ICH BIN ALLEIN

'Cancer is a rare and still scandalous subject for poetry; and it seems unimaginable to aestheticize the disease.'
Susan Sontag, *Illness as Metaphor*

It is in every part. Nothing can be cut off or out.
A steady suddenness.
It isn't Keats
or randomness.
It is this body
nurturing its own determined death.
I will find out how much pain is in this body
and I will not behave myself.
It isn't fit for poetry
but since
poets create their own mythology
there is no choice.
My friends have all gone home.
I'm in the dank half-light. I am alone.

DEATH WHO

The conversation with cancer
begins equitably enough.
You and he are summing each other up,
trading ripostes and *bons mots*
before the soup.
Everything seems ordinary.
There is interest and boredom,
and you've been drinking all afternoon
which could mean that you're depressed
or that you're in good form.

TITLE: ICH BIN ALLEIN: I am alone.

You get each other's measure
and the conversation settles,
subjects divide and increase like cells.
Gradually you realise
that like the background Mozart
all the emotions are involved,
and that you're no longer saying as much.
Put it down to strength of intent.
He's getting aggressive
and you're getting tired. Someone
says he's a conversational bully
but you're fascinated.
He tells you things about yourself,
forgotten things and those not yet found out,
pieces from childhood and the unhealing wound.
It's all there.
Forgetting food, you drink (too much
red wine will encourage nightmares
but that's not a problem now), you marvel.
Isn't he tireless!
A raconteur like something out of Proust.
He blows cigar smoke into your face
and makes a little joke.
It's actually too much.
You're tired and the more you tire
the more the words are everywhere.
You go and recline on the couch,
but he won't shut up. He follows you there
and makes the cushions uncomfortable for you.
It's so unjust.
Your host is in the kitchen,
all the guests have gone
and cancer's got you like conviction
and he's kneeling on your chest,
glaring over you,
pushing a cushion into your face,
talking quietly and automatically,
the words not clear.
He's got you and he's really pushing,
pushing you to death.

SHOOTING THE DOGS

There wasn't much else we could do
that final day on the farm.
We couldn't take them with us into town,
no one round the district needed them
and the new people had their own.
It was one of those things.

You sometimes hear of dogs
who know they're about to be put down
and who look up along the barrel of the rifle
into responsible eyes that never forget
that look and so on,
but our dogs didn't seem to have a clue.

They only stopped for a short while
to look at the Bedford stacked with furniture
not hay
and then cleared off towards the swamp,
plunging through the thick paspalum
noses up, like speedboats.

They weren't without their faults.
The young one liked to terrorise the chooks
and eat the eggs.
Whenever he started doing this
we'd let him have an egg full of chilli paste
and then the chooks would get some peace.

The old one's weakness was rolling in dead sheep.
Sometimes after this he'd sit outside
the kitchen window at dinner time.
The stink would hit us all at once
and we'd grimace like the young dog
discovering what was in the egg.

But basically they were pretty good.
They worked well and added life to the place.
I called them back enthusiastically

and got the old one as he bounded up
and then the young one as he shot off
for his life.

I buried them behind the tool shed.
It was one of the last things I did before
we left.
Each time the gravel slid off the shovel
it sounded like something
trying to hang on by its nails.

MILK CREAM BUTTER

He'd get up every morning before the sun
had cleared the treeline on his neighbour's creek,
and while the sound of magpies trickled in
the slightly opened window of his room
he'd take whatever clothes he'd worn all week,
a tattered pile that mostly smelled of him,
and shake them out and put them on again.
That time of day the paddock by the house
was brittle with a covering of frost
so when he went to get his seven cows
it left a zig-zag trail of darker prints
where the silver grass got crushed beneath his boots.
The cows would wander down along a fence
that led them through a set of open gates
and when they'd turn into the narrow lane
he'd notice how their cautious feet would mince
the gravel-filling with the mud again.
Arriving at the milking shed the queue
of weighted cows would always be the same.
They'd practised twice a day and now they knew
the sequence and the distance off by heart.
They knew the routine of the single bail
and after that how far to keep apart.
So there was nothing much he had to do
except to chain them in and wet the teats
then draw the lines of milk into the pail

between his legs, a tight metallic gasp
that changed into exquisite frothy breaths.
In less than half an hour he'd have them done
and while they sauntered back the way they'd come
he'd go out to the separating room
and tip the previous morning's creamless milk
into two pig troughs that used to be a drum
and then he'd pour each bucketful of warm
fresh milk into a metal cooling dish.
Beside them was a wooden butter-churn
that looked like some sideshow magician's prop.
He'd fill it up with sour cream and turn
the handle steadily until the fat
began to float in globules on the top.
A final rapid stirring firmed them up,
he'd slide a bucket underneath, then pull
the plug and let the buttermilk escape
before he'd fill the small vat nearly full
of water, rinse the butter clean, then add
some salt and take the soapy mixture out
in handfuls, which he'd torture like a rag,
removing with a twist the final drops.
The rest was just a kind of copyright.
He'd press the butter into one-pound pats
with an emu imprinted on the tops
denoting him, and when the job was done
he'd notice that those blocks of golden light
were glowing deeper than the early sun.

AFTER A DRY STRETCH

The rain appears, as always, from the west.
Behind the mountain ranges it seems at first
to be a bigger, purpler, more distant range:
a counterpoint for some corellas, their wings
turning whitenesses on and off, unsynchronised.
Soon, almost quietly going about its business,
a marriage of elements descends the foothill slopes

and settles in for the day on the flat country.
In minutes your field of view is brought up close:
through rain there is only more rain further back
and cow shapes with their colours all washed out.
Reconstituting paddocks, eliminating dust
the rain is what was promised by machines.
Remembering its way by feel down gullies
it gathers colour, plaited milky brown, and reaches
the creek all stirred up, back together at last.
Getting through barricades of its own making,
hastily putting up new ones out of any loose wood,
water-rat-matted coats of dead rushes, bright plastics,
it repeats itself, stuttering in the tight situations
and growing in confidence over the broad deep lengths,
determined not to be drawn out in the next transition.
Now in the paddocks there are frogs, unpuffed,
still sluggish and flecked with dirt. Their credo
is sequential, 'Add water, reproduce, avoid snakes'.
Even the big ones are learning all over again:
they react by mating with the toe of your boot
when you give them a nudge. Their talkback
is regular as the rain, though lower and sharper.
Not far away, in a galvanised machinery shed
diesel is cascading into the tractor already hitched
to a ton and a half of crop seed on wheels.
From inside the amplifying shed it sounds like
hard seed is raining down on the corrugated roof.
A nail hole lets in star-small light, and rain drops.
More bags of seed are ready on a loading platform:
they might be sandbags stacked before a flood.
The farmer looks out at his unwritten paddocks,
relieved that all the weather-chat is finished
and that soon he'll be out there for days on end
filling the fallow space with standard lines.
The yard dog chases the old tab across bags
of seed. They both know it's only a game.
Over at the house too, the rain is happiness
for water is chortling into the big tank,
smoke is unravelling from the year's first fire
and mushrooms are forming in the minds of children.

THE NEW FLOOR

Digging three rows of holes to start with
the remembrance of physical work comes early,
that moment of unguardedness when the load
is shared equally between body and mind,
something it has in common with palpable love:
a design feature to stop the species dying out.
Its symptoms are tentative beads of sweat,
a deeper breathing that falls into step,
and the sensation of having new hands,
of feeling them tighten with plump blood.
Waiting to be remembered after these fade
is the pleasure of knowing how things work
and a reminder of the ordinary details involved.
For instance, the simplicity of your tools:
hammer and nails, chisel, pencil and saw.
And for your measurements not much except
a spirit level and a roll of string.
No amount of big technology could make
the finished floor more level than these can.
It's as good as that other thing, poetry,
which only needs a pencil and some paper.
With love the lines fit into logics of their own:
the first of redgum stumps, then tin caps, bearers,
joists, and finally the bare pine boards.
They lie there at the end of low-tech work,
tongue in groove and side by side as tight
as lines from Dante's faithfully measured book:
an understanding to keep the years together.

A MEMORIAL SERVICE

Emerging from the little church
those muted fifties suits
and wonder-fabric dresses

seem just as sad and lifeless
as when they're hanging up
in varnished ply-wood cupboards

between weddings and funerals
for six months at a stretch—
those crosses on the calendars.

Outside it's past a hundred
and every steering wheel
is too hot to hold.

The farmers and their wives
at first bunch up as tight
as suits and dresses on a rack

to say the same familiar things
to the widow standing there
with children at her side

and then spread slowly out
the way that cows do
when let into a fresh paddock.

There's beer and lemonade
laid out on trestle-tables
in the shade of big redgums

but most of the congregation
is still thinking about
the details of the eulogy,

a list of main events,
both self-imposed and not,
so common they seem clichéd

to those from somewhere else
but which are real enough
for anyone involved with them:

an isolated station childhood,
impulsive under-age enlistment,
imprisonment in Palestine,

a soldier settlement block,
and then the growing parallels
of family and farm

until the common pulse
gave out in a bright room
cluttered with technology.

It makes them think about
their own peculiar list,
how ordinary it would seem

set out on one short slab
of main points and praise
as final as a headstone,

how everything left out
would be as hackneyed
as the flesh off the bone.

Abandoning the main body
a little at a time,
mostly in long-time pairs,

they walk back to their cars
and talk of getting out of
these best clothes at last.

THE PIER

Upset about death you go for a walk
and finish up down at the pier
watching the old men with their long rods

that doodle slowly like distraction.
It's overcast and out there on the bay
squalls are circling like seagulls.

The pier runs a hundred metres into the sea
and you notice that the beams
of Oregon or whatever across the top of it

are weathered as blunt at their ends
as the fingers of those fishermen
and that the big wooden thumbs

where a ship would be tied up
are neatly capped with bird-droppings.
Each time a wave crashes along underneath

there is the rickety sound of train travel
and the two rows of tree trunks
supporting and extending the platform

are worn away a little bit more.
Above the waterline they look complete
but when that line breathes down

it's worrying to see how much
the lower parts have been decayed away
and you imagine it all collapsing in the future.

The further out you go the more
those trunks have been weakened
in the place they most need to be secure

and the deeper the water looks
(so deep it's hard to figure out
just how they would have built the pier)

until on a plank made slippery
with scales and fishgut stains and seaspray
you come to the end.

INDEX OF AUTHORS

INDEX OF TITLES AND FIRST LINES

Poems without a title have been preceded in the text by an image. Such poems are usually referred to by their first line.

INDEX OF TITLES AND FIRST LINES

INDEX OF TITLES AND FIRST LINES

INDEX OF TITLES AND FIRST LINES